Contents

Introduction 11
    The journey 11
    Paradise found 13
    Learning the language of love 14
    Expect irony 16
    The map 17
    Awakening 20
    Freedom, for the sake of freedom 21
    Obstacles on the road to freedom 23
    References to Wikipedia 23
    Bible references 24
    Publisher 24
    Family and friends 24
    BunchOBlokes 24
    Acknowledgements to my teachers and encouragers 25

Prelude: The dream 27
    Dimensions of the Glory of God's Kingdom 29
    Treasure in jars of clay 30
    Jesus, friend of thieves and tax collectors 32
    The Arc of the Universe 33

Chapter 1: Preparations for the road 37
    The zeitgeist 39
    Sharing a secret 42
    Love lost 44
    Is the Golden Rule a placebo or strong medicine? 46
    If only…I had learnt the Golden Rule 47
    The Golden Rule as the ethical foundation
        for a full and satisfying life 50

  The Golden Rule is Christ's command to us 51
  If Jesus' commands are so important,
    why are we not taught them? 52
  Learning hard lessons 54
  The cure. 55
  PS. 61

Chapter 2: What is the Golden Rule? **63**
  Is the Golden Rule good?. 63
  Finding my place 65
  Sola scriptura? 67
  Symbiotic symbolism. 70
  Paradox at the heart of the message 73
  Freedom! 79
  Enforcing equality. 81
  Is the message of Jesus reliable? 88
  Paradise restored 92
  The beginning, middle and end of history. 94
  The cart before the horse 95
  The secret of the ages 97

Chapter 3: Where did the Golden Rule come from? **99**
  Abraham, Moses, the law and the Glory of God. 102
  The Golden Rule recipe (How not to over-egg the cake). . 106
  Is faith good? 108
  What is the highest good?. 110
  Is the Golden Rule, Golden?. 114
  The law of non-contradiction 116
  Jesus' Golden Rule in the Bible 123
  God is love 128

Chapter 4: Who needs the Golden Rule? **129**
  Love hurts. 132
  Faith and works 136
  School Days 141

How Good is the Golden Rule?

LEARNING
THE LANGUAGE
OF LOVE

Warren Mills

Published in Australia by
Freedom Publishing Books
33 Scoresby Road
Bayswater VIC 3153
Australia

ISBN 9780648497769

Copyright © Warren Mills 2019

All rights reserved. Other than for the purposes and subject to the conditions prescribed under the *Copyright Act*, no part of this publication may be reproduced, stored in a retrieval system, or transmitted in any form or by any means, electronic, mechanical, photocopying, recording or otherwise, without the prior permission of the publisher.

Unless otherwise noted, all scripture quotations are from *New International Version* © 1992 by Biblica.

Cataloguing-in-Publication entry is available from the National Library of Australia http:/catalogue.nla.gov.au/.

Illustrations by Brett Cardwell
Text design by Filmshot Graphics (FSG)
Cover design by Ian James – www.jgd.com.au

Printed in Australia

The decline of Christian consensus in the West 143
  Jesus. Lord and Savior 144
  How the West was lost 145
  First things first 148
  Back to the future 149
  The end of the best era in history 151
  Egalitarianism 152
  The rise of the "Nones" 156
  Who cares? 157
  Love your enemies 158
  Justice and love 162
  Redemption and repentance 164
  Choose life 165
  Summary 166

Chapter 5: Progress on the road 167
  Spiritual consciousness 169
  Which spirit? 170
  Binary baloney 173
  Toward the Kingdom 174
  Here be dragons 176
  Spiritual competence 177

Chapter 6: How does the Golden Rule work? 179
  Impossible to ignore, impossible to do 180
  Repentance that requires change 182
  The new law of love 184
  The Golden Rule as dialogue 186
  Get wise 189
  Why is the Golden Rule so hard to do? 193
  Fear God 194
  Love casts out fear 196
  Getting in the zone 197
  Warts and all 198

    The Golden Rule algorithm..........................199
    Table A. Inward Growth 202
    Table B. Outward Growth...........................204
    Small steps 207
    Easy to say. Hard to do 207
    What kind of love?...................................209
    Proof of love..212
    Software for the soul................................214
    The deep mystery behind the Golden Rule 218
    First, do your best 219
    Traditional tosh 220
    Can the Golden Rule work universally? 222
    The Crown 225
    Conclusion 228

Chapter 7: Treat others as you would have them treat you . 231
    The cure to all ills? 233
    Love, manifest in me................................234
    Jesus, take me as I am 235
    Humility and grace 236
    Love others, but don't watch their eyes too carefully 238
    With rhythm and E..................................240
    Whose rules rule?...................................243
    Tell the truth 245
    Failing Forward 245
    Self-control...247
    Honesty begins with "I" 249
    Golden Rule 101 250
    Who teaches the teacher? 250
    Trust and obey 252
    A stitch in time saves nine..........................253
    Competencies of the new covenant...................255
    The paradox of freedom 260
    The reality of freedom 261

Enforcing equality? 262
Course prerequisites 265
Course assessment 266
Patterns of failure 268
The Big Ten sins 269
Solomon's despair 270
What to do when it all goes wrong 271

Chapter 8: ...as you love yourself? ... 273
Love as cosmic glue 274
The Nicene creed 276
Looking at love 282
What does it mean to love yourself? 284
Strength from weakness 285
Did the Golden Rule encourage
    the self-esteem movement? 286
Feel-good faith 288
The self-centered Golden Rule 291
Maslow's hierarchy of needs 292
Personal sovereignty 295
Desire for self-transcendence 295
Compliance as outcome 298
How then should we teach our children? 300

Chapter 9: Ego death ... 303
To thine own self be true 306
Do you love a false image of yourself? 310
Love as a universal force 312
Love is measured as pleasure 313
The inward and outward journey of love 314
Discovering levels of love 316
The inward journey 318
The outward journey 319
Transformation toward the image of God 320

    Born again 321
    Moving from ME to US 322

Chapter 10: Interlude 2 . . . . **325**
    To Do List Christianity 326
    Hot Rod ministry 328

Chapter 11: Are we there yet? **335**
    Strangers preparing for a strange land 340
    The loser who wins 342
    How do I measure success? 344
    Fulfilling human desires 349
    Trust God 350
    Be patient. 351
    The need to be fully human. 354
    Go deep 358

Chapter 12: Conscious Transformation **361**
    Becoming conscious 363
    Conscious competence 365
    Jesus' explicit teaching 367
    Confused by complexity 370
    From the known to the unknown,
        from the simple to the complex. 375
    Freedom and liberation. 376
    What does transformation look like? 378
    Who is God? 379
    Who am I?. 381
    What is my relationship to God? 381
    My purpose is to love God and enjoy him forever 381
    Faith 382
    Hope 383
    Love 383
    Hearing from his word 383
    Process and sequence 385

    First the natural, then the spiritual 385
    Righteousness, peace and joy in the Holy Spirit.........386
    Obstacles to transformation 386
    Life is for living 389
    God is love 391

Chapter 13: My joyful place in the Cosmos 393
    After all 397

INTRODUCTION

The journey

I would like to invite you to accompany me on a journey of discovery- a quest for the source and the purpose of the Golden Rule with this book as our guide. This is a journey like no other because, unless you are very fortunate to have discovered it already, we can catch only a fleeting vision of our destination before we depart. This vision is very real, however, because most of us have a memory of having seen such a place before. It feels strangely like home. It is filled with potential and comfort. It is warm and inviting, encouraging, secure and exciting all at once, like our childhood home or our grandparent's place. However, there is a catch. Although you and I are invited to this mysterious place, before we can get our passports and visas, we must begin to learn a new language, which may come as a surprise because most of us think of ourselves as literate, but we are not. It's not entirely new, but it does have some new rules of grammar, some new words and concepts that we must acquire. It is more a new idiom that changes how we think about a subject that we previously thought we understood. It's like learning technical terms to describe a new job we have just started except that it's not just about learning the meaning of words. It is about experiencing what they mean when they are imprinted upon us like childhood experiences. This is a pre-requisite because, in this case, there is an impenetrable barrier that prevents us from getting to our destination any way other than past the guard at the border (whose name, by the way, is Peter). Regardless, we have both been invited, so let's begin, if you will accompany me.

How Good is the Golden Rule?

Our destination is a place called Paradise. It exists in what religious people blandly call "the Kingdom of God". I say "blandly" not to criticize others' descriptions, but to recognize my own apathy as this place never appeared to me much, until I began to learn this new language in a serious way. Since then I have found this to be a fantastic place – far better than all the brochures of the Maldives you have ever seen; far beyond anything we can imagine – because God dwells there. That's what a kingdom is. It is a place where someone is recognized as king. He has invited us in personally and we can enter, provided we learn the language that we will need both to understand the signposts and directions there and to be able to communicate when we arrive. Paradise is a doubly mysterious place, in fact, because we are already partly in it. But if we cannot speak or read its language properly, we miss many of its meanings, and so we are unaware of the delights awaiting us. It's a bit like being taken to the carnival by our parents when we were small children and falling asleep on the way, then waking up in the middle of the bright lights, music and wonderful sights that we had heard about, but did not know really existed other than in a dream, which has become real.

Fortunately, the process of obtaining a passport and visa is not so difficult. We simply declare our intention to accept the invitation to begin the language and the journey. But this presents another catch, for if we believe that God or Paradise don't exist then we cannot begin, because it is impossible to depart for a place that we know – or think we know – is not real. Nor can you accept an invitation from someone you don't know – or believe does not exist. Fortunately, there is another way to begin. We can take language lessons by distance learning before we apply for our travel credentials. This is very helpful because as we learn, so the signposts and sounds of our vision become clearer. Either way, we must learn the language before we can enter the gate. This is not just a luxury for the rich and famous either. In fact, many would give their fortune just to visit, but money is not its currency as it is open to all comers. Eligibility is determined not by wealth, status, intelligence as the best qualified are children who still believe that such a place exists because it is fresh in their memory.

The language, by the way, is called the language of love which God speaks. So we need to listen carefully in order to hear his voice and hear what he has to tell us.

Paradise found

Learning the language of love does two distinctly different things. First, it helps us understand what it means to be human, because love is what makes sense of the life God has given us because we are made in his image. This life is intensely personal and relational. Just as Adam and Eve walked with God in the cool of the evening in the Garden of Eden, so a restoration of this personal relationship with God and each other is our first goal. When I say restoration, that implies something has been lost, which I think we know intuitively. But now is not the time to regret what might have been, but to begin to take back lost ground. To walk and talk with God in Paradise requires that we learn his language very well to avoid making fools of ourselves, suggesting that we have no right to be there with him.

The reason I suggest that we travel together is that each time I accompany someone like you on this journey I learn something new myself. Plus, one of my great joys is seeing how others react the first time they reach this place. Not just to the delights of discovery, but the promise of more to come. I should warn you however, that there are many bumps in the road. Although many potholes, diversions and dead ends are unavoidable, some of the bumps are not in the road so much as they are in us – we bring them with us. This is a surprise for many people who were born in the modern scientific and technological age, since we rarely assume that *we* are ever the obstacle to progress. This is a problem, though, because it has created an expectation that progress is always easy, linear and predictable. It is not. For example, to learn the language of love, there are some things that we must unlearn. Some of our most precious values that we think of as reliable absolutes are not. Things like selfishness, arrogance, excessive ambition and pride and envy are easy to mistake as self-esteem or self-protection mechanisms, but they are obstacles that we must avoid.

Learning the language of love

The title of this book, "How Good is the Golden Rule?" begs the question of my thesis: that the Golden Rule is not only good, but very good because it was given as a command by the one who I regard as the greatest teacher of human history, Jesus of Nazareth. As I have believed this for most of my life, I can now look back to see how it has worked out in reality. My assessment so far is not bad overall with some successes and failures along the way. What I have found to be true, though, is that the Golden Rule itself is utterly reliable when we understand what it is. This made such an impression on me that I have begun a new career in the past few years writing about the Golden Rule and my experience of it. I have discovered it to be an inexhaustible trove of treasures, the most valuable of which is that it teaches us about love. Not just any old love. It teaches us that because we are made in his image, God's agape love is available to use with each other, and with God. Although I approach this task as a Christian, I am not so arrogant as to say that people from other cultures and religions cannot experience the same thing as we hope to do. However, there is no-one else like Jesus. No-one else ever claimed to be both fully human and fully divine: both the Son of Man and the Son of God. He is distinctive because he is God in the flesh who became the great teacher of humanity whose claims we can test for ourselves.

As I have mentioned, learning the language of love is a journey into a land where things are not always what they seem to be. As

Introduction

we embark, we will discover that some things that we previously thought were good are not, while some things that we thought were bad turn out to be good. It's easy to get into a rut where we don't see the possibility of doing anything differently. For example, we have often thought that getting things done quickly was more important than doing them well and bringing others along with us. Another is the need many people seem to have to "do things their way," regardless of the effect this has on others. We might also discover that money is not the most important goal or even a measure of success. At least, we will discover that some of our ideas about the nature of reality can be misguided, and so we must be prepared to listen and watch carefully, perhaps to hear and see some things differently. Take love itself, for example. There are many possible variations of experience and corresponding definitions of what love is. Some will say that love is an intense feeling, which it can be, but that is not all it is. Nor is it just an emotion, or just a preference for a thing or a person who we would never criticize. The important discovery is that all love emanates from God, because he is love. This means God's love expresses itself as his unconditional desire for our best interests: to want the best of all possible good things for us which he has already made available, expecting nothing in return, other than our acceptance of his offer. In this sense, love and good are synonymous. Then there are other forms and types of love: that between a parent and a child, between siblings, between friends and neighbors and workmates. Then there is passionate erotic love which has an incredible mixture of desire, emotion, passion, physical sensation, anticipation between a man and a woman who were made for each other by him..

I find it interesting that it is only in a family of a man, woman and child that all the different elements of agape love coexist. By themselves, none of the elements of love are the same as agape, because agape is God's love reserved for our benefit and pleasure. They are all, however, derived from God's love for his purposes.

If a particular type of love does not fit into this overarching definition, it is not love. If there is an intent to deceive using love as the cover for a sinister motive, so some types of love are not what they claim to be as they are counterfeit. Agape love has far too many characteristics to mention now, but we can short-list a few so that we will be able to recognize real love when we see it. Agape is, above all else, relational and personal, good and life-giving. It is also reasonable and rational. It is emotional, passionate, physical and sensual. It is transcendent and revitalizing. It is real and not imaginary, although to anticipate agape love is part of the experience. Similarly, other things that are good have the same source and characteristics as agape love. They include life-giving food and drink, which is nourishment for our body, soul and spirit, just like the air we breathe and the warmth of the sun and the beauty of a sunset. It may be a beautiful sound, like music or laughter, or the fragrance of perfume or a garden. Or maybe just a lover's gentle touch.

Expect irony

> *I have always noticed that deeply and truly religious persons are fond of a joke, and I am suspicious of those who aren't.*
>
> A.N. Whitehead. *Church and Home.*

I have discovered another interesting thing about God's love that tells me something about him. God's love always results in joy. He has a wonderful sense of humour and often plays jokes with us. Some of his jokes are like the jokes you would use to make a baby laugh, which to me is evidence of a response to God's goodness in even the smallest of people. Some of his jokes are more serious, so deeply ironic that it takes many years to get them, especially if the joke is about our own pretentious self-righteousness. An example is the way Jesus told parables whose point was not obvious until much later, when he had to explain to his disciples what they meant. Or take the Old Testament story about Ruth in the Book by the same name. She was the foreign daughter-in-law of Naomi, in spite of the biblical injunction against mixed marriages (which, as I will explain in Chapter 5, is one of many examples of deep irony and paradox throughout the Bible). This discovery led me to look for unexpected outcomes in unusual places, especially when there is a possibility that I am setting myself up for a fall. (Like two clowns at the circus, doing silly things behind each other's back, it sometimes turns out that I am both, as it were, playing tricks on myself). One practical effect of expecting irony is humility. It causes me to be cautious about pretending that I always have the answers and, therefore, I have made myself the deluded master of my domain. Expecting irony prevents me from being too dogmatic as there is always the possibility that I have missed some vital clue which, once I have discovered it, will turn my version of reality on its head.

The map

To help us on our journey, I have laid out this book as a map based on my experience. This may not suit everyone, but it is the best I can do as I have followed a very circuitous path myself, one that would be hard to describe other than as a journey and a series of experiences that I understand only with hindsight. You will see that although I am not a scholar, I have done my share of living and reading along the way to make sense of what I have experienced because I believe in Jesus and want to share him with you. To accomplish this, the book is designed to have two major themes. The first theme is the design and function of what the Golden Rule is: what it is for, where it came from, who it applies to and how it works, all presented in overview; then I discuss in more detail what we can expect from it. My claim is that this is no abstract theory. The Golden Rule is our first hand, present tense, concrete encounter with the Divine, the Ancient of Days, Jehovah God. This relationship, I believe, is accomplished by us deciding to follow God's gentle voice and how to speak to him in return about the real stuff of life: how to flourish for ourselves, our families and friends, and for the common good. The second theme is how to prepare for eternity with God, as his sons and daughters who are being equipped to help run the family business. Although I think the two themes are inextricably linked, I have separated them, so I can explain them more clearly, by putting the second theme in the Prologue, Interludes and Postlude in which I will illustrate and describe with awe and wonder my best guess as to what eternity has in store for us. For this almost-impossible task, I use the metaphor, The Arc of the Universe, which is also a map. It is a big-picture description of Paradise and a guide to help us get there. It tells how to know when we have arrived, what to do and where to find things. The Golden Rule, as I have mentioned, is the secret we need to begin this journey. This, and most of the other instructions and guidelines that I have found to be reliable, are from the master map, The Bible. The remarkable fact is that although I have often misunderstood it, the Bible has proven itself time and again as a source of deep wisdom and reality. Often, its wisdom becomes most obvious when I have ignored it, only to find its warnings were right. This is sharply contrasted by the religious impulse to say that because it is the inerrant Word of God (which I believe it to be, although I prefer the words authoritative and reliable to avoid being misunderstood) that I also know exactly what it means by reading it literally. Fortunately, my expectation of irony has become honed over the years as I have discovered new levels of meaning, plus my growing ability to hold apparently contradictory ideas in tension, which I have realized to be an essential life-skill, not exclusively reserved for reading the Bible. As for inerrancy, putting aside misreadings and misunderstandings, how can it be otherwise? If it is the Word of God which it claims to be, and I have found it to be so, it will continue to be proven right and its detractors proven wrong, which I have also discovered to be true.

For many years, the map I was following led me on a path that was a mixture of rough and smooth. It was smooth where I knew to properly apply the Bible and the Golden Rule – in my marriage, for instance – but I completely forgot to apply the same principle that I knew worked so well, such as in dealing with my children or in business, where I would revert to another set of unproven ideas that I understood even less. The discovery that there are many possible paths in life is what we learn as we become adults. The question we must answer, though, is this: Do all paths have the same value? Do we all end up at the same destination? The answer to both those questions is clearly no! I know from my own experience that while some of my ideas and some of the paths I have taken were life-giving, some were life-denying. Even more so, when I look at friends and acquaintances who are now dead or whose lives have been damaged by needless suffering as a result of their poor choices. So, apart from the Golden Rule, how do we make those major life-decisions regarding which path to follow and how to follow it? So much of what I have experienced is a blur – from childhood to adolescence and adulthood. Even a major cultural shift like the sexual revolution of the 1960s was to me, a mixture of radical social change and personal experience that constituted daily life. Although my views were mediated by my continuing faith and church attendance, as I look back, so much of what I thought was OK was self-serving, if not hypocritical.

It was not until I became a grandfather that I began to reflect more deeply on the many available paths that – ostensibly – lead toward beneficial changes for society. Which of these paths complimented my experience of the good life? Which of them involve life-depriving contradictions? While I was asleep in my apathy, my default position had been to inevitably accept that the mainstream views of Western democracy, with its Christian origins, pointed the right way. However, these views have increasingly led to an aggressive form of secular democracy; to an insurgence that is now attempting to expunge God from its history and its place in the public square. In some cases, the highest values of democratic secularism have become a strange brand of "tolerance and diversity", expressing Neo-Marxism and its handmaiden, political correctness. As I become more conscious of this shift away from a Christian consensus toward cultural Marxism, this has become a major focus of my thought, my writing, and my relationships, especially at church.

Awakening

Major elements in my awakening were my retirement from full-time work and my becoming a grandfather, especially when I started to wonder about what sort of world my grandchildren would experience. At about the same time, I became a participant in *The Conversation*, an Internet-based academic forum created here in Melbourne, Australia. This was to be a baptism by fire. I knew my conservative Christian position would not be popular, so to avoid being upset by my opponents calling me names, I established my on-line identity as a "contrarian, grumpy old Bible-basher." Not long after, I encountered my first barrage of ridicule by my interlocuters on TC whose tactics were to dismiss, deny and discredit anything I said. At the same time, I became aware of voices against social "progressivism" from YouTube luminaries such as Professor Jonathan Haidt, TV broadcaster Ben Shapiro, and many others, all of which led me inexorably to Jordan Peterson, a Professor of Psychology from Toronto University. I was conscious that I was both resisting change and contributing to it at the same time, so I took Peterson's advice to "tell the truth scrupulously" and to express my values and ideas as clearly as possible, causing many problems. Having decided over several years that the basis of

Christian ethics was the Golden Rule, I began to be more outspoken, which led to me being formally silenced and leaving the church in which we had been active for 18 years. As a result, I have become a vocal critic of "progressive cultural Marxism" and its influence on the church, on politics, and public life generally, where previously I would have tried to maintain a more accommodating position or have said nothing at all.

Just before you start to doubt my orthodoxy, I would like to say that while I have taken inspiration from many sources, I am really a contrarian, grumpy old Bible-basher who has staked his life on the Lordship of Jesus Christ, but I have discovered many other points of view that send me back to the Bible for re-assurance only to find a much bigger picture than I first imagined.

Freedom, for the sake of freedom

My concern is about what will happen down the track as the influence of Christianity is increasingly forced to the boundaries of mainstream thought and behavior in Western democracies. My concern is not to preserve the features of democracy for its own sake, because I make no claims for it being more than a political system, nor about it being the highest possible form of social organization, as Marxism does, for example. I do, however, find capitalistic democracy to imperfectly align with Christianity as it is a result of freedom, which I understand to be intrinsic and fundamental to the gospel of Jesus Christ who, at the beginning of his mission, stated his purpose in these words: *He has sent me to proclaim freedom for the prisoners and recovery of sight for the blind, to set the oppressed free* (Lk 4:18). Indeed, according to the Apostle Paul, our mission is to give freedom for the sake of freedom. (Gal 5.1) as Jesus said to his fellow Jews who had believed him, "If you hold to my teaching, you are really my disciples. Then you will know the truth, and the truth will set you free. (Jn 8: 31-32). This is the goal and intended outcome of Christianity. It is not just a coincidence for which we must thank democracy, capitalism or some other aspect of the Western lifestyle, although they obviously all play a part. Developed nations that have adopted the patterns of the democratic West – even if not all its values – have increased their citizen's life spans from the biblical standard of three score years and ten, to well over 80 years in most, and as high as 85 years in some. I accept that life-span is not an absolute indicator of freedom, but it does suggest, in my view, that a result of personal, social and political behaviors and structures that I describe as "life giving" do extend the productive and satisfying years of life. I rest my case with the observation that millions of people from what I describe as "oppressed" and non-Christian cultural backgrounds have made it their life goal to escape as refugees to Western democratic countries. Actually, the highest good, as we will discover, is not what we get, but what we give. Nor will we ever discover freedom by asserting our rights. This is not to say that we have no rights to assert, because as I will explain later, my view is that to "love ourselves" as the Golden Rule suggests we must, obliges us to make our point of view known, but to do it in such a way as to add light, rather than darkness. I believe that the arrogant assertion of individual rights is ultimately destructive because my rights may be opposed to yours. The Golden Rule, however, is not the assertion of rights so much as the demand that we individually take the initiative to treat others as we would want to be treated, *if my rights were fully asserted by you.* As you can see, this provides us with many dilemmas that I hope we can resolve together, so that we can apply them to ourselves.

As I promised earlier, my proposal in this book is that we undertake an actual journey toward a real place where we will meet many fellow-travellers. We may also meet a few vagabonds on the road who would distract us if they could, so we need to be aware of their tricks. I also promise that this proposal is a genuine offer of relationship. It is not an ideology or wishful thinking dressed up in other clothes, as so many religions and movements are. Nor am I offering something that is not mine to give. The destination I mentioned – Paradise – is such a good place because of who we meet when we get there. We will be welcomed at the gate by Peter, as I mentioned and then, when we get inside, we will meet Jesus. It is meeting him on arrival that this journey is all about. Certainly, just getting to the place is something to look forward to, but the real objective of the journey is to meet Jesus and his (our) extended family, which we can do along the way.

Obstacles on the road to freedom

My concern is that many of the "progressive" ideas and activities that are aggressively displacing traditional Christian belief and practice have the opposite effect to what they claim for themselves. Plus, they are significantly life-denying. I believe that I have a duty to my grandchildren and my country to warn against what I see as harmful to their best interests, and to encourage them to make choices that will lead to satisfaction and fulfilment with good things. Even so, my objective is not just to prove my case as to the harmfulness of various beliefs or life choices, because the list of them is endless; and as soon as I have eliminated one, another raises its head. Rather, my goal is to put forward an alternative way of thinking and being, a new beginning and a new objective that is not just intellectually sound. I simply ask that you put my proposition of the Golden Rule to the test in your own life.

Oh! I almost forgot. We will have a travelling companion – a very strange and elusive person who seems to come and go unannounced. He told me with a wry look that his name is Smokey, but I think he was joking, so I will just call him S for short.

References and Footnotes

As this is not intended to be a scholarly book my use of references and footnotes does not follow an academic standard. Rather, as the book is an account of my thoughts and life experiences relating to the Golden Rule, references are provided to enable readers to follow my sources.

I frequently use Wikipedia as a source of information and references because I like the succinct way that Wikipedia gets to the point and summarizes complex issues as it reflects a consensus, more than an exact science. Where greater rigour is required, I have tried to use more authoritative sources, or I make it obvious that I am expressing my opinion.

Similarly, I often refer to a YouTube video with just the URL address. This reflects my experience as to how I have done some of my research by watching YouTube. My experience leads me to believe that we have begun a knowledge and communication revolution where I can become a consumer and a creator of on-line content, that will be equal in its effect to the printing press and the Gutenberg Bible.

Bible references

All Bible references are to the New International Version unless otherwise noted.

Publisher

Michael Murphy of Freedom Publishing Books is responsible for this book as he encouraged me to write it. In the ordinary events of life, there can be no greater source of motivation than for someone to believe in us and encourage us to have a go.

Family and friends

Much of this book is about my experience within my family and friends. This is where we learn the real stuff of life so that we equip each other to go into the world and make our own way well enough

Introduction

prepared that we can not only survive but to thrive. My deep gratitude goes to my wife, Elaine, my children Bobbi-Jane, Brock and Cassandra, their spouses, children, in-laws, aunties, uncles, cousins and many others who make up this rich tapestry.

BunchOBlokes

BunchOBlokes is a project to create free, on-line discussion material from men's groups that grew out of what will always be known as Stan's men's group. Stan Hankins was a typically generous North Carolinian expatriate who invited a group of blokes into his home for a Bible/discussion group. The first hour was always spent around the kitchen table laden with food prepared by Gigi, where we discussed sport, politics, work, wisdom etc, and how the Bible makes sense of all these interests. Anyone who benefits from this book owes a debt of gratitude to Stan and Gigi Hankins for starting what became the BunchOBlokes project out of my interest in providing workable answers for this group, from the Bible and the Golden Rule in particular.

Acknowledgements to my teachers and encouragers

Elaine has been my best friend and fellow traveller for almost 55 years. She is Mum to our three children, Bobbi-Jane, Brock and Cassandra and Nana to our five grandchildren. My encouragers and teachers include Julian Clarke, David Wraight and the BunchOBlokes blokes Mal Cocking, Brett Cardwell (who has drawn the pictures in this book) and Ben Pleysier. Others include Bob Pearson, Mal Garvin, Bob Mumford, NT Wright, Dallas Willard, Ben Witherington, Mark Galli, Katrina Lambert, Matt Williams, and many more fellow travellers. I must also mention George Eldon Ladd whose book, A Theology of thr New Testament, I read so long ago I had forgotten it until I recently rediscovered it in my library, and realized the extent to which he has influenced my for the past 30 or so years.

I would like to pay a special tribute to Phil Munday who supported our BunchOBlokes and BunchOKids projects, from which I have learned so much about the Golden Rule. Phil's generosity has encouraged many lives on their journey toward the amazing Kingdom of God, including mine.

Warren Mills
March 2019

Prelude: The Dream

For many years, each Easter, our family used to go camping in the high country of Victoria. I remember fondly how we would sit around the embers of a log fire in the chill air, late at night, drinking Billy tea and eating freshly-made scones with jam and cream. Even later, when the camp was silent apart from the sound of the creek and someone snoring, I would get up to answer nature's call and gaze at the brilliant Easter sky, looking back to the past, and filled with hope for the future. Stargazing while standing in the freezing Easter night became my de facto celebration of Christ's passion.

One of the greatest visions of the future the world has heard was proclaimed in Washington in 1963 when Martin Luther King Jr rallied thousands, demanding jobs and freedom for farm workers. During his speech, King began to flounder with his prepared words when one of his entourage, the world-renowned gospel singer Mahalia Jackson, sensed the moment and shouted, "Tell them about the dream, Martin!" King went on to create history, uttering some of the most powerful and beloved words ever spoken.

> *I still have a dream. It is a dream deeply rooted in the American dream. I have a dream that one day this nation will rise up, live out the true meaning of its creed: I hold these truths to be self-evident, that all men are created equal.*

Mahalia Jackson had supported many of King's rallies and also shared the dream, and with her singer's lyrical instinct, she knew the right words for the occasion, so she encouraged him to say them. Rising to the occasion, King went on to quote words of hope based on Isaiah 40:3-5.

> *I have a dream today...I have a dream that one day every valley shall be raised up, every mountain and hill made low; the rough ground shall become level, the rugged places a plain. And the glory of the* LORD *will be revealed, and all flesh will see it together.*

Five years later on April 3, 1968, at Mason Temple church – the day before he was assassinated in Memphis, Tennessee – Martin Luther King had another vision. He said:

> *Well, I don't know what will happen now. We've got some difficult days ahead. But it really doesn't matter with me now, because I've been to the mountaintop. And I don't mind. Like anybody, I would like to live – a long life; longevity has its place. But I'm not concerned about that now. I just want to do God's will. And He's allowed me to go up to the mountain. And I've looked over. And I've seen the Promised Land. I may not get there with you. But I want you to know tonight, that we, as a people, will get to the Promised Land. So I'm happy, tonight. I'm not worried about anything. I'm not fearing any man. Mine eyes have seen the glory of the coming of the Lord.*

Although King had a prescient awareness of his fate, he was unafraid because he had seen the future, and knew he had a place there. His bold rhetoric and activism were inspired by his faith in the Lordship of Jesus which is established both in history and in the present reality of King's experience. The disparity between the future glory and the current reality of oppression of his people both appalled him and motivated him to continue to act as he did. In so doing, he had integrated the past with the present and the future, using the Bible's account of the Kingdom of God as his framework and his hope.

But this future is not just reserved for a few luminaries such as Martin Luther King. If you and I want to, we also can share it, and feel confident that there is a place in it for us, because we have seen into the past which allows us to see the future. This is not just a matter of "seeing" with an eye of faith in *unseen things hoped for*, of which Hebrews 11:1 assures us. It is more tangible than that. When we gaze into the night sky and see the Milky Way, we are looking back at least 26,000 light years toward the centre of our galaxy. We see only a small part of one system that comprises between 100-400 billion stars, which itself is part of another cluster of galaxies. The awesome beauty of the night sky is wonderful enough; but now we can see images from the Hubble telescope of incomprehensible grandeur. This vision – which has existed, so we are told, for billions of years – should reassure us that we can expect it to continue for a few billion years more, or perhaps, for all eternity.

Dimensions of the Glory of God's Kingdom

Despite its unfathomable grandeur, the physical scope of the universe is only one aspect of the wondrousness of God's Kingdom; for God exists outside time and space, and his glory has dimensions which, though they are beyond the grasp of our limited understanding, still somehow reach into our needy hearts.

In view of this overwhelming beauty and wonder, how do we make our way in the material world of the 21st century? – a time in which we seem to think we already know almost everything worth knowing with the aid of science when our position should be our increasing awe at the complexity and scope of the universe. My view of reality is like Martin Luther King's in that, on one hand, the world seems to be in a state of growing confusion and despair while, on the other, we can see a tiny glimpse of God's grandeur and goodness manifest in his handiwork in time and space, and in human hearts. If we agree that the material world is complex, what thought do we give to complexity of the human body, soul and spirit?

But none of this wonderment about the physical world of time and space represents anything like the totality of who God is, how he acts, or what his purposes are. We have been invited now to engage with him and experience his love and transforming power in many ways for the benefit of the totality of our being. According to 2 Cor 4: 6-7

> *For God, who said, "Let light shine out of darkness," made his light shine in our hearts to give us the light of the knowledge of God's glory displayed in the face of Christ. But we have this treasure in jars of clay to show that this all-surpassing power is from God and not from us.*

Treasure in jars of clay

Even as we admit our limitations as "treasure in jars of clay," we wonder what to do. If we cannot fully comprehend the extent of reality that we can see, is it then necessary to rely upon God, who we cannot see, to determine if our hope will be fulfilled? Is he our best bet? We already know without having to be reminded that we as individuals cannot solve our problems alone. We are social beings who need to relate to others to live productive and fulfilling lives. So, who will help us? How do we resolve this dilemma without faith, without trusting in someone or something greater than us? Must this remain wishful thinking, something that I can ignore, satisfying myself with naïve ignorance? No! We do not need to resort to vague notions or leaps of faith. Rather, as we take each small risk that faith demands, so we can *taste and see that the Lord is good*, by responding to his invitation and trusting him, one small step of faith at a time.

Such difficult questions were enough to motivate Martin Luther King to the point that he was prepared to invest his life in pursuit of a dream for the benefit of other people, because he could look back on what he had gained so far as a measure of what was possible, and yet to come. He realized an almost incomprehensible truth: that the greatest goal a person can aspire to is to commit his whole life to a cause – a vision so fantastic, and so improbable, that it would change the course of history. I believe that King glimpsed the infinitude and grandeur of the elements and scope of God's Kingdom through what I describe as the Arc of the Universe. For when I grasp these by faith and by sight, I have made progress in my relationship to God as I recognize that I can trust him totally as the source of goodness and love.

Even as I make this confession, my sense of purposefulness is rising as I connect with an intrinsic need within me – especially when I re-read the Apostle's words:

> ...*the knowledge of God's glory displayed in the face of Christ,* and I realize what Paul also knew: *To them God has chosen to make known… the glorious riches of this mystery, which is Christ in you, the hope of glory* (Col 1:27).

This is not just an imagination of a deity that I trust in. It is a real historical person who laughed and wept and enjoyed food and drink and the company of his friends.

Now I am really on the horns of a dilemma. To have hope, I must invest myself in the God of my dreams. For my hope to be realized, I must trust what the Bible meant for the men and women of history who invested their trust in the God of their dreams. What do my instincts tell me to do? I am going to go with Jesus, the great teacher of human history, because I trust in him, his history and his word. How can I be certain unless I test him and his promises, by obeying him and doing what he commanded us to do?

> *To love God with our heart, mind, soul and strength, and my neighbor as myself.*

Jesus, friend of thieves and tax collectors

But wait! Just before I take the next step, I must disclose my lingering doubts. It is one thing for me to put my faith in Jesus; but do I know what I am getting into? I am not the sharpest knife in the drawer. Am I up to the standards he requires? Can I meet the test? The answer is both *no* and *yes*. He does not expect me to be what I am not. Despite this, he offers me the opportunity to become like him, to *share the mind of Christ* (Phil 2:1-3) by a process of transformation that he supervises and empowers by his spirit, subject to my willingness to take each lesson. I am encouraged when I remember that Jesus was accused of being a friend of thieves and outcasts, (Matt 9:10-11) provided they were willing to accept his invitation on his terms. Plus, we know that his disciples have not always been saints. Martin Luther King was an adulterer who gave his enemies plenty of reasons to doubt his bona fides, while his namesake, the great reformer of the church, Martin Luther, declared himself to be *Against the Murderous, Thieving Hordes of Peasants,* and was perhaps responsible for their revolt and the death of many.[1] It is when I take this last step of faith in Jesus that my dream begins to materialize. Then, my dream of the Arc of the Universe and the Glory of God reaching down to include me becomes true – a dream inspired by Martin Luther King that also applies to me and you, with all our faults.

---

1 https://en.wikipedia.org/wiki/Against_the_Murderous,_Thieving_Hordes_of_Peasants

Prelude: The dream

The Arc of the Universe

The Arc of the Universe is a re-occurring theme that has captivated me for many years. I first became aware of the concept from the writings of the mathematician, philosopher and theologian A.N. Whitehead, who proposed that our relationship with God involves a process of "teleological" or purposeful activities through which we participate in God's emerging creation. Whitehead's "process theology" proposes a symbiotically creative relationship between God and humankind in which we create the future together, within God's teleological framework.[2] After studying this idea for many years, I became aware that its modern interpretation is pantheistic with no room for the crucified Jesus of my childhood, so I stopped reading and thinking about it. However, I have continued to wonder about Whitehead himself, comparing him to current advocates of process theology. For example, I find that Whitehead's paper "Religion in the Making"[3] assists my understanding of how we respond to God – to my great personal benefit, because he expanded my vision of what the Bible suggests God has in store for us. I hope that you may also catch glimpses of his thought in these pages.

> *As I approached the top of this arc, it was as if time stood still, and I was flooded with both emotion and awareness.*
>
> Ron Garan.

My thinking about Whitehead and others like him does not provide me with every solution to the imponderables of Christian faith because, in my view, there are many questions that cannot be answered rationally; they can only begin to be answered by faith. Whitehead does provide, however – as does Jordan Peterson –

---

2 AN Whitehead, *Process and Reality*.
3 alfrednorthwhitehead.wwwhubs.com/ritm1.htm

another point of view or way for us to see ourselves in relationship to each other and to God, which I will examine in more detail in Interlude 1.

I experience the Arc of the Universe as the largest possible picture of the material, temporal and spatial reality that I can hold in my imagination. The Bible describes it magnificently in many places such as in Isaiah 43:24-25:

> *I am the* LORD, *the Maker of all things, who stretches out the heavens, who spreads out the earth by myself, who foils the signs of false prophets and makes fools of diviners, who overthrows the learning of the wise and turns it into nonsense...*

Martin Luther King Jr also said, "The arc of the moral Universe is long and it bends toward justice".[1] Perhaps the most powerful words used to describe this concept are those of an astronaut, Ron Garan, who, following a 2008 space-walk said:

---

[1] From an article by Martin Luther King, Jr. printed in "The Gospel Messenger" periodical in 1958.

Prelude: The dream

As I approached the top of this arc, it was as if time stood still, and I was flooded with both emotion and awareness. But as I looked down at the Earth-this stunning, fragile oasis, this island that has been given to us and that has protected all life from the harshness of space-a sadness came over me and I was hit in the gut with an undeniable, sobering contradiction.[2]

This is the "overview effect", and it has been reported by an astonishing number of visitors to space.[3] The best expression of this vision of the universe, though, is not found in words but in photos of ultra-deep space from the Hubble Space Telescope showing thousands of colorful lights resembling M&M chocolate buttons against the canvas of the black sky. At first glance, we might assume that the buttons are planets, but they are not; they are far-off galaxies, of which there are countless millions. Maybe billions. This is an image of wonder, hope and awe, or possibly of fear. It gives us the sense that the material world of time and space we can see with our eyes is so immense and incomprehensibly beautiful and apparently fragile and yet enduring, so infinitely complex, and so perfectly organized to provide every condition and circumstance necessary to sustain life, that even the great atheist Richard Dawkins agrees that the Cosmos "appears to be fine-tuned to support life".[4] Indeed. But if the material world is so complex, how can we dismiss the complexity of human body, soul and spirit so easily when there is so much evidence to the contrary?

Each chapter of this book contains a progressive reference to and illustration of the Arc of the Universe as I attempt to explain how we become sons and daughters of God and begin to participate in his creative process. This is illustrated by my friend and colleague

---

2 Ron Garan, *The Orbital Perspective*.
3 *The Weekend Australian Review*, December 2-3 2017.
4 REF

Brett Cardwell, who interprets the strange workings of my mind better than I do. As the Arc of the Universe is an aside from the Golden Rule, the concept and its relationship to the Golden Rule are summarized in the Interludes and Postlude, rather than in the body of the text.

1
PREPARATIONS FOR THE ROAD

The longest journey begins with a single step.

—Laozi

In this year, 2019, when we have achieved the dream of global communication and instant access to the inventory of human knowledge, I have written this book in the hope that this wonderful world will be as kind to my grandchildren as it has been to me and my wife Elaine, our children and their spouses: Bobbi and Ben, Brock and Michelle and Cassandra and Karl. I hope that 70 years from now, Chase, Hamish, Taylor, Sara and Josephine, and maybe others yet to arrive, will be able to say that they too have been privileged to live in the best period of history, having experienced the benefits of relative peace, amazing scientific and technological progress, and almost complete freedom to form relationships, to learn, to travel, to dream, to discover, and to design and build businesses, houses, works of art and architecture and machines, as I and my generation have. However, I fear that these freedoms and opportunities are at risk of being diminished because their source in Christian faith and Christ's teaching of his Golden Rule has been displaced from our consciousness due to a host of modern distractions.

I hope that my grandchildren, in the twilight of their lives, will not wonder in despair at the meaning of it all, yearning nostalgically for the golden age of their parents and grandparents, comparing what they have lost to what existed previously. I hope they will always be free to make their own discoveries of love and all good things, experienced and gained by striving, learning, working and cooperating for the common good. I hope that they will be free to learn that progress is not just the result of material wealth, science and technology, since it also requires particular attitudes, values and insights to be rewarding and satisfying, such that each of us might say *life is good* as we drink deeply from its fountain. I am concerned for them and their generation because there are some ominous signs on the horizon that the freedoms I have enjoyed are being reduced, ironically, in the interests of "diversity," "tolerance," "safety" and "equity". I hope that they discover that progress is not guaranteed unless they build their lives on the same foundation of love that I have experienced not just in my family, but in society as a whole. I hope that love will equip them to resist the challenges of selfishness and alternative ideologies that seek to redefine humanity – unless, of course, they discover something better than what human experience has produced so far. But this is something for which I see no evidence and hold no hope.

As G.K. Chesterton reminds us, when we lose our religion, it is not as though we believe in nothing, but we will make anything into an object of worship. This current Western generation is no different. As we abandon formal religion, we invent new religions, often a projection of our ego as our object of worship. Of course, just as most atheists deny that they are religious, so do the so-called "Nones" who say they have no religion, spiritual, secular or otherwise. But you don't have to dig too far to see that they satisfy the non-spiritual definition of religion by revering and arguing about what they value most, which in my opinion, defines religion. Atheists, who believe that there are no gods, generally believe in the ultimacy of science or natural causes for the existence of the material world of time and space which in my view, is the religion you have when you don't have a religion.

Before we rush to judgement to say how pathetic it is to deny one form of religion while creating another with ourselves as its god, we should remember that this applies to all of us, religious or otherwise. Christian religion in its halcyon days in the first few centuries of the Christian era, is full of human frailty. Even now, while some Christians worship money and accomplishment, some others at the opposite end of the spectrum worship self-deprivation and the sacrifice of service, while others invent new sects by claiming that they alone have all the missing ingredients. Even among the mainstream of Christian traditions, there are those who "venerate" images of humans, status or grand ceremony as the central focus of their worship, contrary to the clear instructions of scripture. We all do it, some more than others to our greater or lesser harm. This phenomenon is beautifully explained by Ben Witherington in his YouTube video, *What's wrong with evangelical theology?* where he reflects on this effect within evangelical traditions. I particularly appreciate his statement that the very thing that makes each tradition distinctive, has the least of exegetical and theological support among what Christians share in common according to standards like the Nicene creed.[1]

The zeitgeist

I first began to think about this about seven years ago when I read what I have come to see as a prophetic article written by the

---

1 https://youtu.be/ndJd1XFihe8

Melbourne Herald-Sun newspaper columnist Jill Singer, in which she questioned the value of the extended family. Her question was something to the effect that "If the experience of grandparenthood is so good, where are its advocates?" As I had just become a grandfather for the first time, I had begun to experience some amazing, and unanticipated effects of deep gratitude towards my daughter Bobbi and her husband Ben for being so kind as to give this old man a grandson. Fortunately, I share the joy with my wife of almost 50 years, Elaine, with a real sense of having completed the circle of life together by producing children with productive independent lives, who have produced their own children.

Back to my story – Singer, who has since died at age 60 of AL Amyloidosis, was an award-winning journalist and outspoken feminist critic of the Christian religion; and so it did not surprise me that she would also question another great institution that I hold more and more dear. Although I thought to write a response to her column, I didn't – perhaps because I didn't know whether my experience was just a rush of grandfatherly hormones to the brain or something more profound. But then I remembered my mate from South Australia, Wally Beattie, making similar observations about himself when he became a grandad for the first time. As this new experience grew, I felt more and more that it was I, perhaps, who was a bit unusual, because not many men of my age had remained married long enough to enjoy its fruits with the bride of their youth. As I reflected on the contrast between Singer's cynicism and my enjoyment, I resolved to answer her question by becoming an advocate of this tremendously satisfying experience of life – of being highly invested in passionate family relationships, of the joys of Christian faith, of the value of marriage, and the sheer pleasure that these things bring to a grandfather, and as an explainer of the reasons why these exquisite joys are possible.

I have benefited from many good relationships in my life, from my relationship with my deceased parents and their families, to my relationship with my wife, her parents and her family, plus our extended family, friends and neighbors. All of these relationships enabled me to appreciate this new, unanticipated phase of life. When I reacted to Jill Singer's article, I didn't think she was making a derogatory comment about marriage on philosophical grounds as I thought she was asking a genuine question – perhaps out of her poor experience of family life. Whatever her motivation, I have since discovered that radical feminist rhetoric intends to destroy families and to bring down "patriarchy", ostensibly to elevate the interests of women. Despite all the evidence regarding what's good for individuals and families pointing in the opposite direction, the feminist agenda has been to promote transgressive sexuality. According to Mallory Millett, the sister of a feminist pioneer, Kate Millett, the feminists' strategy is implemented by *"promoting promiscuity, eroticism, prostitution and homosexuality!"*[1] If the only evidence we were to consider is the rise in abortions, then we must acknowledge their success.

My concern is not just to debunk feminism or socialist ideals, or to advocate Western Capitalistic Democracy. Rather, my aim is to warn about what is being lost to "progressive, politically correct" ideologies which, incredibly, have become the "zeitgeist" or the prevailing worldview in Western democracies, displacing a traditional Christian consensus. My purpose is to encourage a fresh understanding of how all relationships are intended to work within the framework of a Christian society and culture – that is, one whose principles are found in the teachings of Jesus Christ. My fear is that modernity, for all its benefits, has obscured these principles and brought us to the point where we are looking over a precipice. Today, we risk losing the best of what humanity has gained.

---

1 *Marxist Feminism's Ruined Lives* by Mallory Millett, http://mallorymillett.com/?p=37

Sharing a secret

This book is a call to people of goodwill to take the initiative to not just curse what they fear as the darkness of the age, but to boldly light a candle of hope by applying the one life-giving principle from which I have benefited and derived so much fulfillment and enjoyment.

My goal is to encourage you to make the same discovery that I and many millions of people have made before me: that the secret of a satisfying life is contained within Christ's Golden Rule, *to treat others as you would want to be treated.* I suggest that this memorably simple challenge – which we already teach our children – contains a profound secret, and that it is impossibly hard to achieve without some serious assistance. I have come to see the Golden Rule as a process of learning about myself, my relationships, my place in the world, and what I should do with my life to make it resolute enough to face inevitable challenges and ultimately satisfy my human needs and potential. In short, the Golden Rule is the way we learn the language of love, the essential elixir of life.

My proposal to accept the challenge offered by the Golden Rule, however, is just a beginning – it is a gradual awakening to the fact that life offers so much more than a series of momentary or even extended pleasures. I believe that we are being prepared for a future that very few of us can comprehend. As the British historian Arnold Toynbee observes in his mammoth study of history, "It is a paradoxical but profoundly true and important principle of life that the most likely way to reach a goal is to be aiming not at that goal itself but at some more ambitious goal beyond it."[1] Do we have such a transcendent goal that will help us to get through the hardships of life? Is there light at the end of the tunnel that will enable us to see the different phases of life from childhood to adulthood and to retirement, each with their different passions, motivations and troubles, so that we don't get to 70, still driven by a pathetic need to demonstrate the sexual prowess of our youth? How do we prepare ourselves to deal with the limits of time and space with the certainty that one day we are going to die? How does my life prepare me for death? Am I living each day thinking that my present life is all that there is? Or do I have a sense that my life now counts toward another far more fulfilling future existence? Furthermore, if I am preparing for a time yet to come, what do I do for such a possibility? If there is an impediment in me that might prevent it, how do I deal with that part of myself that I must destroy if I am to learn to live fully, both now and in a time yet to come?

I intend to paint the biggest possible picture of life and show that we are part of an unimaginable Divine plan in which there is a place for you and me in the unfolding purpose of the cosmos. This book is an invitation to you to engage in a vision that is so big, so fantastic, and so unbelievable that you will need faith to even begin to contemplate it. Not just faith, in fact, but *faith, hope* and *love*. Applying the Golden Rule is hard enough to begin; it is even harder to stay the course if you do not know where you are going.

---

1 Arnold Toynbee, *Mankind and Mother Earth*.

When this hoped-for destination begins to emerge more clearly, the steps on the path and the difficulties that we face become easier and more manageable, if we help each other. This is not just a matter of cooperation, which is fundamental to all relationships, it is also about community; a sense of widely shared responsibility for the welfare of individuals among the group which will emerge as a secondary theme. As we proceed, we become increasingly conscious of who we are, where we live, what we have accomplished, where we are going, who our friends and enemies are, and how to deal with the obstacles we must face along the way. Consciousness, though, can be a burden and lead us to despair if there is not someone there to guide and encourage us. Amazingly, these resources are freely available from other fellow travellers, some of whom I will introduce you to. Some of them you already know. They are your friends, family and others who care for you and with whom you have already had a glimpse of freedom. This is the same vision that inspired Billy Graham, John Wesley, Martin Luther King, Florence Nightingale, Martin Luther, Teresa of Avila, Thomas Aquinas, Augustine of Hippo, Tertullian, Paul the Apostle, Mary, Jesus, Solomon, David, Ruth, Moses, Abraham, Noah, Adam, Lisa Simpson (Bart's sister) and many others. It is this faith, hope and love that liberates us and enables us to fulfil God's law of love, not by grudging compliance or obligation, but as an outcome that is experienced as a result of joy and gratitude.

Love lost

Tragically, some have already lost the ability to see that love is what makes life worth living – love that is experienced in intimate relationships, the joy of loving and being loved in return. Consequently, we are now also at risk of losing the very thing that is the essence and fabric of life. If love is lost, we will not just lose the possibility of full relationship with God and our intimate partners. We will eventually also lose all hope, all beauty, all optimism, all enterprise, all discovery, all courage, all purpose and the ability to choose the good that gives life, as against counterfeit good which is in reality, the knowledge of evil, which promises much but delivers nothing but despair. Most egregiously, atheists add insult to injury when they deny the existence of God because God is love, and we are made in His image. By denying God in one gesture of willful ignorance or defiance, they disconnect themselves from the possibility of ever experiencing love in its fullness, because you cannot experience what you don't believe to be possible. God is not just the source of love, but the very essence of it. Without God, there is no love and no life and no hope. The faint glimmer of love that God-deniers experience is an afterglow, the small deposit left in every being made in his image. This residue of love is a mere flickering candle remaining from past generations who experienced it abundantly – men and women who were inspired by their encounter with love to invest their lives in experiencing all that it had to offer, and who gave their lives for the benefit of others, just as God gave himself to reconcile us to himself.

By any reckoning, we are entering a post-Christian age, as is reflected in the decline of church attendance and Christian influence in Western social and political culture. The grand cathedrals of Europe are empty. Local church buildings have been sold due to lack of use; some are now restaurants, others have become warehouses. Many Christian institutions from past generations struggle in tired despair or have abandoned their Christian roots to become secular, social welfare organizations. Current generations are becoming known as "nones" to indicate their lack of faith in anything religious. Rather, their confidence is in the rationality of science and technology to answer the questions of life. Many are blindly confident that their loss of faith will not cause the gains made previously to be lost, but history suggests otherwise. Am I over-reacting in my assessment? Should I not be more optimistically inclusive, more open to equality and the "progressive agenda," more opposed to "oppressive patriarchy" and more supportive of sexual and gender diversity? I confess that I don't consider abortion, the sexual revolution, the trivialization of marriage, the abuse of children, gender diversity, the legalization of marijuana or the "Ice" epidemic to be progress. By my definition, what is required are clearly described guidelines with enduring benefits for individuals, families and for the common good of society. I contend that they are found in the stories of the Bible, the Ten Commandments and the teachings of Jesus in particular.

Is the Golden Rule a placebo or strong medicine?

One indication as to how greatly the Golden Rule is misunderstood and trivialized is that many people have not even considered what it is; whether it is simply a placebo which pretends to cure and illness or instead a strong medicine which does cure. For example, a regular criticism of the Golden Rule advanced by sceptics is that it represents an imposition of one person's will upon that of another and, as such, that it is a façade of doing the right thing to hide an ulterior motive.

Inversely, when Christians apply the Golden Rule, they assume that because they have good intentions both toward themselves and the other person, the other will automatically be grateful and responsive. A proper understanding of both situations, though, reveals that a person holding either view has yet to begin to understand what the Golden Rule really is and how it works. My experience of applying it is always different from what I first thought it would be because my perception of reality and my consideration of other people is so limited. If I am experienced with the Golden Rule, I will not jump to conclusions as to how it should work for others, or what the results will be in the short term. Rather, I will expect some irony, if not some paradox in the way that my attempt will unfold. Accordingly, with experience, I will be less inclined to jump to conclusions, and be more inclined to trust the process and wait to see what the result will be. An instance of irony is the effect that the Golden Rule has on the assertion of individual rights, which, in many cases, are in direct conflict with the rights of others. When I begin to apply the Golden Rule in its complexity, I realize that as much as my rights are important, they are not absolute. Therefore, I must at least weigh my rights against yours, even when they are in tension, if I am to make any progress at all. Usually, but not always, I will defer to you and allow your rights to predominate over mine, as this is what love requires.

If only…I had learnt the Golden Rule

If you listened to rock-and-roll as a child, you may be familiar with Chuck Berry's 1957 hit LP record, *School Days*, in which learning the Golden Rule is described as equally essential to an education as history and practical math:

> *Up in the morning and out to school*
> *The teacher is teaching the Golden Rule*

How Good is the Golden Rule?

> *American history and practical math*
> *You studying hard and hoping to pass*
> *Working your fingers right down to the bone*
> *And the guy behind you won't leave you alone*
> *Ring, ring goes the bell...*
>
> *...Hail, hail rock and roll*
> *Deliver me from the days of old*
> *Long live rock and roll*
> *The beat of the drums, loud and bold*
> *Rock, rock, rock and roll*
> *The feeling is there, body and soul.*[1]

There is no doubt that the rock-and-roll generation, of which I am part, made good use of our school days, becoming the most highly educated people in history. But one thing is certain. We did not really learn to apply the Golden Rule. If only we had, things might have turned out differently than they have. Certainly, if I had learned more "Golden Rule lessons" earlier in life, I might have avoided repeating some of the mistakes that I have made over and over.

The American philosopher and linguist Noam Chomsky says that the Golden Rule is a "...double universal. Everybody says they believe in it, but nobody does it".[2] Chomsky is suggesting that this universal maxim, best summarized by Jesus' saying, *treat others as you want to be treated,* has never fulfilled its promise as the basis of good relationships between people in all situations of life because although it is acknowledged as a good idea, people don't commit themselves to its use because it is hard to do and if they had, history

---

1 Songwriter: Chuck Berry. School Days lyrics © Universal Music Publishing Group

2 Noam Chomsky. *The Golden Rule* YouTube. https://youtu.be/6Jq0q6fTKo4

would have turned out differently. So where does the problem lie: with the principle or with us?

My question is this. If we had learned the Golden Rule and shared it with others, which demands personal accountability to acknowledge the ultimate value of each person expecting nothing in return, by extending fairness, empathy, tolerance and dignity, sharing more of the abundance of the world's resources more equally, how would the world have turned out different than it is today? In the past 300 years since the enlightenment began, there has been an endless continuity of experiments to achieve this goal, but none has succeeded in creating the sort of paradise they promised. Although they promised to save the world, they did exactly the opposite, and resulted in the deaths of many millions of people. But still we persist with "progressive" ideologies, many from the enlightenment period when the religious "superstitions" of history were replaced with new ideas that would revolutionize human existence. Despite knowing from recent history that these ideas did not work, we still persist. Why is this so? Why do modern societies continue down this path, despite new ideology, science, reason and politics repeatedly failing to provide a solution to the problems faced by humanity? Are we not proving Albert Einstein's statement that madness is to do the same thing repeatedly, while expecting a different result?

What then is this thing that everyone knows, but nobody does? As I will explain in Chapter 2, there are many versions of the Golden Rule from many diverse cultures. The one that interests me most is attributed to Jesus Christ and appears in several versions in the Bible. The most common is *to treat others as you would have them treat you*. I contend that all biblical examples are variations on *the law of love*, as this law summarizes the essential nature of God as the source and essence of love, as well as his relationship to us and what he expects of us, his creation.

The Golden Rule as the ethical foundation for a full and satisfying life.

Using the Golden Rule as an approach to life, love and hope was developed by myself and my friend David Wraight, as the basis for writing our BunchOBlokes series of men's group discussion guides.[1] We began with the Golden Rule to encourage men to improve their relationships and to find their way into the gospel of Jesus. Of course, there is more to discovering the gospel than just the Golden Rule, so our focus here must include discussion about our need for reconciliation with God by our acceptance of Jesus and our transformation into his likeness.

BunchOBlokes discussions are guided by the Golden Rule, presented as an ethical, spiritual and behavioral foundation for life and the way a good life is realized. It consists of the ordinary aspirations and pleasures of living: relationships, marriage, sex, children, families, fun, food, wine, learning, music, art, work, creativity, innovation, exploration, discovery, health, wealth, comfort, entertainment and sleep. However, if life does not include love, then none of it is meaningful or satisfying. Love is enjoyed in relationships including marriage, family, friends and neighbors where daily routines come alive with purpose and satisfaction. However, love transcends our individual passions and aspirations when we discover love for God which emanates from loving others as we love ourselves, because love is the glue that keeps the Cosmos together. This is a mystery that has taken me a lifetime to understand and a whole book to explain that ultimately, the message of Jesus is to find our place in God's purpose for his creation. The Golden Rule is how we discover the mechanism and scope of this wonderful good news. It is therefore also a corrective to the post-modern malaise of nihilism which denies God's existence, his ultimate reality and his truth and any sense of

---

[1] www.bunchoblokes.org

a purpose in life other than wealth, power, pleasure, comfort and advantage, while aggressively protecting our increasingly fragile self-esteem. This book, then, is not a sociological, psychological or even a religious analysis. It is a plea to come to Jesus and obey his commands because in doing so, we discover life in its fullness.

The Golden Rule is Christ's command to us

The Golden Rule is nothing less than a method by which we obediently, purposefully and consciously begin to rediscover and restore our place in God's kingdom by relearning the language of love. It is what John meant when he said;

> God is love and he who abides in love abides in God and God abides in Him (1 Jn 14 :6).

It is Jesus' Great Commandment, in which he says so clearly;

> Love the Lord your God with all your heart and with all your soul and with all your mind. This is the first and greatest commandment. And the second is like it: Love your neighbor as yourself. All the Law and the Prophets hang on these two commandments (Matt 26: 37-40).

I hope to convince you that this statement is the greatest unmediated, unconditional, objective, imperative, and explicit command from Jesus, who is God incarnate. It was given to his disciples (including us) for our personal acceptance and decision to begin to practise the Golden Rule and to persistently apply it to every person to whom we relate and will relate in the future. To achieve this goal, I pray that the Golden Rule will become the conscious principle that guides every Christian's thought, utterance and action. If this were the case, the Christian church, and therefore the whole world, would become radically transformed, renewed and revitalized. I am not claiming that to consciously apply the Golden Rule is the only way we can come to God and find a place of fulfilment and purpose, as I know there are other paths, as God *rewards those who seek him* (Heb 11:6). However, if we are conscious that this is God's command, then it is the path we must take.

Our goal in life, then, should be to prepare ourselves as much as we can contribute to a relationship with God, which results in nothing less than our transformation into the image of Christ by the renewal of our minds. In other words, our obedience to the Golden Rule is how we enter a process of incarnation, and become like Jesus, who died for us. However, several people have ,perhaps unwisely, said to me that they already love God, or that when they love God, they will be able to love others, but John reverses this claim and says;

> *Whoever claims to love God yet hates a brother or sister is a liar. For whoever does not love their brother and sister, whom they have seen, cannot love God, whom they have not seen* (1 Jn 4:20).

Even allowing for some hyperbole in these words, if we think that we already love God or are already remade into the image of Christ, we should be very careful about making the claim that we love God as Jesus said we must, *with all our heart, soul, mind and strength,* because the implication of this love, is that we are prepared to come and die with him. This suggests to me, that while I should desire to love God and become like Jesus, I should allow him to lead me as I follow obediently, rather than to make claims I am not qualified to make.

If Jesus' commands are so important, why are we not taught them?

The powers of evil have an investment in ensuring that we do not discover God's love. I am aware that even this statement will be objectionable to many because the possibility of there being evil forces has been discredited by secular and some religious teaching. However, I will attempt to show you that the disfunction in society and the malevolence in individual people is an evil force that seeks to influence us. I am motivated to address the general ignorance and misunderstanding of both the source of evil and Christ's remedy for it within the Christian church because I know what ignorance feels like. Despite Jesus making the Golden Rule his great command, the church has paid it insufficient attention as a foundation for teaching and preaching, and therefore, as our strategy for spiritual growth against evil. My interest in the Golden Rule grew over many years, during which I barked up a few wrong religious trees before I tried to prioritize the same things that Jesus prioritized. Often, when discussing this view with fellow Christians, I found a strange resistance to the suggestion that the Golden Rule is even important by comparison to Bible knowledge, prayer and devotion, evangelism and the like. This observation is supported by the lack of sermons I have heard on the Golden Rule as compared to sermons and books about faith, for example. A brief search of a preaching resource site, sermoncentral.com, is instructive. The topic on "Faith" gets 109,475 hits, "prayer", 66,101 hits, "prosperity", 9330, "missions", 21,247, and the "Golden Rule" – a mere 31 hits. I find this to be perplexing as Jesus warned specifically against the perils related to evangelism, missions, false discipleship, prayer, tithing and other subjects that we accept unquestioningly as being part of the Christian agenda. We should notice, however, that Jesus never speaks against the one thing that he said contained

"the whole of the law and prophets" (Matt 22:40).

Widespread ignorance concerning the Golden Rule has allowed it to be misused by the opponents of religion. Often their reference to the Golden Rule indicates to me a lack of understanding as to its meaning, mainly because of the redefinition of the word "love", which I believe has been used to undermine the foundations of society. My view, as I will explain in Chapter 5, is that the post-modern, politically correct view of love, though it refers to "inclusiveness", "fairness" " tolerance" and "equity", is almost the polar opposite of what it claims to be. Fairness and equity are only available when we, as individuals, accept responsibility for our lives and make ourselves accountable to God by implementing Christ's Golden Rule personally and socially, even if imperfectly, and understand the meaning of love as Christ intended it.

In my view, every sermon and every word of teaching spoken in a Christian church should be summarized or prefaced, either implicitly or explicitly, with reference to the Golden Rule rather than the socially just, politically correct, feel good, get rich and become famous pernicious waffle by which we have been seduced into a post-Christian stupor. Neither must we return to the "Judeo-Christian tradition" or "family values," but to the life-transforming message of Jesus that allows us to

> *"be contented with so much liberty against other men, as he would allow other men against himself,"* (which Thomas Hobbes) *"...used as the basic principle for a peaceful society."* [1]

Learning hard lessons

Separation of church and state is an important idea that prevents the tyranny of absolute power as Lord Acton noted. However, secularists, in their misplaced zeal to enforce this separation, have created a false divide whereby every truth identified by religion is diminished and dismissed out of hand, and replaced with a half-baked secular facsimile. This must stop if we are to regain

---

1   Jeffrey Wattles, *The Golden Rule*, quoting Thomas Hobbes. p. 77.

our rapidly diminishing freedom to choose love for ourselves and for society. We should not return to the previous situation of the church having authority over the state; but the voice of faith, hope and love should be given equal status to rationality in the public square. One of the most difficult lessons to learn is that life is difficult and made more so by the extent to which Christians are held in self-imposed delusion as captives to our secular culture. A we will examine in Chapter 6, we have a fundamental problem accepting hardship, particularly when we need to learn hard lessons about ourselves. I believe that perhaps the greatest difference that the Golden Rule makes to us is that it teaches us about the need for trust, obedience, humility and self-sacrifice. But it is not what we think. The challenge is not to do with fasting, self-discipline, tithing or giving to the poor, as important as these things are. Rather, it is related to our preparedness to face the deceptions of our own ego and willingly submit to what I describe as "ego death". This is a powerful and subtle irony. The very thing about ourselves that we consider a strength is a weakness. The thing that we consider to be a weakness is in fact a strength – if we can learn this difficult lesson as an outcome of Divine inspiration, or as a result of obedience to God. This lesson, I believe, cannot be learned any other way. In later chapters, I will explain in more detail how our engagement with the Golden Rule enables us to face our human limitations and failings, not just to overcome them with self-discipline as we should, but to gain the humility required to see our desperate need for transformation into the image of Christ to do what we cannot do alone. We know that God's grace comes to us only when we are humble enough to receive it, as it is by the power of his Spirit and by his grace that we are transformed into His image.

The cure

A wise teacher once said to me that *"things always get better and worse at the same time"*, which I have found to be true. We are currently witnessing unbelievable progress in the science and technology of knowledge and communications, medicine and health, transport and travel, as well as rapid advances in food production and distribution that are helping to reduce malnutrition in the developing world. However, amid this progress, the first world is showing signs of stress and decline, particularly regarding the failure of relationships within families and in the wider culture where mental disorders, suicide, security threats, despair and nihilism infiltrate daily life. Many other changes widely considered as "progress", such as those to abortion, euthanasia laws and gender confusion, suggest to me that we are losing a sense of the value and sanctity of human life and of our accountability to God. This is because the most fundamental principles of humanity are not determined by science. They are exclusively related to the condition of the human soul and our relationship to God and to each other.

The solution to this malaise, so desperately needed in my view, is to go back to the point of departure – to when we began to lose the sense of value of relationships – and begin again by reinvesting in the Golden Rule. Most people of my generation who have lived in the Western democratic world have had access to wonderful opportunities based upon our Judeo-Christian heritage that permitted such progress because, according to the philosopher, A.N. Whitehead,

> *"We have discovered an orderly and purposeful creation because we believed in an orderly and purposeful creator",*[1]

a creator whose being defines the source and reality of all good by his declaration of his love for us. I believe that each generation must discover for itself that love is an essential universal force for the good, as essential to life as gravity. I believe that the modern

---

1 AN Whitehead, *Process and Reality*.

quest to dispense with God has resulted in a plethora of alternative beliefs. And now, in the interest of accommodating all of them, we are increasingly being restricted as to how much we say about this one source of goodness, as it is undemocratically exclusive, blocking the possibility of alternative sources of wisdom and challenging the notion that there can be only one God and one definition of "the good". If I am right, the risk is that as love is lost, so many other competing ideologies emerge as faith in God moves down the hierarchy of popular values, each one a further dilution of its predecessor, each one leading us one step closer to despair.

I believe that we have left behind the one godly command that we need for our individual and universal satisfaction and fulfilment. The Golden Rule. And if we understand its value, we will recapture it not just by becoming conscious of what we have lost, but by doing what it requires without delay. First, we need to repair our most personal intimate relationships so that we have less regret about lost opportunities, lost family and friends and, if possible, fewer enemies, or people who hate us. This does not mean that we need only to apologize for all that we have done wrong, because words are cheap. It does mean, however, that we have to act differently toward each other, especially toward family members and friends who already care for us. If we can accomplish this, then we need to turn our vision further outward and to include our enemies—not necessarily to agree with them, but to want what we think of as being good for ourselves to apply to them.

This is no easy solution. In fact, in some cases it will not work at all, but that is the reality we have to accept after we have given it our best shot. This is not blind obedience to God that many have already rejected as a fait accompli. Rather, it is the first reasonable step in a process of learning how to be on good terms with each other and within ourselves, as an antidote to self-loathing and despair. Our engagement with the Golden Rule will lead us further and deeper toward discovering that it not only works because it helps us to understand ourselves and our world more, but because it leads us to the source of life, and to the realization that God is love.

I am not advocating a return to a notion of Christendom where the church rules the state. Far from it, because I know that power corrupts, even despite our best intentions. I agree with the Australian Aboriginal leader, Noel Pearson, who points to Martin Luther's doctrine of the two kingdoms as the basis for *"the modern model that distinguishes theocracy from pluralist democracy"*. In my view, the two ideologies must be held in tension to keep each other in check.[1] In keeping with this necessary tension between the two kingdoms, I intend both to warn and to encourage my audience. Even though I don't want to be a purveyor of doom, I believe I

---

1 Between the church and the state, let's value common decency. The Weekend Australian October 13-14 2018.

Preparations for the road

must ring the bell of warning to face a challenge as old as humanity itself. As much as this generation is ignorant of the biblical concept of sin and denies the reality of it being the manifestation of evil in us, I believe we are witnessing humankind's continuing fall from grace, which began in the Garden of Eden. This breach in the relationship between us and God occurs daily, and in every dark corner of society, because, as Aleksandr I. Solzhenitsyn writes, *"the line dividing good and evil cuts through the heart of every human being"*.[2] If this is true, then the solution I am proposing depends on what you and I do next, because there is no other universal solution to our predicament than to treat each other as children of the same father. There is no possibility of us being redeemed as a culture or as a group, because salvation is exclusively one person at a time. A spiritual awakening may be a big event within a society, but if it is to be useful, its result must be an aggregation of individual souls responding to their maker's intended purpose for their lives.

The Golden Rule in its simplest form is *to treat others as we would have them treat us.* Although several variations have appeared

---

2 The Gulag Archipelago 1918-1956.

in the cultures and religions of human history, it reaches its apogee as a maxim in Jesus' teachings, known as the Great Command. Despite Jesus' endorsement of it, however, the Golden Rule in its most basic form is non-religious and may be implemented initially without reference to God. Based on my seven decades' experience as a Christian and my understanding of the Bible, history and contemporary thinking, I argue that the Golden Rule is a universal divine command which provides the ethical foundation for all relationships and human aspiration. I propose that we must become more conscious of natural laws that govern the human soul so that we can observe and reflect God's purposes revealed historically and personally in his interaction with us. As we become aware of the integration of compassion, mercy and justice in God's character, so we realize that this is the basis of all relationships and the means of resolution of good and evil in our personal and social lives. Moral principles that emerge in this way are not mere abstractions. Rather, they are concrete beliefs and decisions guided by God's commands and verified by our small steps of faith. The Golden Rule is the most fundamental ethical formula that contradicts the common belief that our behavior is just the result of evolution, or that the good is an accumulation of human wisdom.

If, on the other hand, we choose to ignore the Golden Rule, we will experience increasing life-denying disintegration, confusion, despair, and eventually the death of the human soul. The Golden Rule is therefore an antidote to our anxiety and accelerating despair resulting from the loss of Christian heritage as it is displaced by nihilism in its many forms. By consciously applying the Golden Rule we learn about our relationship to God as an extension of our relationship with each other which is the basis of all human satisfaction and hope.

PS.

I thought you might enjoy an irony to close this chapter. I recently met Geoff King on his daily walk into the city. He asked me what I did, so I told him. The next day, he sent me the following letter to the editor of the Herald-Sun newspaper, commenting on a recent national enquiry regarding the behavior of Australia's biggest banks. It is headed: **Golden rule fits all.**

> *I'm appalled at the comment from a NAB CEO (National Australia Bank) that "it all depends on your definition of ethics." I'm a few years older than him, but I am sure he would have heard of the golden rule that may be paraphrased here: "Do to others as you would have them do to you." This has been and still remains the core of judgement in our societal (which includes business) behavior. It is also the common thread through the majority of religions. It is not the golden rule as per Aluddin where the thief says to Aladdin the golden rule is "he who owns the gold rules." Maybe our CEO has been watching too much Aladdin. Would the CEO be happy and satisfied to have done to him what his bank has done to customers? I think not.*

Doug Read, Heathmont. Herald-Sun. Thursday November 29, 2018

2

What is the Golden Rule?

The glory of God is a human being fully alive; and to be alive consists in beholding God.

—Irenaeus of Lyons

Is the Golden Rule good?

To save you a lot of reading, the short answer to the question posed by the title of this book, *How good is the Golden Rule?,* is that it is very good. Good beyond comprehension. Beyond our wildest dreams. I hope to show you that the Golden Rule is good because it is designed by God to reveal his goodness to us, not just as an intellectual concept, but as a foundational experience of life where we engage symbiotically as we are enabled and guided by God's spirit to discover his goodness for our benefit. When we discover that the Golden Rule is nothing less than a relationship with God for our good, we become fully alive, fulfilling our God-given human purpose with great joy and excitement. However, if you are satisfied with this answer and don't continue to read and test this claim, you may never discover just how good the Golden Rule and God's grace is. This is because your discovery of the Golden Rule depends upon your humble acceptance of God's offer of grace to become one of his Blessed Ones.

There is nothing new in this claim about God's goodness as it was established by the first words of the Bible, in Genesis Chapter 1. As God watched his creation unfold to his command, he observed at each successive step that his creation is *good*, until at last he created breath in living creatures. *God saw all that he had made, and it was very good* (Gen 1:31). I think this means that God's spirit, which creates the breath of life in us, makes what is good, very good. That's right, isn't it? We know from our experience that life itself is very good. Then it is enhanced by our experience of those natural phenomena of creation – light and darkness, water and land, vegetation, night and day – which were all made for our sustenance, use and enjoyment. Living things that have the breath of life in them contribute even further to making life very good as they perform many additional functions that benefit us and the whole of creation. Think about how you interact with your pet dog, or cat. When we experience the beauty and wondrous complexity of life and enjoy it within the limits for which it was designed, we recognize its goodness.

When God rested from his creative work on the seventh day, he sent water for shrubs and plants to grow and to perpetuate life. God saw that there was no-one to take care of his new creation, so he made humankind in his own image to care for and enjoy his work. Seemingly, God prefers a manicured garden to a tangled mess, as most of us do also. This story casts men and women as God's highest accomplishment. Adam and Eve walked with God in the Garden of Eden in the cool of the evening to chat with him, thriving in each other's presence in the beauty and purposefulness of God's handiwork. However, their assignment was to manage God's creation within the imposed limits of one rule: not to eat of the tree of knowledge of good and evil. Now we know the tragic story of Adam and Eve's sin and fall from grace and relationship with God to the lasting harm within his creation.

Finding my place

I spent much of my early life as though I was attending a church picnic while looking through the fence at a football match next door. I was engaged with the Christian faith from birth and had retained what I thought were Christian ideals and appearances of conformity (some of the time). But my real attention was often elsewhere. My family were all members of the Open Brethren movement, which follows the teachings of an Anglo-Irish clergyman, John Nelson Darby, whose austere characteristics were similarly reflected among the Brethren. As a group, they were committed to a form of strict belief and practice which they imagined the original Christians had followed. The Brethren had no clergy, no creeds or liturgy, and no instrumental music was performed during their worship services, at which no women (who also never wore makeup) would ever speak. Remarkably, many intelligent women waited in silence for men, including young boys like me, to speak, as women were not permitted to do so. Rejecting most external religious trappings, the Brethren often met in bare-boarded Gospel Halls, convinced by their almost total rejection of Anglican and other denominational practices that they were the only true Christians.

As if to demonstrate his intellectual superiority and Divine calling as a reformer, Darby developed an almost incomprehensible and innovative eschatology by reinterpreting Christian doctrines as a series of "dispensations" or eras relating to biblical history, which he discerned by "rightly dividing" the scriptures, an expression Darby borrowed from 2 Tim 2:15 (where it means "correct teaching") to give himself license to reinterpret the Bible by dividing it up to accommodate his new way of understanding the current and future role of his faithful flock. The Brethren thus assumed the position as the *"Blessed ones of God,"* a position previously held by the Jewish nation of Israel. Darby reasoned that because the Kingdom of God was yet to come, most of the teachings of Jesus were "Kingdom Truths" and applicable only in heaven, or after the "rapture" or removal of the church from the world. The rapture was to be the beginning of a "time of tribulation" for those who remained on earth awaiting the return of Jesus to usher in the "millennial reign", after which Jesus would return to judge the living and the dead. At least that is how I understood it.

Brethren men and women, though, were good at Bible knowledge. My mother was a modern woman who balanced her knowledge of the Bible against philosophers such as Sigmund Freud and had rejected the most extreme Brethren views. She encouraged me to think for myself, for which I am very grateful as it is the source of my slightly unusual point of view. One consequence of my Brethren background, however, was that I was more familiar with the teachings of the Apostle Paul than the teachings of Jesus. I was more a Paulian than a Christian because the Brethren said Jesus was talking of an age yet to come, while Paul taught the "plain truth" that applied here and now. In fact, the worst of Brethren teaching was a return to the bondage of legalism, reflecting Paul's dealings with matters of church administration in his very idiosyncratic manner rather than the more ironic teachings of Jesus. Just as many Christians before me, I have since learned that the Kingdom comes as implied by the Lord's Prayer; *now and not yet*. I hope to explain this ironic mystery in the following chapters.

One of my greatest early insights into scripture was the result of a Bible study led by a dentist, John Messer, who asked, *"What do you do when you find scripture confusing or contradictory?"* His answer stuck in my 16 year old brain and has served me well; *"Keep reading."* I have come to see that this is pure wisdom and an act of faith; to suspend judgement until I have gained more knowledge and experience because;

> *"...faith is the substance of things hoped for, the evidence of things not yet seen."* (Heb 11:1)

My act of faith has been to persevere with what my parents told me was true, and hope against hope that my faith would be rewarded when I have seen the reality that I have seen. Risky, I know, but unbelievably satisfying. Just as if to remind me not to be too clever, I recently a watched a dispensationalist, Robert Breaker, on YouTube, explaining his theory about "rightly dividing the word of truth" with charts covered with circles and arrows, emphasizing that he possesses the truth, and others including me, do not. The problem is that he reminds me of myself. [1]

Sola scriptura?

It is also strange, though, how beliefs that I thought I rejected in my late teenage years still have a certain hold on me more than 50 years later, as I still struggle to resolve convoluted doctrinal abstractions about obscure Bible verses. For the record, I think I have found my place as an evangelical Christian (in the Australian, rather than American political sense) who errs on the side of a pragmatic Wesleyan, rather than an expert view in my understanding of scripture. I see myself as having wrestled with the biblical text and

---

[1] https://www.youtube.com/watch?v=vFoe1kF4K5o

church history to resolve the problem of biblical literalism, where I prefer to attempt to discern the spirit of the law from the text and the context, plus my experience rather than extract the literal letter of the law from an imagined "plain reading" of the text alone. I have a reasonably developed understanding of the literary genres of scripture plus as I have mentioned, I expect the meaning of the text and its context to be ironic, if not paradoxical.

I do believe that I have secured a place in the Kingdom of God as a blessed one, motivated by my desire to do God's will because of my experience of his love and grace, rather than by my compliance with legalistic requirements. As a result, the older I get, the more impatient I become with literalistic, dogmatic religious theories, and the more interested I become in observing the human outcomes of all types of belief and practice, especially my own and those I can observe first hand. However, I believe that faithful Christians do begin to comply with God's law because of our transformation into Christ's image by the power of his love, not by our compliance with Luther's insistence on Sola Scriptura – the doctrine that scripture alone is the source of authority for faith. I am very much encouraged in this view by Jesus who, while excoriating the Pharisees, said;

> *You study the Scriptures diligently because you think that in them you have eternal life. These are the very Scriptures that testify about me, yet you refuse to come to me to have life* (Jn 5:39-40).

I think Jesus is asking us about the source of our values, inspiration and ultimate meaning. Do we rely entirely upon an ancient book as some biblical literalists would have us believe they do? My answer is no. We rely on the Bible as we rely on history as a source of information about God and his encounters with men and women, albeit a Divinely inspired, amazingly complex and yet integrated source. But the Bible does not save us, nor does our faith in the words of the Bible alone. It is in observing what the Bible teaches us to do because of our faith in and relationship to Jesus that we find salvation. When we trust in Jesus as our savior and the one who sends us his Spirit, at that moment, our belief and relationship to the Bible and to Jesus is transformed through an intellectual and emotional act of will to become a dynamic relationship of symbiotic interaction as the Spirit begins to influence every aspect of our being if we allow it to be so. I prefer to take the approach recommended by our vicar at St James Old Cathedral, Matt Williams, who says that we must try to make a *"righteous reading of the text"* to discern what Jesus and others meant and how that might apply in our situation as we apply all the resources of scholarship, wisdom and insight that we can muster while keeping the definition and demands of "righteous relationships" in mind. Otherwise, we tend toward the default position of reading literally and legalistically and not relationally as the Golden Rule suggests we must. Having said all of this, however, I do accept that the Bible is authoritative as it has the last word over and above all other sources of knowledge and wisdom, because it is the word of God.

The big remaining obstacle for me in my adulthood, however, was to take Jesus at his word in all areas of life, because in many ways, my mind still belonged to the "chosen few" of the Brethren. Although I left their fellowship, I still felt that I was somehow "entitled" to special status conferred by my heritage and Bible knowledge, which I believed put me in a different camp to ordinary Christians. I noticed this more in recent years when I came to know a man named Paul, an exemplary Jehovah's Witness in whom I saw several strange characteristics that I also recognized in myself. Paul, whom I admire for his diligence, has accepted the proposition that the leaders of the Jehovah's Witnesses (called "The Faithful Slave) are Divinely appointed and therefore able to reinterpret the Bible and history to align with their view that they are the only true members of God's Kingdom. This favored position of the Jehovah's

Witnesses (who emerged from the same period and with some of the same influences as the Brethren) is maintained not by their reliance upon God's love and grace as revealed in scripture, but by their absolute obedience to the Faithful Slave's interpretation of a raft of obscure Bible passages that they use to qualify themselves for the role. As a footnote, my criticisms of the Brethren are in most cases no longer valid, as they also have moved on to occupy the middle ground of orthodox evangelical Christian belief and practice, having abandoned many of their distinctive teachings of dispensationalism to the dust of history. It is ironic to me that my wife and I now worship at the St James "Old Cathedral", the first Anglican cathedral in Melbourne, where we relish the tradition and liturgy that our Brethren forebears rejected.

Symbiotic symbolism

It remains for me, though, to attempt to confront the necessary tension between literal compliance with the written biblical law, on the one hand, and obedience to God's Living word (in Christ) on the other (which I characterize as the *Letter of the law versus the spirit of the law or law versus grace*). 1 Sam 15:22 reminds me that *Obedience is better than sacrifice,* suggesting that my sacrifice or supreme effort accounts for nothing by comparison to my willingness to be obedient to the still, small voice of God's Spirit, revealed in scripture and confirmed in my mind and conscience by my relationship to Jesus Christ. This view is summarized for me in the refrain of the old Hymn, *Trust and obey, for there's no other way to be happy in Jesus, than to trust and obey.* Taken together, they resolve my anxious striving or complacent entitlement with the simple acceptance that faith in God is a necessary precondition to all progress in relation to him. The question of faith is resolved not by my dogmatic certainties, but by my experience, where what I do and say must be closely aligned with the evidence of faith, hope and love manifest in me, rather than some intellectual "objective proof" regarding the truth or reliability of the biblical stories about God. In this view, our reconciliation with God is an ongoing process that begins with God's Spirit calling us into a relationship by an act of legal settlement known as justification, whereby we become spiritually "born again" as we respond to the Spirit's call to accept Jesus as Lord and Savior based on his sacrifice on the cross; a relationship that I believe to be truly symbiotic, which I must now explain. Symbiosis is a term from biology referring to two interdependent bodies "living together." It has its origin in scripture in the symbol of the serpent that Moses held up to heal anyone who looked at it. (Num 21:8) It is later used in the Gospel of John which says;

Just as Moses lifted up the snake in the wilderness,
so the Son of Man must be lifted up. (Jn 3:14)

The symbol of Moses lifting the snake, is replicated by Jesus being lifted up on the cross for all who will to look at him and receive life, resulting in Christ dwelling in me, in the person of his Holy Spirit.

To them God has chosen to make known among the Gentiles
the glorious riches of this mystery, which is Christ in you,
the hope of glory (Col 1:27).

By this I mean that the mysterious relationship between God and us does not rely on the initiative of just one or the other. I know it is true that God can impose his will upon us at any time, but he usually does not. With very few exceptions, God only ever invites us into a relationship with him which we can always accept or reject. If we reject him, God respects our bad decision, at least for the time being. If we accept, then we begin a dance where he leads, and we follow in a truly intertwined relationship of love, where the Spirit is ever-present in us, even when are not always conscious of it. As our conscious minds become renewed, so we will more readily know what God requires of us as against what our unrepentant ego may still desire for itself. The still, small voice of the Spirit remains in us, but we don't always listen carefully enough to hear what he says, or what he wants us to do to bring us further into his Kingdom within time and space. The event of justification is a beginningof this process that needs to be backed up by our conscious spiritual growth as we mature in our faith and face the challenges of life. Although this may make my Christian identity sound tenuous, it is not. Rather, my faith is constantly tested, causing it to grow and flourish as I respond to God's offer of grace. As I write this book, my assurance of my faith in God and my place in his Kingdom has been reinforced by my deepening understanding that God is love. My position is made secure by his grace, if I continue to desire to receive it as my behavior confirms the change that has occurred in me. My hope is that I have found a secure place in God's kingdom, since I recognize God as the ultimate Sovereign and make myself accountable to him. God has revealed himself to us in his son Jesus Christ, who now asks us to trust and obey his great command, to love him and our neighbor as ourselves, as the Golden Rule requires. If I have responded to God with my whole being; body, soul and spirit to the extent that I can for the moment, then I have entered a new reality of God's Kingdom.

Paradox at the heart of the message

I believe that perhaps the greatest complicating factor in a more advanced reading of scripture, is that the Christian message is fundamentally paradoxical, and so is the biblical account of it. This has caused many to avoid certain parts of scripture as being truth only in a time yet to come. Others have used obscurity for the creation of new doctrines, that always seem to favor their own interpretation of exclusive insight. I have been interested in the concept of paradox for most of my adult life because I thought that the main teachings of Jesus were paradoxical, and therefore, must be understood this way.

Perhaps it is this orientation that has attracted me to Kierkegaard's teaching of Christian existentialism, despite not really knowing what it was until recently. According to Wikipedia:

> *Kierkegaard argued that the universe is fundamentally paradoxical, and that its greatest paradox is the transcendent union of God and humans in the person of Jesus Christ. He also posited having a personal relationship with God that supersedes all prescribed moralities, social structures and communal norms, since he asserted that following social conventions is essentially a personal aesthetic choice made by individuals. Kierkegaard proposed that each person must make independent choices, which then constitute his existence. Each person suffers from the anguish of indecision (whether knowingly or unknowingly) until he commits to a particular choice about the way to live. Kierkegaard also proposed three rubrics with which to understand the conditions that issue from distinct life choices: the aesthetic, the ethical, and the religious.* [1]

---

1 https://en.wikipedia.org/wiki/Christian_existentialism

This disposition has gotten me into a lot of trouble with Christian friends who tended toward a literalistic or legalistic view of scripture. It seems to me, that people who look for absolute certainty in the text cannot tolerate any suggestion of ambiguity, whether it is deliberate or not. I continue to find it amazing that the Bible, which led the great theologian, Karl Barth to summarize his faith as "Jesus loves me this I know, for the Bible tells me so" that a child can understand, is also capable of seeming unlimited, transcendent explanations of life with amazing complexity and unprecedented reliability.[1]

In my view, there are many manifestations of paradox in the Bible, especially in the teachings of Jesus and his parables in particular. The word "parable" is derived from "parabola," a mathematical concept meaning a "U" shaped curve with symmetry around an axis. A parable, then, is an analogy which has two different meanings, so that if you understand one, then the second is more understandable. A paradox is defined as an apparent contradiction, where a second true meaning is initially obscure and can only be fleshed out by looking below the superficial meaning. This, in my view, is a very important idea that we must apply to our reading of scripture and our dealing with the spirit of God by always looking below the surface for another, often ironic meaning – something that I characterize with the slogan "Expect Irony" which I believe should always be applied when reading scripture or dealing with the spirit of God, because the alternative is arrogant ignorance. My interest led me to read *The Promise of Paradox*, by Parker J Palmer in the early 1980's and to reflect on his statement that *"...paradox is the tension of opposites."*[2] This realization, in my experience, is a necessary part of a process of faith and growth. Not that we are satisfied with paradox or contradiction, nor can we always resolve

---

1 https://emailmeditations.wordpress.com/2014/07/03/448-the-story-behind-jesus-loves-me/
2 Parker J Palmer, *The Promise of Paradox*, Ave Maria Press.

it until we allow it to be played out and realize, that only in our relationship to God, who sacrificed himself for our sake, is there any possibility of resolution, as I hope to explain.

In broad terms, the biblical paradox is reflected in the difference between Old Testament law and New Testament grace, which our freedom in Christ is intended to resolve. However, this distinction is usually obscured by religious tradition and dogma, both new and old. Tradition or dogma should not be allowed to intrude into our understanding of scripture if it prevents us from feeling the weight of important issues. To foreshadow an example of my point: *Freedom requires that we as individuals work together to discern and understand the meaning of the Bible and the Word of God.*

When we become energized as enquiring Christian believers, we are faced with a plethora of religious traditions, teachings, dogma, doctrine and emerging trends competing for our attention and allegiance. We must then ask ourselves, *what is the purpose of my relationship to Christ?* Great care must be taken, because it is possible to leave behind the spiritual bondage (or apathy) of one kind only to become ensnared in another kind of religious slavery. Paul uses extreme hyperbole (another mathematical concept related to paradox) to express the wish that teachers who advocate religious circumcision of new believers castrate themselves:

> *You, my brothers and sisters, were called to be free* (from religious law). *But do not use your freedom to indulge the flesh; rather, serve one another humbly in love. For the entire law is fulfilled in keeping this one command: "Love your neighbor as yourself"* (Gal 5:12-14).

To drive his point home, Paul quotes the most concise of all versions of the Golden Rule to remind us that Christ's Great Command is intended to be the major orientation of our lives –

not some dogmatic religious practice, tradition or belief, but our relationship with each other and with God. He continues...

> *I say, walk by the Spirit, and you will not gratify the desires of the flesh.* (Gal 5:16).

Paul lists the corrupted desires of humanity that we already know can enslave us if we do not constrain them – or rather, if we don't put them to some better use, some higher purpose.

> *The acts of the flesh are obvious* (or at least, they should be): *sexual immorality, impurity and debauchery; idolatry and witchcraft; hatred, discord, jealousy, fits of rage, selfish ambition, dissensions, factions and envy; drunkenness, orgies, and the like. I warn you, as I did before, that those who live like this will not inherit the kingdom of God* (Gal 5:19-21).

Serious stuff! Paul then contrasts the flesh with the spirit by listing the outcomes of the Golden Rule:

> *But the fruit of the Spirit is love, joy, peace, forbearance, kindness, goodness, faithfulness, gentleness and self-control. Against such things there is no law* (Gal 5:22).

In view of such clarity, I find it galling that any Christian teacher should take it on themselves to condemn another religious teacher, other than to properly criticize them or their doctrines against scripture and sound reason, without resorting to personal attacks, ridicule and condemnation. An example of this is John MacArthur, the well-known Calvinist, dispensationalist writer, teacher and pastor from Grace Community Church in Sun Valley California, whose specialty is to condemn Christians he disagrees with including all Pentecostals, Roman Catholics, Billy Graham and NT Wright and many others. MacArthur goes to the extent of running Strange Fire conferences designed specifically to condemn all Pentecostals and Charismatics on the basis of his Calvinist, cessationist and dispensationalist prejudice. Even if he claims to have ultimate scriptural authority, I am sure he would not want his frequently-used misrepresentations and *ad hominem* attacks used against him in such a judgmental and merciless way.[1] If critics like John MacArthur were to apply the Golden Rule to such matters, then they would be free to properly criticize others in the same way that they would be prepared to be criticized. More seriously, I wonder if MacArthur is prepared to have mercy given to him as he has given it to others.

Rigorous criticism is necessary in my view, because just to say what I think is true – just as I am doing now – often requires that I compare myself against another person or doctrine to make my point clear and relevant. For example, criticism may be applied to Joel Osteen's overly simple prosperity gospel message of "Your best life now", for which he and others have been criticized because it makes the gospel seem like a certain path to personal, material and financial success with statements such as:

> "Start calling yourself healed, happy, whole, blessed, and prosperous. Stop talking to God about how big your mountains are, and start talking to your mountains about how big your God is!"[2]

I have no argument with having high aspirations, though. Brian Houston is the founder and leader of the Hillsong international church who has moved away from the prosperity

---

1 https://www.christianpost.com/news/john-macarthur-responds-to-critics-who-believe-his-strange-fire-conference-is-divisive-unloving-107051/.

2 Joel Osteen, *Your Best Life Now: 7 Steps to Living at Your Full Potential*.

message and now says more clearly: "*God does not expect us to be mediocre*". Amen to that. To not be mediocre includes, in my view, to have the highest possible aspirations, for yourself and others. Osteen is not the most strident of the prosperity preachers, nor is his definition of success only about money. But he does seem to be saying that personal success should be at the top of our priorities. If he means self-love, then all he would have to do is to quote the Golden Rule, which has an immediate corrective for selfishness. This raises the question, then, whether living by the Golden Rule must be our first use of freedom, above and beyond all other more instinctive and primal human drives? Speaking as one who has at different times been highly motivated by things other than the Golden Rule or obedience to Christ, the answer is an emphatic yes! I would like to repeat the whole of the quote from Galatians 5 to which I alluded before; *It is for freedom Christ has set us free,* which, I believe, includes me being free to experience the best that is possible and to make my own errors and for you to lovingly correct me or vice versa rather than to bind myself in selfishness or by attacking another person without considering their point of view and best interests.

I am suspicious of any religion, doctrine or tradition that removes or obscures the central message of love or the Golden Rule. But just before you accuse me of hypocrisy because I am doing what I am accusing others of doing, can I ask you to consider if we humans are all wrong and all in need of God's mercy – some more than others. As none of us has completely pure motives, we all should be a lot more careful and loving in our criticisms, especially of our enemies. As for those who exclude themselves from this limitation to criticizing others by aligning themselves with Jesus who excoriated the pharisees and called them "snakes," I suggest that there is a bit of difference. For a start, Jesus was without sin, and perfect, because he is God. Secondly...well, there's no need for a second reason. This is exactly the point at which dogmatic hard-liners of every kind go wrong; they allow God's mercy for themselves, but not for others outside their group. By comparison, Jesus offers mercy to all who will give it to others.

Although it is tempting for me to get on my self-righteous religious high-horse and say, *"yes, of course, you must give your life in total obedience to Christ,"* I am reminded of my wife Elaine's fears of her father's dream to send her to darkest Africa as a missionary dressed in a white cotton dress with a bonnet and lace-up boots. Her 16-year-old response was to dye her hair purple and to take me, a wild-eyed car hound as her boyfriend. I do believe that God expects us to have high aspirations for ourselves as our first duty. This is why the Golden Rule says, *treat others as you want to be treated*. Plus, Jesus' words about freedom refer to freedom for its own sake: not to be selfish, or to obtain immediate perfection, but to be fully human and to align our values, drives, instincts, passions and priorities in proper order as we mature and change with time and circumstances, while we ensure that we are *no longer slaves to sin* as Paul demands.

Freedom!

Western culture offers a formula to achieve success in a more generalized version of Joel Osteen's dream of freedom. This is realized by individuals using existing freedoms to access their inherited democratic rights of liberty, equality and to pursue prosperity and personal success, and to encourage our children to harness the possibility of social mobility – all of which can be achieved through personal education, goal setting, self-discipline, competence and hard work in a society with very few barriers. Although this has proved to be a reliable path to success, and despite our access to free education and choice, it is becoming less an option, let alone an answer, for some who do not want to, or cannot begin this path. Increasingly, too, there are those who take this path, only to founder on the rocks when they achieve what appears to be *too much* success. In the pursuit of alternatives, many acknowledge that the search for freedom requires us to bark up a few wrong trees or go down blind alleys before we find a satisfying road. There are now enough doubts circulating about the implied promises of Western Democracy to suggest that while it has given the world the most productive environment and the most sought-after opportunities of all socio-political ideologies, democracy is not perfect. What does seem to be more universally appealing, though, is the quest for freedom. Even then, we need to be careful. As Jesus reminds us,

> *What good will it be for someone to gain the whole world, yet forfeit their soul?* (Matt 16:26)

I would like to present what I think is at once the most ironic, powerful, difficult and important of all Jesus' teachings on love and the Golden Rule. It is important because if we do not grasp it then we will not understand how agape love applies to us as the means by which God reveals himself to us. We all desire freedom, but we go looking for it in all the wrong places. Often, we think of freedom in negative terms, as *freedom from* such things as pain, poverty and hunger, because fear is a very strong source of motivation to avoid pain and discomfort. The opposite is the *freedom to do* a range of activities that used to be considered as the preserve of the rich where we can now indulge ourselves in luxuries related to food, power, comfort, security and travel. However, there is nothing more pathetic than a person who has grasped at freedom from pain and suffering by taking what they thought was a cure, only for it to have the opposite effect to what they were expecting and to find themselves in bondage to an ideology, or worse. As an aside, it is our high degree of God-given freedom that permits the possibility of evil. If we were not free, we could be restrained from evil. If we are free, we can be evil. So also, is the evil of natural events both a sign of the possibility of evil (that we call the fall) and the radical freedom we enjoy to do good or ill.

Despite its potential pit-falls, I suggest that our quest for freedom is right because, according to the Gospel, Jesus;

> ...*came to set the captives free and give sight to the blind* (Lk 4:18).

We could say that this type of freedom is a metaphor for a spiritual freedom that is, according to some, unmeasurable, and therefore illusory. But research confirms that real quality-of-life measures, such as life span, health, wealth and happiness, seem to accrue to people of religious faith.[1]

Enforcing equality

The modern notion is that freedom requires social equity. This has come to mean that no one in an equal society should ever have to experience discrimination or inequity. This idea has the same biblical origins as the Golden Rule, as it is implicit in the command to "*love your neighbor as yourself.*" This is meant to include anybody with whom we have day-to-day contact – especially family members. Jesus' brother James makes this command into a serious duty by elevating what we understand as an obligation of equity based on love to the extreme of an ultimate accountability to God. James opens his argument by saying: *My brothers and sisters, believers in our glorious Lord Jesus Christ must not show favoritism.* He prosecutes the case that improper belief in Jesus' teaching of the Golden Rule may result in our becoming guilty of evil:

> *Suppose a man comes into your meeting wearing a gold ring and fine clothes, and a poor man in filthy old clothes also comes in. If you show special attention to the man wearing fine clothes and*

---

1 https://en.wikipedia.org/wiki/Quality_of_life

> say, "Here's a good seat for you," but say to the poor man, "You stand there" or "Sit on the floor by my feet," have you not discriminated among yourselves and become judges with evil thoughts? (Jas 2:1-12).

Although the Gospel of Jesus and the Golden Rule are characterized as the law of love, James is giving another meaning to the word "law," in contrast to what Paul said by referring to Jesus' statement that the Golden Rule is a *summary of the law and prophets*. Then he agrees with Paul by saying that there are severe consequences for those who ignore its demands. In my view, this suggests that all law is fulfilled not by our self-disciplined compliance with it, but by our being transformed by love. To heighten this paradox, Jesus said in another place:

> *"I did not come to bring peace, but a sword* (Matt 10:34).

This is an allegorical "sword" that Jesus, the "Prince of Peace", wields not to bring peace on earth to make everybody happy, but rather as a weapon to wage war against sin and evil where a man's enemies may be his own family, because of his allegiance to Jesus. Jesus drives this point home with the ironic statement, *Let the dead bury the dead."* (Lk 9:60)

Jesus rejects the excuse of family obligation to avoid the duty of Christian discipleship and re-emphasizes the serious consequences of neglecting the law of love. James then really tips the acid on his audience:

> *Listen, my dear brothers and sisters: Has not God chosen those who are poor in the eyes of the world to be rich in faith and to inherit the kingdom he promised those who love him? But you have dishonored the poor. Is it not the rich who*

> *are exploiting you? Are they not the ones who are dragging you into court? Are they not the ones who are blaspheming the noble name of him to whom you belong? If you really keep the royal law found in Scripture, "Love your neighbor as yourself," you are doing right. But if you show favoritism, you sin and are convicted by the law as lawbreakers. For whoever keeps the whole law and yet stumbles at just one point is guilty of breaking all of it. For he who said, "You shall not commit adultery," also said, "You shall not murder." If you do not commit adultery but do commit murder, you have become a lawbreaker. Speak and act as those who are going to be judged by the law that gives freedom, because judgment without mercy will be shown to anyone who has not been merciful. Mercy triumphs over judgment.*
> (Jas 2:1-13)

The penultimate sentence reflects the end of the Lord's prayer, where it says: *and forgive us our trespasses as we forgive those who trespass against us.* The seriousness of this statement cannot be over emphasized. It means that if we are not obedient in being merciful to others, then we should not expect God's mercy when we face his judgement. Does this threaten our place in the Kingdom of God? Yes, according to Paul, who says; *So, if you think you are standing firm, be careful that you don't fall!* (1 Cor 10:12). However, none of what I have said above implies the modern idea of equality of outcome, where all of us are different for many reasons. Scripture is adamant about equity as it states we are all equal in God's sight. But this is not equality of outcome. On the contrary, it is equality of opportunity.

As I have mentioned, I think that many biblical uses of words and concepts related to law, grace, salvation and freedom are often so deeply complex that they are intentionally paradoxical; their meanings are not always what we first imagined them to be. I hope you agree with me because, if we are too certain, or too confused and bogged down by controversies and irrelevancies, we are prevented from struggling to understand the scriptures together, as we should. This prevents us from properly resolving important matters, such as trusting and obeying God as individuals and in relationships.

I would like to conclude by recommending an approach that has served me well: Not every doctrine is equally important. Test all important matters against scripture as much as possible by being skeptical (but not cynical) of a doctrinal emphasis that does not have constant clear support in scripture, that is consistent other similar scriptures. This is what our pastor Matt Williams means by a "righteous reading of scripture," that it is consistent with God's love, and the Golden Rule.

Above all, whenever you must trust scripture or rely on the Holy Spirit, expect irony.

To summarize, my points are three-fold.

First. The Golden Rule is the non-negotiable requirement of obedience for Christians who claim to follow the teachings of Jesus. It is not the basis of justification (salvation), as we are justified by faith alone. It is, however, the basis of sanctification or transformation into the image of Jesus by the renewal of our minds, which requires a conscious act of obedience to Jesus.

Second. The requirement of obedience to the Golden Rule is stringent and utterly dependent upon our transformation by the spirit of Christ. It is ludicrous to pretend that equity can be established by any means other than by the salvation and transformation of souls by the power of God's love, which is manifest in Jesus.

Third. We cannot interpret or understand the Bible or the Kingdom of God alone. We need each other to discern and work out their meaning together.

What is the Golden Rule?

To finish my rant about paradox and irony, I was fascinated to discover that John MacArthur presents a view of the Golden Rule called; *The most misunderstood parable*. He begins by telling the parable of the Good Samaritan, claiming that its meaning is hidden, and not correctly understood because it is often interpreted in support of social justice, with which I agree. MacArthur analyzes the story to show that the love displayed by the Good Samaritan, is impossible for us to emulate because we do not *"Love God with all of our heart, and our neighbor as ourselves, because we cannot,"* which I also think is true. He goes on to say that we cannot begin to love others in the way that the parable demands until we are saved and begin to love others as we love ourselves as we move toward perfection in God's sight. So far, so good because I agree with what he says, but there is a difference between his attitude to the text and mine. MacArthur sees the parable as a story of exclusion from the Kingdom, rather than a means by which we can commence a process of becoming part of it, by our obedience to Christ's command. MacArthur explains the parable by saying; *"Jesus sticks the knife in,* (demanding that we) *love God and love everybody like that."* (the example of the Samaritan) He continues; *"The parable is designed to make us feel guilty for not loving God and others perfectly, until we have pleaded for God to give us his mercy God demands perfection according to the law Hard for religious people to see their religion as sin."* He concludes, *"The lawyer never asks Jesus for his mercy and grace. Righteousness is the issue,* (the lawyer should have) *come* (to Jesus) *for mercy and grace."*

MacArthur describes his view of salvation where he implies that sanctification (transformation) is an automatic process inspired by the Spirit. This seems to be the standard Calvinist doctrine, which I confess to not understand at all. Rather, transformation, as I have described in this book is by no means automatic. It is always, or at least usually, the result of my conscious obedience to Jesus' command. Rigorous, but careful criticism of MacArthur's view is necessary because just to speak the truth in love about my own interests often requires that I compare myself against another person or doctrine to make my point clear and relevant, without being a hypocrite. According to the Golden Rule, while we should not engage in self-indulgence, to explain our point of view is essential to loving ourselves. Nor can there be any abuse, coercion or manipulation in any criticism, as Paul demonstrates. As we have seen, the Golden Rule summarizes a group of Jesus' sayings which he requires us to take seriously, including his command to *Love God with all your heart, soul and strength, and your neighbor as yourself.* The Golden Rule then, is the tip of a biblical iceberg which reveals more of the identity of God as the essence and source of love as it becomes our path into God's Kingdom as we learn about the nature and language of love from one another.

Tellingly, Jesus further summarized the Golden Rule as: *Do to others as you would have them do to you* (Lk 6:31).

The premise of this book is that to be an effective Christian disciple requires an obedient return to his explicit teaching, to the extent that we can understand it. If we trust and obey, we will be successful not only in our Christian role and mission, but in the whole of life. I am aware that I am entering the lion's den as I say this but, in my view, obedience to Jesus' teaching is required to achieve our highest human potential as it is realized in fulfilling and satisfying relationships. If we do not obey him, then we will fail in our life mission regardless of how we define success, as I will explain in Chapter 8. Although I am aware that this is a debatable idea among Christians and secular people alike, I will try to show that as a Christian, consensus of obedience to Jesus permeates a culture, then the culture benefits in ways that it does not notice as having Christian origins. It is always necessary, however, for the leading edge of the faithful few to be exemplars of obedience for "common grace" to have its effect. Many modern religious and secular people scoff at the idea of obedience regarding any religious leader or ideal. Either that, or they quake in fear at the prospect that such a leader is a despot, as many are and have been. However, I contend that obedience to Jesus' instruction to *love your neighbor and your enemies* is free of risk in the real sense, because Jesus is God incarnate, called the Son of God. He is not only our savior and Redeemer, but also the perfect human called the Son of Man, who leads us into the highest possible human experience. Jesus wants us to emulate him by our acceptance of his invitation to recognize him as creator, lawgiver, judge, Lord and coming King. But there is a catch. We cannot pull ourselves up by our bootstraps. We cannot do what the Golden Rule requires of us by ourselves, as we need each other plus divine help to do it. The irony in my experience is that we do have to begin to try to make it alone, if only to realize that we *cannot*. This is what I call the GR Catch, which suggests that I must usually do everything I possibly can before I finally give up and let God be God and do what he does best, which is to transform us into his image.

Jeffrey Wattles says in the Preface to his book *The Golden Rule*, "In my intellectual and personal adventure, I sought and I found, but I did not find by seeking, and now I know why it is said that you only understand the Golden Rule by living it."[1] I agree with Wattles, but my aim is to go a step further by attempting to convince you to discover for yourself that trust in and obedience to Christ is necessary to discover and experience the mystery of living a fully satisfying human life. Not only is your satisfaction and fulfillment as an individual dependent upon it, but so too is that of humanity, for all time and eternity.

---

1   Jeffrey Wattles, *The Golden Rule*, Oxford University Press New York. 1996.

Is the message of Jesus reliable?

In my view, the historical person and message of Jesus Christ is more reliable than those of other ancient and modern religious leaders, religions, theories or ideologies of any kind. The number and the nature of the claims of those who lived with him and those who later wrote about him are totally different from all other claims of spiritual insight. Their writings encompass a unique combination of actual events involving real people, places and times, infused with a narrative of gritty everyday activities, hardship, hope, love, joy, sorrow and failure, and every other human quality that gives life its rich meaning. Many Christian historians and apologists maintain that the best evidence for both the historicity and the truth claims of the biblical account of the life, death and resurrection of Jesus is the effect he had on the Roman Empire. Their reasoning is that if the disciples and followers of Jesus had any doubts about the accuracy of events described by the New Testament and the claims that Jesus made for them, then the Christian movement would never have gotten off the ground. They contend that, considering how many disciples died for their faith in Jesus, if there had been the slightest doubt about the authenticity of the events or his claim to be the resurrected Son of Man and therefore the Messiah, then the movement would not have survived beyond his death, let alone to change the history of the world. Comparison of this phenomenon to more recent religious movements such as Islam or Mormonism are not valid because they both promised material, sexual and political success, positioning themselves in the slipstream of Judeo-Christian teaching and history. By contrast, Christianity promised (and still does, as we shall see) hardship and persecution in this material life. Furthermore, the biblical record is very much contemporary to the events it describes. For instance, the Apostle Paul goes to great lengths to validate the historicity of what he taught about Jesus. Writing 1 Corinthians 15:3-5 in AD 55, Paul includes a creed affirming Christ's resurrection, as he also does in Galatians, which was most likely written in AD 48. Given that Jesus was crucified in about AD 30, these letters are quoting creeds that confirm eye witness accounts of events that happened as recently as 18 years earlier.[1]

After their initial doubts, early Christians came to believe so strongly that Jesus rose from the dead that they gave their lives in obedience to him as their long-awaited Messiah. However, believing in the resurrection of Jesus was one thing; being obedient to his commands was another thing entirely, because it was what people did that cost them their lives, not just what they thought or said in private. When Christians first sought to obey Jesus, one of the first and most distinctive things they did was to apply the Golden Rule. Evidence of this is the way Christians were

---

1   https://www.bethinking.org/did-jesus-rise-from-the-dead/the-resurrection-of-jesus-and-the-witness-of-paul

described by non-Christian historians, who remarked that they did not just care for the needs of their own people, but for the needs of non-believers too. Fantastically, and incredibly, they obeyed Jesus command to *Love their enemies*.[1]

The witness of Christian converts from the time of Christ is verifiable history, because it is established and demonstrated, not just by what people say, but by a continuation of people who believe in his resurrection and have testified as to his power to inspire and to transform their lives ever since, including mine. I believe that Christians who have treated the "righteous sayings" of Jesus seriously, demonstrated this transformation to this day, allowing us to say that the best proof of Christian faith is the transformed lives of true believers.

Also remarkable is the way that the Christian faith has continued to reform itself, correcting dilution, corruption and exaggeration caused by religious accretions or cultural baggage any human activity inevitably acquires along the way. However, I appreciate the way Christianity has penetrated and changed some cultures as it picks up some new beneficial nuances. Most famously, Christianity became the religion of African slaves who, when abducted to the new world, adopted the religion of their abductors. Not only did they adopt it, but they transformed it to become the movement that then transformed Christianity in the last century. In 1906, at a revival meeting in what had been a horse stable at Azusa Street, Los Angeles, California, an African-American preacher, William J. Seymour, began a multi-racial Pentecostal revival, mimicking in many ways the original event of the Spirit coming to all recorded in Acts 2. This phenomenon, which became known as the Azusa Street Revival, was accompanied by miracles of physical healing, soulish and emotional utterances in "Unknown tongues", combined with a capella worship songs and stories of oppression as

---

1 https://en.wikipedia.org/wiki/Early_Christianity

slaves as they identified with the one who became a slave for our benefit.[2]

In 2006, I was in Los Angeles, travelling with an old school mate who had reached the end of his emotional tether dealing with lifelong bipolar disorder, hoping that he might enjoy an epic road trip to explore our shared interest in motor racing. When we arrived in LA, we met people on the bus from all over the USA who were in town for the Spirit 2006 conference to celebrate the centenary of the Azusa Street revival. As I already knew of this history, I was keen to attend the conference and participate in it, but my mate was not in the least interested, so I reluctantly deferred to him. It was fascinating, though, to meet people on the bus and in our hotel in LA who were there to celebrate this event which has changed the face of Christianity, making it a more multiethnic and multicultural movement, as well as less formal and less bound by the fading formal culture of Europe. As I will explain later, if I had not experienced my own deeply significant Pentecostal experience earlier in my life, it is unlikely that I would have maintained my Christian faith.

Tragically, but predictably, the spiritual fire sparked by the resurrection of Jesus has gone out in many parts of the sophisticated Western world. Each generation has become complacent and satisfied by their own achievements in the modern world, without acknowledging the need to maintain the influence of Christianity. The extent to which Christians no longer take the truth of the resurrection to heart or the words of Jesus Christ to be serious commands reflects the extent to which Christian faith and its influence is in decline. This is most obvious in the "progressive" wing of the church, which has abandoned such "primitive and unnecessary" beliefs as the biblical claims about miracles. This results in an unconvincing message that has no power to save

---

2 http://enrichmentjournal.ag.org/200602/200602_142_Legacies.cfm

people from their sins or to transform their lives. Rather, as their alternative message provides a political answer to a spiritual question they resort to political activism, which effectively denies the power of salvation by the power of finished work of the risen Christ. Without conversions and baptisms, these churches are in universal decline, as evidenced by the empty cathedrals and churches of Europe and Britain, and now America and Australia. The Christian church must restore itself from further loss of faith and obedience if it is to play a role in the next phase of Western civilization, if there is to be one.

Paradise restored

The vision that I hope to present is an experience of life that few modern people share in its fullness. This is the "abundant life" that Jesus promised to those "blessed ones" who earnestly seek Him. This is a story that most people today dismiss as a religious delusion, a figment of an over-active imagination or wishful thinking—the same criticisms used to condemn Azusa Street by the established religious and cultural order, some of which were valid. Abundant life, however, is by degree and not an all-or-nothing proposition. According to many historians, modern people – especially those living in Western democracies – are all beneficiaries of the Christian faith, whether they acknowledge it or not. Rodney Stark argues that the liberal Western democratic world emerged from Christian principles founded 2,000 years ago.[1] Similarly, Greg Sheridan, in his book *God is Good for You*, quotes an article entitled "The First Sexual Revolution" by Kyle Harper, which claims that the Christianization of the Roman Empire was the result of "*infusing marriage with the idea of mutual love and reciprocal and equal obligation and by constraining sexuality through higher morality,*

---

1 Rodney Stark, *The Triumph of Christianity. How The Jesus Movement Became the World's Largest Religion*, Harper One.

Christianity creating far better relationships between men, women and girls." ² It was also much better for slaves, whose owners previously felt no compunction about using them in any way they liked. In that environment, the ideas of Christianity were novel, fresh and exciting. Now they are stale and dull resulting in society becoming inoculated against any but the most powerful strains of Christian teaching, including the Pentecostal revival at Azusa St..

Assisted by several books by Rodney Stark, (listed in the Bibliography) my understanding is that Christian concept of abundant life resulted from the social, philosophical, theological and psychological progress, building upon a Jewish foundation. Abundance was achievable by all, rich and poor alike, because Christians recognized that the basis of society was the biblical warrant of the absolute value and dignity of each individual person being free, but accountable to God and to each other. Not by money or power, but by other, less obvious qualities, relating to righteousness, peace and joy, that always apply to the genuine experience of freedom regardless of individual circumstances. Many of the freedoms we enjoy from the British system of government, justice, the rule of law and related principles, were drawn directly from Christian teaching in the Bible. Following abuses of religious freedom where people were forced to escape religious tyranny to the New World, these principles became enshrined in the constitutions of the United States of America, Canada, Australia and other new nations, as the basis of our unhindered liberty to enjoy life and practice our faith. While not everybody was a Christian or obedient to Jesus, general political and religious freedoms became widely available in what is called "common or prevenient grace" in which we all share.

The Christian concept of human dignity is not a collective assessment of value, as in socialism, or a utilitarian concept which

---

2 Greg Sheridan, *God is Good for You. A defense of Christianity in Troubled Times*, Allen and Unwin.

says that the highest good is what benefits most of the people most of the time. Rather, it is an aggregation of the intrinsic value of every individual person, as each of us is a bearer of the image of our creator, God. However, this relationship and these freedoms depend upon our individual obedience to God – or in this case, to Jesus Christ. As I will explain in Chapter 5, Jesus' teaching of the Golden Rule makes democratic freedom possible because it is a point of entry to what I call the "Law of Love". It is made explicit in the famous verse John 3:16: *For God so loved the world that he gave his one and only Son, that whoever believes in him shall not perish but have eternal life.* This means that the benefits of abundant life are freely available for our acceptance, provided we allow ourselves to be transformed by our conscious obedience to the Golden Rule.

The beginning, middle and end of history

The Bible describes humans as body, soul and spirit, each of us occupying a specific moment in history. We each have a beginning and will experience an end in time and space. However, beyond these already unfathomable limits, there is another dimension of spiritual reality that has been revealed to us historically by ordinary people, prophets and teachers of the Bible. Our destiny, in this view, is to experience all that life has to offer in this incomparably beautiful blue planet, Earth, which is filled with goodness, peace and satisfying relationships for our enjoyment and pleasure, along with some difficulties to be overcome. This vision of our place in time and space is available to us now in the ordinary events of life, but we then transcend its limits by joining forces with the creator, God, who promises us a place in eternity. He can do this because he is the eternal spirit, the law giver and the judge of good and evil, who dwells outside of time and space waiting for us to enjoy him and his creation forever.

Despite the best efforts of science to prove otherwise, Earth appears to be the only place in the entire Cosmos where there is evidence of conscious life. As far as we can tell at present, it is here that God has established life and is making his kingdom among those who have accepted his invitation to join with him in this transcendent enterprise. To accomplish this, we are invited to become his adopted sons and daughters and to join him in the family business called the *Kingdom of God,* which, according to Jesus, is already amongus.

> *The kingdom of God will not come with observable signs. Nor will people say, 'Look, here it is,' or 'There it is.' For you see, the kingdom of God is in your midst'* (Lk 17: 20-21).

His rule and Kingdom are manifest within our existing beings as we accept this proposition of the Kingdom of God by faith and begin to become transformed into his image by our obedience to him. Not just as individuals either, because according to the Golden Rule, our relationship with God depends upon our relationship to each other which implies our relationship to a community who are essential to the development and testing of our faith. This promise of transformation is not something new; it is what God promised Abraham and Moses according to the Old Testament account. It is the promise for us to return to our originally intended human purpose, identity and place which we have lost. It can be regained in its fullness only by the transforming renewal of our minds and our increasing cooperation with God's elusive but ever-present Spirit.

The cart before the horse

I am concerned that some of the models of faith promoted by modern Christians often put the cart before the horse. We have been told that we can be self-sacrificial, non-judgmental, peace loving, and spiritually, emotionally and morally sound by rejigging the social order. However, we have not been told how to learn these things which are the very essence of life. Some rely upon a convoluted interpretation of "biblical truths" or unachievable "To Do" lists of what good Christians must be or do. We are given conflicting messages about "behaving well" and to "rely upon God's grace with fellowship, prayer and Bible study" to comply with God's law – often before we even understand what these concepts mean. In my view, it is essential to know that God's grace is not automatic, even for sincere believers. There are many things that facilitate grace, including fellowship, prayer, Bible reading and dedicated study, but even these things can lead us astray, as they do within the many Christian cults and sects that each claim to own the franchise on truth. Ultimately, the grace that we seek requires our conscious desire, our seeking after, yearning, hungering and thirsting for cooperation with the one they called "Teacher" and his servant, the Holy Spirit, and a strong intention to learn from him by our obedience, not just sincerity or sacrifice alone.

The secret of the ages

I am convinced that rather than continue to allow Christians to drift into complacency or become apathetic, self-defeated hypocrites or self-loathing failures, we need to begin again by taking the words of Jesus seriously when he gives us what he calls a new commandment:

> *To love one another, as I have loved you* (Jn 13:34-35).

Which we already know is beyond us. However, this is not an impossible task because he also gave us his Great Command:

> *To treat others as you would like to be treated,*

which we can begin to do now.

This is the secret of the ages; it is the means by which we learn to love, and it is what we must now rediscover. It is also, properly understood, an antidote to our sin and failure, because the Golden Rule provides the means and the process by which we learn about ourselves, our relationships with each other, and with God that allows us to grow in grace. This process is perhaps not as tidy and as predictable as we might hope, but it is reliable, provided we stick at it.

Is the Golden Rule good? Yes and amen.

3

WHERE DID THE GOLDEN RULE COME FROM?

Whoever does not love, does not know God, because God is love. 1 John 4:8.

I am sure you have met someone who has offered you something too good to be true. It may have been a used car, a house or a horse, or someone like a "rock solid investment in pine tree plantations", as happened to my wife and I. (In our case, we were fortunate to notice that the proposal still had the name of the last person who had been offered this "iron clad" investment, suggesting that he had not researched our "risk profile" as well as he claimed.) If we are wise, this sort of experience leads us to apply the rule, *If an offer is too good to be true, it probably is.* In cases where we suspect that someone has put lipstick on a pig to make it look good, we should question their motives to see whether they really do have our best interests at heart, or whether they want to get their hands on our money – or perhaps, more importantly, on our soul. Of course, we don't want to be cynical about every offer; but neither do we want to be duped into being a fool who is easily parted from our money, or our soul. Relationships of all kinds are built upon trust, and this requires that what we say to each other is identical with our motives toward the other. When trust breaks down, especially in intimate relationships, we are in deep trouble. So how can we tell whether a person is worthy of our trust? One thing is that they would not ever ask us for payment before we have seen and tested the goods. They would be happy for us to "try before we buy", especially if it's a used car. Of course, there are some instances where it is not possible to get an absolute assurance of another person's offer of goods or their motives toward us, so we need to take a small risk to see if a bigger risk is worth taking. It is the same where there is a lot at stake, such as with an offer of happiness or success in life. We need to check the bona fides of the person making an offer before we accept it.

I suggest that you should consider the Golden Rule in the same cautious way: because it promises so much, you should be wary about who is making the offer, and whether can you test the product before you sign the contract. I would like to remind you that although it is God who desires only good things for us and who ultimately provides us an abundant and fulfilling life, we still need to check the bona fides of his agent who is making the offer. How can we check the product that Jesus says is the secret to life? How can we be sure that the preacher's motives are consistent with what he says? In fact, the whole biblical narrative about Jesus confirms that he is trustworthy, because what he says and what he does are consistent to the extent that he gave his life for us, as the text at the start of this chapter, John 10:9, suggests. But we still need to be cautious about who will benefit from our venture of faith in God.

Amazingly, the Golden Rule has an inbuilt detector for bad smelling untruths. It is always necessary for us to judge every application of it by our own standard of integrity, because the

Golden Rule requires that you treat others as you would want to be treated. This is important as it achieves a couple of things at the same time. First, it allows you to take the initiative to be in control and sit behind the wheel during the test drive to control the many variables. Second, it allows you to determine for yourself if the product – the Golden Rule itself – is what you have been led to believe it is. If we seek assurance as to the pedigree of the Golden Rule, we need to go no further than the Hebrew Bible that we call the Old Testament. As we will see later in this chapter, similar statements appear in other religions and philosophies that may be attributed to human wisdom. But this is not the case with the Biblical Golden Rule which claims to be an intrinsic part of God's revelation to the Jewish nation.

According to the theologian N.T. Wright, the entire story of the Bible begins with this narrative of God's creative acts and our fall from intimate relationship with him. The remainder of the Bible story is about God's plan to put "the world to rights". By this Wright means that God's entire purpose is to restore our relationship with him and prepare us to find our place in God's Kingdom, known as Paradise.[1] I will attempt to explain how God accomplishes his purposes by his glory, which he described as the scope of his character – his love, grace, mercy and justice. God's Glory is the means of reconciliation between us and God, as first revealed to Moses on Mt Sinai when God gave him the Ten Commandments, written on stone tablets by God's hand. The Ten Commandments, then, are a manifestation of the Glory of God, but they are not its totality. Rather, the Ten Commandments and the Bible as a whole are signposts pointing us to God. They also help us to know what direction to travel in and when we have arrived in God's Kingdom because we will see God's law manifest within us as an outcome of his Glory, which I will try to explain

---

1   http://ntwrightpage.com/2016/05/06/putting-the-world-to-rights/

first hand. Good relationships are the key to my discovery of God's purposes for me in his creation. When relationships go well, life is good, purposeful and satisfying. When relationships fail, life is not so good. The Apostle Paul describes this ideal state as *God being in Christ, reconciling the world to himself* (2 Cor 5:19). Our task, I believe, is to achieve reconciliation between ourselves first as this enables the possibility of a renewed relationship between us and God. Having commenced this way, we can then begin further preparation for an experience of unimaginable glory which we only catch a glimpse in the wonders of creation and the beauty of the cosmos. I hope to demonstrate that this is what the Golden Rule both teaches us and prepares us to enjoy on an increasing scale. This is the means by which we re-discover our place in paradise. Nothing more, and nothing less.

Abraham, Moses, the law and the Glory of God

According to the Old Testament, the people of Israel held a unique relationship with God as his chosen and favored people, and thus serve as a model for all other people. If they continued to reciprocate his love and obey his commands, God would bless the Israelites and cause them to flourish as a nation. However, they began to see God's law as an imposition and a restriction to their freedom rather than a spiritual, moral and behavioral restraint and guidance for their own benefit. The law came to be seen not as the key to receiving and remaining in God's love and mercy, but instead a necessary duty which they mistakenly thought entitled them to God's favor. The story of the Exodus explains that when Moses, who had led the Israelites out of captivity in Egypt into the desert, went to receive the Ten Commandments from God on Mt Sinai, the Israelites became impatient with his absence and created a Golden Calf which they worshipped in a frenzied orgy. Utterly frustrated with the rebellion and hard-heartedness of his people, Moses demanded God to reveal himself so that people would know who it is that they are following. However, Moses was not to see the full revelation of God's face; instead, this would have to wait until the advent of Jesus, the Living Word of God made into human flesh.

> *Then the* LORD *came down in the cloud and stood there with him and proclaimed his name, the Lord. And he passed in front of Moses, proclaiming, "The* LORD, *the* LORD, *the compassionate and gracious God, slow to anger, abounding in love and faithfulness, maintaining love to thousands, and forgiving wickedness, rebellion and sin. Yet he does not leave the guilty unpunished..."* (Ex 34:5-7).

About 1400 years later, Jesus was born as the incarnation of God, and proclaimed that the Golden Rule is a summary of God's Old Testament laws and the teachings of the prophets as a revelation of God's love for his creation. God's gift of the Ten Commandments to Moses was evidence that God loved them as his chosen people and has *willed the highest good for them*, which, according to Thomas Aquinas, is the definition of love.[1]

Israel's common religious view became that God's favor must be gained by complying with the law as summarized by the Ten Commandments. Faithful Israelites should have known better as they recited the Shema every day and said:

> *"Hear oh Israel, the Lord our God is One"* ...
> *"Love the Lord your God with all your heart, soul and strength"* (Deut 6:5).

We recognize this as the first of two parts of the Golden Rule, that is also known as the law of love. Israel's view of God's demand

---

1 Thomas Aquinas, *Summa Theologica*.

for compliance, however, is a misreading of God's intention as he yearned for their love and relationship, not just their compliance with the letter of the law. It remained for Jesus to correct Israel's failed relationship with God by adding a second part to their daily reminder of how to relate to Him:

> *You must not hate your brother in your heart. You must surely reprove your fellow citizen so that you do not incur sin on account of him. You must not take vengeance or bear a grudge against the children of your people, but you must love your neighbor as yourself. I am the* LORD (Lev 19:17-18).

Of course, it is these two combined and summarized that we know as the Great Commandment or as the Golden Rule which is recorded in the first three Gospels, most comprehensively by Mark:

> *And one of the scribes came up and heard them disputing with one another, and seeing that he answered them well, asked him, "Which commandment is the most important of all?" Jesus answered, "The most important is, 'Hear, O Israel: The Lord our God, the Lord is one. And you shall love the Lord your God with all your heart and with all your soul and with all your mind and with all your strength.' The second is this: 'You shall love your neighbor as yourself.' There is no other commandment greater than these"* (Mk 12:28-31).

John's Gospel records it slightly differently as he is inclined to do, as the New Commandment.

When he had gone out, Jesus said, "Now is the Son of Man glorified, and God is glorified in him. If God is glorified in him, God will also glorify him in himself, and glorify him at once. Little children, yet a little while I am with you. You will seek me, and just as I said to the Jews, so now I also say to you, 'Where I am going you cannot come.' A new commandment I give to you, that you love one another: just as I have loved you, you also are to love one another. By this all people will know that you are my disciples, if you have love for one another" (Jn 13:31-35).

The main point of the New Testament is that Jesus took these words as the central message of God to humanity to its logical conclusion because he loved us. Jesus offered himself to atone for the sins of humanity, thus allowing all who want to experience God's love and blessing to do so, provided they recognize Jesus' sacrifice of love. Jesus prepared us for this at the commencement of his ministry, when he said, *I have come not to abolish the law, but to fulfill it* (Matt 5:17 paraphrased), which brings God's giving of the law to Moses back into view. Jesus later declares that the Golden Rule fulfils the requirements of the law and the prophets as we have just seen. Incredibly, many of us continue to make the same mistake as the Israelites at the foot of Mt Sinai when we understand God's commands as a limitation on our freedom rather than a path towards it, because we prefer rebellion and sin to the benefits of obedience to God. I will develop this theme further in Chapter 7, where I show how the 10 Commandments and Jesus' New Covenant of Love, is part of a much larger statement regarding God's love, which is fulfilled and enabled by the Golden Rule.

The Golden Rule recipe (How not to over-egg the cake)

Success is usually the result of a process of applying what we have learned and believe to be true when faced with different problems or opportunities, using what I will call, for the sake of discussion, an algorithm. My son Brock, who designs computer systems using algorithms, says they are more like a recipe, or a series of recipes, than a formula. Someone else said that an algorithm is a mathematical proof that your opinion is correct. I think we will go with the recipe idea for the time being. A recipe, of course, contains several components in a mixture that must be added in at the right time in the right proportion for a cake to be satisfying. Similarly, the recipe for a happy life contains several ingredients that I consider to be essential, things that we must properly select and mix in carefully to ensure that life is not spoiled, such as "faith," "hope," "love," remembering that it is possible to over-egg the cake with too much of one thing, and not enough of another.

Jeffery Wattles examines the Golden Rule from many points of view including that it could be the necessary and sufficient foundation of a universal religion of all human ethics which requires no other references to *"controversial axioms"* that is *"invulnerable to counterexamples"* presented against it. (p 4) He observes that *"philosophers and professionals"* are embarrassed when the Golden Rule is taken with *"philosophical seriousness,"* "because of its religious origins (p 6). Wattles resolves this esoteric debate masterfully, concluding that *"...only a principle so flexible can serve as the moral ladder for all mankind,"* and *"Whoever practices the*

Golden Rule opens him/herself to a process of change." (p 188) The Golden Rule. Jeffrey Wattles.

The Golden Rule is usually considered a sort of wise saying, or an ethical principle or a maxim. And it is. But I have found it to be far more than this, too. In fact, I hope to convince you that the Golden Rule is the Secret of the Ages because it teaches us about what love is, and how love works in our relationships – with God and with each other. Despite my use of the word "love," I suggest that in this context this word has a far more practical meaning than we would normally apply to it. Consider, if you will, that God is the designer and creator of all things and we are his creation, made in his image. If this is so, then we should seek to understand what his original design purposes were for human beings, and whether we are using our opportunities in a way that is "fit for our intended purpose". This, in my view, is not an unreasonable goal. The discoveries of science have revealed the incredible complexity of the universe, and its widely acknowledged "fine tuning" to support life. I suggest that if we understand our design purposes better, we will discover that we – in our bodies, souls and spirits – are similarly fine-tuned for specific purposes. Some of these functions, such as love, have always been known instinctively as poets and songwriters have so beautifully expressed; but some other aspects and functions of our being are just beginning to be discovered, such as DNA and its role in the human genome. I propose that what we are beginning to see is that our relationship to God should be one of awe and enquiry; that same recognition which led the Psalmist to say:

> *I praise you because I am fearfully and wonderfully made; your works are wonderful, I know that full well* (Ps 149:13).

Accordingly, we should be doing all we can to understand this complexity as it applies to us, not just of our physical bodies, but also that of our souls and spirits to understand whether what we are doing is the "highest good" for ourselves, as this is the definition of love which I believe unlocks our human potential, enabled by the Golden Rule. I consider the Golden Rule to be an algorithm, or I should say, recipe, that is designed to perform exactly such a function – to enable us to continue to learn, first about ourselves, then about our relationship to others, and finally, about God and how we relate to him to find our destined place and purpose in His Kingdom. Another way of looking at this puzzle is to ask what we can learn from the Golden Rule about our personal enlightenment, our transition from a limited place in a material world to an important role in an everlasting transcendent world of faith, hope, love. This is a big question that the Golden Rule answers by providing process for our transition from the material and temporal world to a spiritual and eternal reality. According to the Christian apologist William Lane Craig, Anselm of Canterbury proposed that God is the highest good that can be imagined – a principle encapsulated in Anselm's ontological argument.[1] Regardless of whether you accept Anselm's argument or not, it is reasonable, in my view, to hold that God is the first cause of all matter, energy, time and space, including the laws which control the universe. Although I would not claim this to be a "proof", because such a proof is not possible, I would say that it is reasonable on the balance of probabilities, for the same reasons that CS Lewis holds: because it helps us to make sense of many of those realities that are not explicable by science, such as the basic concepts of time, space, and energy, to say nothing of faith, hope and love.

Is faith good?

You may have questions about the necessity and reliability of faith, such as, Is it necessary for enlightenment? And if so, why is it that it can be so easily be manipulated and misused by charlatans? This is a good question, and one that we must answer. To begin, it does

---

1   https://www.iep.utm.edu/ont-arg/

seem a little strange to suggest that enlightenment needs anything more than knowledge, considering the advances made by science in improving life for the majority of humanity. But you don't know what you don't know. Scientific knowledge can answer lots of technical questions as to how things work, but it cannot solve everything, such as offering ethical solutions to the problems. So we need another way of probing what we don't know and cannot yet discover by science. This is the role of faith; and it is worth noting that even science proceeds in this way – by intuition (if you prefer this to using the "f" word). I suggest that faith, according to the biblical definition, is essential to the discovery of things that we can only hope are true until we have evidence that they are, or are not.

As for the possibility that faith can be misused, so can anything else that we consider to be good. Everything essential for life, such as fire, water, and winds both hot and cold, can be harmful if it is deliberately misused or too strongly emphasized at the cost of other considerations. Faith, according to the Bible, is the *substance of what we hope for, the evidence of things yet unseen* (Heb 11). In other words, faith is what we hope is true, consistent with what we have experienced so far. Faith temporarily fills in the gaps in our knowledge until we have gained knowledge to understand the visible world we live in, and the unseen world yet to come. Faith is not a blind leap, as Richard Dawkins says it is, nor is it mere superstition or a dread fear of the unknown. Rather, faith, as properly defined, is a series of small reasonable steps that we take in the direction of what we believe and hope for, and what makes sense to us, because we experience it as bringing rewards. This is not the "God of the gaps" that atheists scorn. Rather, it is a tentative venture into the unknown based on the best available evidence, just like the experiments that scientists perform. It is therefore a search for confirmation that what we hope is true is reliable, as it is confirmed by experience.

It is not just religious dreamers who depend upon faith. Scientists rely upon it so they can apply themselves toward a particular discovery that they hope will be manifest by following experiments whose truth can only be "proven" by the fact that it works reliably. I will later make exactly the same claim for Christian faith. The American novelist Mark Twain said that *"faith is believing in what you know ain't so"*.[1] Twain also said, "Twenty years from now you will be more disappointed by the things that you didn't do than by the ones you did do. So throw off the bowlines. Sail away from the safe harbor. Catch the trade winds in your sails. Explore. Dream. Discover." (Source uncertain) Mark Twain's mistake was to confuse categories. On one hand, he is suggesting that faith is exclusively a religious impulse to believe something that is not real. On the other hand, he is saying that the zest and vitality for adventure in life is something different, when in my view they are both the same thing. The Bible explains that faith does not rely upon the certainty of knowledge or sight. In fact, it says that when something is "seen," then faith is no longer required. So then, faith is always applied to something that we hope for or anticipate highly because it is an essential source of motivation that leads us down a path we hope is worth following.

What is the highest good?

As Christian faith is related to love and hope, so it should always involve seeking the greatest good, or at least things that are objectively life-giving. This is another reason for the importance of the Golden Rule. By following it, we learn about values more objectively. Business also has a way of learning about and measuring value – usually in the more limited sense of monetary value. People usually go into business to make money, so they embark on their

---

[1] *Following the Equator*, Pudd'nhead Wilson's Calendar by Mark Twain.

venture in the hope that it will be successful. This success is generally measured by how much money they make compared to what they have invested. Maybe you have heard a businessperson saying that their most valuable asset is people; but you know this is not true because of the abysmal way they treat people to make more money. If we were in business and wanted to avoid the mistake of valuing money more than people, then we invest in the Golden Rule rather than a purely financial undertaking. This process of learning about value begins with us because, initially, like all healthy people, we should value ourselves and our activities and undertakings highly. This, however, does not imply unquestioning self-approval because if we are realistic, we are only beginning to be aware of our faulty values.

Paul, the Apostle of Jesus, best captures the human experience of love in 1 Corinthians 13, frequently used at weddings to express loves' highest ideal. Paul presents faith as an element of God's love that he has made available to each of us, according to his own definition. Faith relates to love because they interact and depend upon one another as they must in a marriage for the marriage to survive. When it does, it leads us to say both idealistically and from experience that love is the highest good because it is one of God's good gifts that we have used as it was intended. The passage finishes with the conclusion:

> *And now these three remain: faith, hope and love.*
> *But the greatest of these is love* (1 Cor 13:13).

You will recognize that I use this summary as our responsibility toward our relationship with God. Faith, hope and love are his gift toward us that we must invest and return to him, so that our relationship grows when we treat him as we would like to be treated, if we were God. We can say then that the Golden Rule is how we learn God's language of love and discover our place in his Kingdom, which is the thesis of this book: That we invest God-given faith, hope and love back toward God, in obedience to the Golden Rule, because it leads us to discover life in its abundance. I am aware that the Golden Rule has many more purposes than this, plus, our application of it is not the only way we can relate to God, but my purpose in this chapter, is to describe where the Golden Rule came from and what its purpose is in our relationship with God and with each other.

Provided we have a framework for objective learning about reality, such as the Golden Rule, we begin our quest by considering what we think to be true, and then, as we proceed step-by-step, we discover what is really true; we learn that while money, for instance, is important, it is not as important as relationships. The process required by the Golden Rule, plus our sense of accountability to God, helps to put our values in the proper order, with the things of highest value at the top, and the things we value least at the bottom. This process of enlightenment guides us to make good decisions based on real values. Eventually, we will see that the highest value of all is love, and then we learn to order our lives around this new reality. Although we like to think of this search for the greatest good as a modern phenomenon, similar quests for meaning are surprisingly ancient. Most modern searches and solutions are simply a rehashing of things that have been tried hundreds, and in some cases thousands, of years ago. The most ancient examples are recorded in primitive art discovered in caves across the world, particularly in Australia, Indonesia and Europe – paintings that have been determined by carbon dating to be perhaps 40,000 years old.[1] Such records of human expression are often depictions of recognizable animals, or a stencil outline of a human hand painted in white pigment that suggests "I was here", "this is my home", or "I belong here". Other more religious images of ghostly non-human spirit figures suggest that early superstitions

---

1 https://www.livescience.com/48199-worlds-oldest-cave-art-photos.html

were not restricted to material reality, but consciousness of ghosts and gods, both good and evil.

Over the past two thousand years or so, possibly for much longer, we have seen the strong emergence of the abuse of human aspiration and motivation, particularly regarding money, sex and power. The proper use of them is necessary for human flourishing, provided they are pursued within proper limits. This was especially the case with the mythological gods of ancient Greece who were like personifications of human passion, ambition and rivalry, along with other human traits which in no way expressed God's love as we now understand it. Some philosophies which emerged during this period continue today, such as honouring the gods of Epicure who delighted in the sensual pleasures of food and wine, or the god Eros, who found the ultimate expression of pleasure and meaning in sexual experiences. Later still, in about 480 BC, political and military power were celebrated in a book called *The Art of War* by Sun Tzu. Niccolò Machiavelli's book, *The Prince,* has become a standard text about how to gain and use military and political power for personal advantage since it was published 400 years ago. While perhaps not admitting to following Machiavelli as their guide, many people now practice ???? the same deceptions and corruptions of power consciously, justifying their actions with the rationale that if they don't take advantage of another person, someone else will, and so to not do so means that one is likely to become a victim of illegitimate power. This approach to power is often justified in highly competitive activities such as sport, business, and global politics. Such a "win at all costs" mentality reveals the deep arrogance of some people. The problem, I think, reveals the excessively high value competitive influences have in some relationships. Survival, in my view, must favor cooperation, not competition. Other texts have idealized the pursuit of human desire, including the ancient Hindu sex manual, the Kama Sutra, and its modern equivalent, Internet pornography, as an imagined source of liberation from oppressive religious impositions. In modern "enlightened" times where we think we have made progress away from primitive superstitions, we find our tastes returning to epicurean evaluation of food and wine on social media or the Internet obsession with pornography. Of our most primal motivations, sex is the one that most often gets out of control today in this technological age because it is so easily available and immediately satisfying – or at least, so we think.

Many current pursuits bear the signs of the quest for the ultimate lifestyle that is realized in terms of money, power, material goods, emotional and sensual experience. Examples range from the Playboy philosophy to the emergence of new religions such as Mormonism and Scientology, all of which try to answer the same questions about the ultimate life, somewhat cynically. For instance, Joseph Smith, the founder of Mormonism, had the same prurient interest in sex as did Hugh Hefner, the founder of Playboy Magazine. L Ron Hubbard declared that his motivation for starting Scientology was "to make money." Meanwhile, the rest of the world seems to be trying to emulate the success of Western Capitalism, with or without political democracy, as we observe the rise of Japan or China, largely mimicking what they think is the financial success formula of the West, promising to provide access to wealth, comfort and continual improvement resulting from our harnessing of science and technology with an apparent high degree of success. Despite the relentless search, U2 singer Bono expresses our lonely restlessness by saying that we *still haven't found what we're looking for.*

Is the Golden Rule, Golden?

In this secular age, the Golden Rule and similar principles are often discounted because of their association with religion. According to many critics, because of the harm that has been done by religion, it has become necessary to separate religious principles from the values and laws of modern secular states to avoid its contaminating effects. Even the faintest suggestion of the possibility of Divine revelation interfering with philosophy and politics, or discussions about what is a good person, are not admitted unless caveats are made to include the possibility of "good atheists," for instance. An example of this is the philosopher Alain de Botton's "Atheist Ten Commandments," in which he attempts to prove that ethics are not dependent upon religion. Apart from him eliminating the need to acknowledge the ultimacy of God, most of de Botton's "top ten" are poor facsimiles of the originals, or second order injunctions that provide no new insights as to what morality is or how it is determined.

I believe that if the Golden Rule is once again made central to the life, teaching and witness of the church, it will have a radical effect – on the church first of all, and then upon society as a whole, because it has happened before since the beginning of the Christian era and in Britain and in the USA, as a major social movement during the 20th Century. The current conditions of the Western world demand that such a reformation needs to happen again to revitalize the church, and for churches to perform their intended role in society, not just as a protector of religious doctrine, but rather as an example of what society should become. However, the Golden Rule is not just a religious theory. Whether or not it is a divinely revealed principle should make no difference to our acceptance or rejection of it within secular society. Close examination of the history, nature, function and applicability of the Golden Rule will show that it is highly practical and useful because it is conceptually simple, and able to be taught to children and practiced by them. When it is used as a serious ethical principle by adults as well as children, it begins to affect individual relationships in a remarkable and observable way that would, I believe, satisfy the demands of scientific rigor. I will later demonstrate that the Golden Rule has a powerful transformative effect when it is seriously applied by individuals who want to improve their relationships and the quality of their lives. However, it is also apparent that the Golden Rule is difficult to implement because it challenges the essence of who we are and the perceived rights and entitlements of individuals in society.

We will see that the Golden Rule is most effective when it takes root in circumstances conducive to good relationships, such as in a marriage, where if it is well applied, it causes people to thrive for many reasons. One important reason is the reciprocal effect it has on both the person who initiates it and the person who receives it. This, however, is not a calculated reciprocity based on the principle of "I'll scratch your back if you'll scratch mine". Although so-called altruistic reciprocity improves relationships, it does not compare with Christ's Golden Rule, which carries the authority of a commandment of God. Most importantly, the Golden Rule responds exactly to the innate human need that is satisfied by loving relationships. Especially when they are filled with rational purpose and meaning and are supportive of our individual roles in society and in God's spiritual kingdom.

The law of non-contradiction

The universality of the Golden Rule has its origin in logic and mathematics. This is important because, despite our human need for certainty, we know that most arguments about history, religion and philosophy cannot be proven in any absolute sense because they are not measurable scientifically. Certainly, evidence can be provided to support almost any point of view in any field, but the scientific proof that modern people desire is not readily available where ethical questions are concerned. Theories in mathematics, on the other hand, can be proven because they work so consistently. If proofs are conducted according to mathematical principles, it is possible for different people to follow the same procedure and come up with the same answer, which is the test that science requires of itself. I propose that the Golden Rule is exceptional in philosophy and religion because it is based on the Law of Non-Contradiction, which makes it verifiable according to the laws of logic. This gives us an additional level of assurance that the Golden Rule's logical conclusions are more reliable than other forms of religious or philosophical speculation. The Law of Non-Contradiction is a foundational natural law. It was first used when Adam and Eve were asked by God to name the animals. For this task to be possible, a basic system of taxonomy was required which systematically classifies animals into logical "kinds" which God had already specified so Adam could distinguish one animal species from another.

The Law of Non-Contradiction states that: something cannot be both A and non A at the same time and place. The logic of how the Law of Non-Contradiction apples to the Golden Rule can be conceptualized by the following diagrams: If God loves me unconditionally, then he loves you unconditionally also. If I know that God loves me giving me a high self-regard, then I love myself and seek the good for myself. If I love myself, it then follows logically that I must then love both God and you.

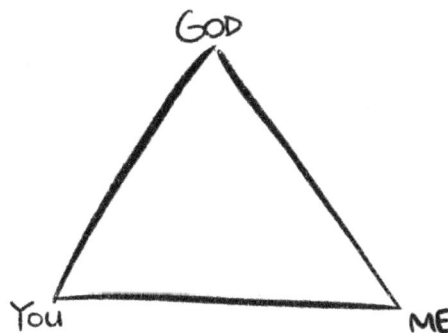

God loves you and me, because he made us in his image

I love God in return for his love to me. This eventually requires that I will love what God loves and hate what he hates. Therefor, I must love you because God loves you as much as he loves me.

Put another way, the logic of the Law of Non-Contradiction as it applies to the Golden Rule is as follows:

- God is love. He is the source of love and the essence of love
- God's act of creation is motivated by his love for his creatures
- God loves me because I am part of his creation
- If God loves me, He also loves you because we were both made in his image
- Because God loves me, I also love myself because I am uniquely valuable to Him
- God's love for me is reflected in my love for myself
- If God loves me, then I love God because He first loved me
- Because God loves me, I must also love you

As the law of non-contradiction is the basis of human conscious thought, speech, grammar, mathematics and cooperative behavior, it is the foundation of human consciousness. As such, it is the basis of orderly thinking, and without it we would not possess the human characteristics that separate us from other animals. The law of non-contradiction holds that something cannot be A and non A at one and the same time and in the same respect. This logical truth underpins our most basic thinking, since it allows us to separate one thing from another. For example, when we say "apple", we mean something distinctly different to the word "orange". An apple cannot be both an apple and an orange at one and the same time, in the same respect, and so on. If we were not able to make this distinction, then language could not convey the meaning required for human understanding and interaction. In other words, for speech to be comprehensible, it must be reasonable, logical and non-contradictory.

Logical thinking, then, is based upon the universal principle of non-contradiction. This is true of all human thought and language, which explains why it is possible for human languages to be learned and translated, because the logical or syntactic structures behind all human languages are similar. Any exceptions to the rule, such as the concept of paradox, which is an apparent contradiction, are usually intentional or employed for the purpose of provocation, or perhaps to suggest a mystery. Often, though, the use of paradox is an implied admission of ignorance where the speaker lacks sufficient knowledge to explain some obscure concept. I am not trying to confuse you with pseudo-intellectual language. My point is to share with you what I have discovered in relation to the Golden Rule and the law of non-contradiction – something that has re-assured me of its profound significance to human interactions. But it is not the intellectual or philosophical background of this argument that is most important. Rather, the crucial point of this argument is that the Golden Rule is essentially practical, because it is based in the foundations of human understanding and behavior. This reliance upon logic and knowledge, however, does not mean that they are always sufficient to explain all phenomena. I will explain later that reason alone, as important as it is to humanity, is insufficient because the reality in which we live is not limited just to a material world of time, space, energy and matter. There are other dimensions of human experience and capability that are also necessary for human flourishing, including considerations of the human soul and spirit in addition to our material bodies. Once again, the existence of a conscious mind alone suggests that there is more at play than meets the eye. The experience of human soul and spirit, which includes the realities of faith, hope reveals an appreciation of a dimension beyond the limitations of reason.

I am reassured in my belief about the veracity of the Golden Rule and its relationship to the Law of Non-Contradiction by the work of the mathematician, philosopher and theologian Alfred North Whitehead, who, with his student Bertrand Russell, wrote the *Principia Mathematica* – a book in which the law of non-contradiction is explained mathematically by the formula:

$$*3 \cdot 24. \quad \vdash . \sim (p . \sim p)$$

I have no idea what this means mathematically as I think of it as a beautiful artifact that I invite you to accept by faith as I have done. The Golden Rule, *To treat others as I would want to be treated*, requires me to truly believe that any treatment, favor or advantage that I might want for myself I should also want for you, since we are both made in God's image and have equal status before him. To not believe this and live accordingly is a contradiction, and therefore should be regarded as a sin: to have fallen short of what God requires of us. Sin, as we know, separates us from God and from each other.

Further evidence that this is a universal principle is reflected in the fact that the Golden Rule, or at least variations of the concept, exist in many different cultural formulations, as shown in the below table outlining the "positive" and "negative" versions of it. I describe a formulation of the Golden Rule "negative" if it is presented as an injunction *not* to do something harmful to another. A positive version of the Golden Rule, by contrast, involves an instruction or command to do something positive toward another person, for their benefit.

Ancient and Modern Versions of the Golden Rule[1]	
Version	**Distinctive features**
Egyptian. Middle Kingdom	Two versions, one positive, one negative
Ancient India, Sanskrit Tamil	Positive Negative, extensive positive commentary
Hinduism	Negative
Buddhism	Negative

---

1 This table is compiled from Wikipedia, *The Golden Rule*. https://en.wikipedia.org/wiki/Golden_Rule

Where did the Golden Rule come from?

Ancient Greece.	
Thales	Negative
Sextus	Negative
Isocrates	Negative
Ancient Persia Zoroastrianism	Negative
Confucianism	Negative
Ancient Rome Seneca	Positive (relating only to treatment of slaves)
Judaism	Positive imperative command of God. Several positive references: Lev 19:18, 19:34.
Christianity	Positive imperative command of Jesus, adopted from the Old Testament. Matt 7:12, Mark 12:29-30 Luke 6:31.
Islam	Both negative and positive. Hadith
Humanism	Negative

The "Golden Rule" is given by Jesus of Nazareth in Matt 7:12, Mark 12: 29-30 and Luke 6:31. The common version is;

> *Do unto others as you would have them do unto you*
> is also stated positively in the Old Testament: Lev 19:18: *Do not seek revenge or bear a grudge against anyone among your people, but love your neighbor as yourself. I am the* LORD, and Lev 19:34: *The foreigner residing among you must be treated as your native-born. Love them as yourself, for you were foreigners in Egypt. I am the* LORD *your God.*

The table above shows consistent use of the more common negative version of the Golden Rule throughout history suggesting that humankind has recognized the concept since there have been written records of human consciousness. Whether or not this is a process of discovery by human intelligence or by Divine revelation is a matter of conjecture. Jordan Peterson, representing the scientific/evolutionary view, suggests the former. Rodney Stark, the prolific sociologist who writes mainly about the sociology of religion, proposes that there is evidence of God's revelation throughout human history, which has been corrupted or lost to a greater or lesser degree, as ancient cultures put their own spin on things they don't properly understand. Stark says that the Jews became known as the People of the Book because they were uniquely ethnically homogenous as they traced their lineage to Abraham, who was the recipient of God's promise of continuing relationship between him and them. The Jews uniquely preserved their written records of the revelation of their monotheistic God, sometimes to the point of death.[1]

Regardless of their source, the negative versions of the Golden Rule pale by comparison with the positive Judeo-Christian version. Even the difference between the Old Testament version and the New Testament teachings of Jesus are profound. Although Jesus draws on the Old Testament law for his version of the Golden Rule, its importance is almost lost within in the hundreds of laws given by Moses to the people of Israel. By comparison, Jesus claims that the Golden Rule summarizes the whole of the "law and the prophets." I find it amazing that there is confusion surrounding the Golden Rule, as both the traditional negative versions and Jesus' positive version are sometimes conflated with the law of reciprocity. This, to my mind, suggests at least a lack of insight into how effective the different versions have been within their cultures, to say nothing of their difference in intellectual rigor. In

---

1 Rodney Stark, *Discovering God*, p. 63, 169.

my view, the negative versions of the rule and the law of reciprocity presented as ideologies, have little force other than as an appeal to polite fairness, rather than a demand for accountability to God, as stated by Jesus.

Jesus' Golden Rule in the Bible

Putting aside the belief that the Bible is the product of Divine revelation, Alfred North Whitehead claims that it is not just a collection of abstract theological statements as other religions tend to be. It is according to him a series of historical events that occur to people in their relationships with each other and with God, from which theology may be derived.[2] This is a very important distinction that many have lost sight of, because the usual presentation of biblical events by preachers is intended to convey some increasingly abstract theological and sometimes spurious point. While I am not denying Divine revelation, it is useful to think that the Golden Rule also follows this pattern of theory being derived from practice, in that what we are given is not a theory so much as a framework for a process that requires our trust and obedience. Apart from the existence and influence of God, the Bible makes very few grand claims for itself, other than to provide a model of what relationships are intended to be, with Christs' obedience to his father God as our example. Another example of such pragmatism is the several versions of the Golden Rule in scripture, which Jesus summarizes as *treat others as you would be treated*. This statement is obviously not all that there is to know about the subject of *the law and the prophets*, but Jesus expresses it simply so that it can be remembered and applied by children in the hope that if they take notice of it, they will discover its complexity later in life, as we are now doing.

---

2 AN Whitehead, *Religion in the making.* http://alfrednorthwhitehead.wwwhubs.com/ritm1.htm.

According to the Philosopher, Dallas Willard, *All God's laws are relational.* This suggests to me why Jesus would claim that the Golden Rule summarized all of the Old Testament law and prophets.[1] When Jesus claims he intends to fulfil the law (Matt 5:17), he does not present God's laws as burdens imposed by God, for their own sake. Rather, they are presented as delightful outcomes of a faithful life, where compliance with laws is not imposed, but as the outcome of our free choice because, by faith, we see that God's laws are good for us because it is through them that we experience our relationship to Jesus and one another. In the New Testament story, Jesus begins to attract his disciples by teaching them a new commandment of love, which became known as the Great Commandment. This law is not one that calls for grudging compliance as the old laws were. Rather, it is more clearly seen as the outcome of our love for our neighbor and God. This is at once the foundation, the process, and the outcome of the Golden Rule.

The following table shows the development of the Golden Rule in the Bible:

Biblical Variants of the Golden Rule
The overarching summary statement of the Bible narrative is that God is Love.
Dear friends, let us love one another, for love comes from God. Everyone who loves has been born of God and knows God. ⁸ Whoever does not love does not know God, because God is love (1 Jn 4:7-21).

---

[1] Dallas Willard, *The Divine Conspiracy.* Also http://www.soulshepherding.org/2015/05/bible-study-and-quotes-on-hearing-god-by-dallas-willard/

1. God's love expressed in creation.	God spoke the world into being and saw that it was good (Gen 1). God made man in his image and saw that it was not good for man to be alone (Gen 2).
2. God's love is characterized by his mercy and justice.	God said to Moses, *I am compassionate, I am merciful, but the unjust will not go unpunished.* Paraphrased. (Ex 33, 34).
3. Moses' summary of Israel's orientation to God.	*Hear O Israel, the Lord your God is one. Love the LORD your God with all your heart and with all your soul and with all your strength* Deut 6:4-5 (Recited daily by faithful Jews as the Shemah Yisrael-daily prayer)
4. Moses instructs the Levite priests in God's command.	*Love your neighbor as yourself.* I am the LORD. (Lev 19: 17-18).
5. Jesus' mission.	Do not think that I have come to abolish the Law or the Prophets; *I have not come to abolish them but to fulfill them.* (Matt 5:17, 22:37-40).
6. Jesus' summary of the law and prophets.	So in everything, *do to others what you would have them do to you,* for this sums up the Law and the Prophets. (Matt 7:12). This has the same meaning as 4, because what we would want for ourselves defines what we think love is. Also Matthew 9:19, Mark 12:31, Luke 6:27, 6:32, 6:35, 10:27.
7. As the father loved me, so I love you.	Jesus says, "as the Father loved me, so I love you". (Jn 15: 9-10, 12:33).

8. Jesus' Great Command.	"The most important one (law)" answered Jesus, "is this: 'Hear, O Israel: The LORD our God, the LORD is one. ³⁰Love the LORD your God with all your heart and with all your soul and with all your mind and with all your strength.' ³¹The second is this: 'Love your neighbor as yourself.' There is no commandment greater than these" (Mk 12:28-33).
9. Jesus' summary of His Golden Rule	"Do to others what you would want them to do to you" (Lk 6:31). Ditto 7 and 8.
10. The Apostle Paul's summary of the Golden Rule	"Love your neighbor as yourself" (Rom 13: 8-10, Gal 5:14).
11. James' Royal Law and Perfect Law	If you really keep the royal law found in Scripture, "Love your neighbor as yourself," you are doing right (Jas 2:8). ...law that gives you freedom (Jas 1:25).
12. Christ's new command; the law of love.	"A new command I give you: Love one another. As I have loved you, so you must love one another. By this all men will know that you are my disciples, if you love one another" (Jn 13:34–35).
13. Reaping and sowing	The concept of what we sow in others, we will reap in ourselves (Lk 19:20-21, Gal 6:7, 2 Cor 5:10, 2 Cor 5:6).
14. The logical conclusion of Christ's command	"Love your enemies" (Matt 5:44, 5:46, Lk 6:27).
15. John's summary of God's purposes in Christ.	"For God so loved the world that he gave his one and only Son, that whoever believes in him shall not perish but have eternal life" (Jn 3:16).

Where did the Golden Rule come from?

16. Peter's injunction to love.	*"...obeying the truth so that you have sincere love for the brothers, love one another deeply, from the heart."* (1 Pt 1:22).
17. Hebrews discussion re the New Covenant and reminder of the purpose of the new covenant.	(Heb 8, Heb 9:15). *"And let us consider how we may spur one another on toward love and good deeds,"* (Heb 10:24).
18. The conclusion in Revelation of the purposes of God's love, manifest in Jesus' sacrifice.	*...from Jesus Christ, who is the faithful witness, the firstborn from the dead, and the ruler of the kings of the earth. To him who loves us and has freed us from our sins by his blood* (Rev 1:5).

The purpose of this table is to illustrate the continuity of the themes of the Golden Rule throughout the Bible. The detail of God's manifestation of Himself and His law is explained by Moses as a summary of all the events of the historical relationship between God and the Jews, from Abraham forward. God summarizes His own Glory in Exodus 33 and 34: *I am compassionate, I am merciful, but the unjust will not go unpunished.* (Ex 33, 34 paraphrased). God's glory is his characteristics of compassion, his grace and mercy, and his justice, which are manifest either explicitly or by implication throughout scripture and is fundamental to a proper understanding of our relationship with God. Jesus' statement that he has come to fulfil the law is finally completed on the cross as he invests all that he has in his relationship with his father, God.

God's compassion, grace, mercy and justice are demonstrated by Jesus in his love of God, which facilitates God's reconciliation of the world to Himself as suggested in John 3:16, which we will return to later. This compilation suggests to me that the statements of Moses, Jesus, the Apostles, Paul, John, James and Peter and the writer of Hebrews had this consistent theme in mind. Later biblical writings needed only to imply the new covenant of love, because by then it was so well established among them.

God is love

The foundation of the Golden Rule is the law of love, also known as the New Covenant. This, in turn, reflects the nature of God, as God is love. As all love comes from God, then if you have experienced it, you have experienced the presence of God. And having experienced it, you may it seek it further.

The Golden Rule is not the definition of love. It is a process of entering a relationship with God that requires we enter a relationship with each other. Its purpose is to teach us that God is love and that he desires good things for us.

In this chapter, I have tried to convince you that the author of the Golden Rule is God, and that it is a universal ethical injunction deeply embedded in the foundations upon which human societies exist. I hope I have also convinced you that Jesus of Nazareth had a unique take on the Golden Rule, not just as a trustworthy all-encompassing statement of Old Testament law, but as providing a radical new insight into the law of love that is the basis of the new Covenant between God and humankind with Jesus as its mediator because of his obedience to his father and his sacrifice at Calvary. As we progress on our journey, we will gain many more insights and learn many more applications of the Golden Rule that I contend are unique in human history and experience as the path toward a full and satisfying life, both now and in eternity.

4

WHO NEEDS THE GOLDEN RULE?

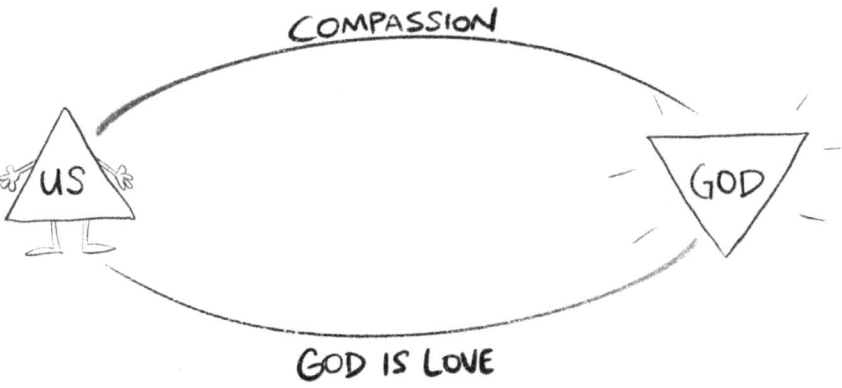

*The Christian ideal has not been tried and found wanting;
it has been found difficult and left untried.*

— G.K. Chesterton.

The point of the Golden Rule, I believe, is to enable us to learn about God's love for us. This is first a message for the faithful. It is also a message for unbelievers, if they are interested in living a fulfilled and satisfying life of enjoyment and purpose, on good terms with other people with whom they work, play, live and love.

Despite the religious implications and the biblical origins of this statement, the utility of the Golden Rule is not dependent upon a religious context for it to be effective as a universal ethical principle. It is, however, greatly enhanced if its Judeo-Christian origins are referenced as they are in the full version of Christ's Great Commandment, to *Love the Lord your God with all your heart, mind soul and strength, and your neighbor as yourself.* In either case, it doesn't function as a law for simple compliance by which we gain credit, but as a complex process by which we learn something about ourselves in relationship to others. In the secular case, our learning would be more a moral-intellectual discipline and an emotional undertaking. The biblical alternative is all these things, plus the potential of being accountable and Divinely inspired by faith in God and the powerful enabling presence of God's holy spirit, especially if we engage as an act of obedience to Jesus Christ.

The scope of the Golden Rule was summarized by the Ten Commandments. The purpose of the Old Testament law was to benefit humanity; to help us and not to harm us. God's expectations were expressed as law to ensure that there could be no misunderstanding as to what we were required to know and do in response to him. However, as we know from the Bible and from the history of humankind, we have continually failed to meet his standards because perversely, to make something wrong often makes it desirable. From God's initial giving of a law to Adam and Eve not to eat of the one tree in the Garden of Eden, his purposes for us are always thwarted by our desire and ability to mis-use our freedom. Following repeated failures of his chosen people, Israel, to obey him, God's ultimate gift of Jesus was intended to overcome the power and the consequences of human sin, once and for all. This suggests that no matter what conditions and expectations God may have had, he realized that we were always going to misuse our freedom and fall short of his expectations. Christ's incarnation is God playing his best hand by declaring his love for us so clearly, that there could be no mistake as to his intentions or to his solution to sin and rebellion. His most explicit declaration of his motivation is perhaps the best-known verse in the Bible: *For God so loved the world, that he gave his one and only Son, that whoever believes in him shall not perish but have eternal life* (Jn 3:16). God is motivated by love, because he is love. The death and resurrection of Christ dispensed with the need for our compliance with the law to earn favor with God and replaced it with his offer of grace for our acceptance. The Golden rule is the one requirement which summarizes the law with one new commandment, to which we are still free to respond or not. If we should choose to not accept God's offer of grace, then God does not immediately impose his judgement against us. Rather, he allows us to suffer the consequences of our choice by the adverse effect our sin has on human relationships and our separation from him. This is not God's retribution against us nor is it a contradiction of his love because it is the result of our freedom. However, our continual rejection of God or our misconstruing his intentions as something other than loving kindness, ultimately results in his justice being exercised against us causing eternal separation between us as a result of our choices. I believe that this is absolute in the sense that God does not then change his mind and make us part of his Kingdom against our will.

The concept of a loving God who incarnates himself and then sacrifices himself for us is so implausible that it is rejected by most people, including his chosen ones, the Jews. Nonetheless, this is the story of the Bible. *That God was in Christ, reconciling the world to himself*, according to 2 Cor 5:19. The Golden Rule, also perhaps implausibly, summarizes and fulfils the totality of God's law. It is not something that can be observed superficially nor can God's love be understood by our agreement with just a concept. It is only when we engage with it and its giver, that the power and complexity of the Golden Rule becomes apparent as both a revelation of our entrenched sinfulness and as an antidote to sin that finally enables us to keep God's law; by the power of his love, not by our compliance. The more we engage, the more we discover that rather than just another of many laws, following the Golden Rule involves a process in which we discover each day how much he loves us, and how we can experience his love in real relationships that makes an immediate difference to us and our neighbors, family and friends, the common good and eventually, to God himself. If this is true as I claim it is, then I cannot imagine a single person who would not benefit from applying the Golden Rule in their lives—unless of course, their motives are contrary to God's, and their intention is not to help but to harm us and him. The Golden Rule, then, at its most basic level requires me to apply my mind to both my own and to your situation. As I do so, I begin to see that my unrestrained ego is selfish and prevents me from loving you, and therefore, from loving God. I further believe that an unbeliever's pursuit of the Golden Rule, leads them to see the reality of God's good creation and how they should respond to God's intended purpose for them, for their and God's shared pleasure.

Love hurts

A couple of years ago, the magnificently politically incorrect comedian, Bill Maher, who hosts an HBO talk show, *Real Time with Bill Maher*, presented a segment entitled 'The Hypocrisy of Evangelical Christians', which I invite you to watch, if you dare. If you demur, he points out that most evangelical Christians (more a political identification in the USA than in other countries) fail to obey Jesus, as they are more fans than followers. He says "*if you ignore everything you are commanded to do, you're not a Christian, you're just auditing.*"[1] Ouch! Maher is putting his finger in the eye of evangelical Christians who are the first to complain about a range of political, moral and social issues, but who are often slow in providing solutions, other than to criticize others. Consequently, Christians in Western Democracies are often hard to distinguish from our secular neighbors, apart from some harsh political views about law and order, abortion and sexual behavior, based on which Bill Maher makes his case about Christians being hypocrites. It is ironic that of all the observers of Christianity, it is an atheist comedian who cuts to the heart of the Christian church's malaise,

---

1 https://youtu.be/Ao_PdmERD_U

observing that we don't do what we say should be done. What has gone wrong with us that we are easily criticized as self-righteous hypocrites who have failed to do the one thing that Jesus presents as his universal *"new commandment?"*

Despite all I have just said in favor of the Golden Rule, I do not suggest that intellectual acceptance of any one precept (including Christ's Great Commandment) is all that is required of us in order to become disciples of Christ. I am very conscious, for instance, that *God rewards those who diligently seek him* (Heb 11:6) which may include situations and conditions far beyond my experience or imagination. I think of the apostle Peter as an example of flawed and impoverished faith and misunderstanding, who with others, went on to change the world as he became transformed into the image of Christ despite his many errors and false starts. Another example is a primitive person who has never heard the Christian gospel. I believe they are not condemned for what they don't know, according to my understanding of Romans 2, which says that the God judges ignorant people by their conscience.

It is not as though no-one on our side of the religious fence is making the same observations of Christian weakness, but they just don't have the cut-through and exposure of a late-night TV host. But I am baffled by Christians who reject out of hand sincere attempts by fellow-Christians to say the same thing that Bill Maher has said. In almost every case, I have noticed a barrage of objections against any attempted criticism of Christian hypocrisy and our failure to treat the Golden Rule seriously, ranging from outright refusal to engage in discussion, to disagreement about doctrinal priorities, which in my view, entirely misses the point of the Great Commandment. When we were first developing the BunchOBlokes project, I visited a pastor whom I recognized as a leader of the men's ministry to ask him to join forces with us in running a men's conference. Although he graciously agreed, his response to our adoption of the Golden Rule as the central pillar was a dismissive. *"That's Old Testament,"* he said, aligning Christ's New Commandment with the superseded Old Testament law from which it came. I could be wrong, but I suspect that Christians are far too sensitive to criticism, and too defensive of their denominational emphasis in the face of any suggestion that we have failed to respond to Jesus' commands or that our doctrinal priorities are disordered. It also seems to me that we love complexity and distrust simple answers. In our rejection of even the possibility of criticism, we have become entrenched in our incompetence, unable to see that we have not yet learned the baby steps required to follow the Golden Rule. Our problem is not a lack of information, but rather our lack of conscious effort in applying what we already know to be true. Admittedly, the Bible can be a confusing book especially if we try to explain it from a dogmatic sectarian point of view, such as to say that all believers must be Pentecostals, or all believers must not be Pentecostals. The only way to carve scripture up in this way, is to ignore the parts that don't fit our doctrine.

In the 2,000 years of the Christian era, we have had many sectarian variations and corruptions of the Christian theme, beginning with the cautions raised by the Apostle Paul, who declared himself against those who sought to negate his central gospel message with their requirements to return to compliance with the Hebrew law such as Pharisees insisting on circumcision. Then we have had several great convocations of the church where important aspects of the emerging Christian faith were resolved, such as the Council of Nicaea, from which the Nicene Creed emerged. Regretfully, we have also had cycles of the abuse of power by the institutional church, such as the Crusades to recapture the Holy Land and the Spanish Inquisition to enforce orthodoxy. However, following each aberration, there has been a correction back to the narrow path of Christian faith led by the great reformers such as John Wycliffe, Jan Hus, William Tyndale, Martin Luther, John Calvin, the Wesley brothers, and many others.

Tragically, even these reforms have gone on to become a distortion of orthodoxy themselves. The thing that encourages me most of all is that we have the scriptures to guide us back to the teachings of the prophets, Jesus and the apostles, if only we would take the trouble to carefully read them and the related history of the outcomes of their faith. I do not intend to create a diatribe against all denominations and distinctive Christian doctrines, as most have been important as a corrective at some point in time. But I do advocate in favor of proper prioritization of principles and teaching of "Beautiful Orthodoxy" of the true, the good and the beautiful, a term coined by Mark Galli of *Christianity Today* magazine to reflect Biblical Christian faith across the board sweep of history and human experience.

About three years ago, a Roman Catholic man named Michael Murphy joined our men's small group so that we could make him into a good Baptist. Michael introduced me to many of his influences including Bishop Robert Barron, the Catholic magazine *First Things*, and now to Pope Benedict's Encyclical Letter, *Deus Caritas Est: On Christian Love*, which has changed my view of the scope of what it means to be a Christian by overcoming some of my prejudice and seeing truth emerging from unfamiliar places. Most particularly, though, my prejudices are challenged by individual people whose faith is tangible and exemplary. I am not a Catholic, nor am I sympathetic to some Catholic teaching, such as papal infallibility, but Pope Benedict's book has newly informed my understanding of the Christian gospel as it is a masterpiece of simplicity and depth. Reading each page has caused me to stop and reflect on things that I thought I already understood. Pope Benedict has provided me with new certainty regarding the pre-eminence of the Golden Rule with statements such as this:

> *The transition which he (Jesus) makes from the Law and the Prophets to the twofold commandment of love of God and of neighbor, and his grounding of*

> the whole life of faith on this central precept, is not simply a matter of morality-something that could exist apart from and alongside faith in Christ and its sacramental re-actualization. (*Deus Caritas Est. On Christian Love.* Pope Benedict XVI. St Pauls Publications).

Regardless of whether we listen to Bill Maher or Pope Benedict, we can all come to the same conclusion: that Christians need to apply the Golden Rule to ourselves – on the one hand to avoid hypocrisy, and on the other, to see and experience the reality of what we claim to be true.

Faith and works

Some important applications of the Golden Rule appear not to be obvious to Christians. This is a concern because until recently, I was unaware of a strong Christian tradition that makes the Golden Rule a primary teaching. Each denomination has its own emphasis, depending upon its history and its perceived contribution to the Christian church. The Roman Catholics focus upon their longevity and authority and the centrality of the Mass as a manifestation of grace. Methodists have a strong social justice emphasis, after the Wesley Brothers. Lutherans maintain the reforms attributable to Martin Luther. Presbyterians follow the reformed Calvinist tradition. Pentecostals, to whom most of church growth in the past century is properly attributed, emphasize miraculous gifts and increasingly health, wealth and prosperity. I am now aware that the Anglican church, of which we have recently become members, do have a strong tradition amongst other things of reiterating and teaching the Golden Rule as the means of God's grace being manifest. Certainly, it is contained in the major creeds that many traditions recognize, but anything that demands primary attention must have regular and primary prominence if it is to be an ethical and doctrinal reference and consciously practised as Christ's Great Command. For this reason, I recently wrote a BunchOBlokes guide called *Conditions for Grace* as I believed that our role in facilitating God's grace for ourselves and others, is a very clear function of the Golden Rule. And vice versa. If we consciously practise the Golden Rule, we will also become more aware of the availability and many benefits of God's grace. To my surprise, when I circulated drafts of the guide, I ran into opposition to the suggestion that there could be any conditions to grace. However, a reference to James 4:7-8 – a passage that I remember from childhood, suggests otherwise. It says:

> *Submit yourselves, then, to God. Resist the devil, and he will flee from you. Come near to God and he will come near to you.*
>
> The KJV says: *Wash your hands, you sinners, and purify your hearts, you double-minded. But he giveth more grace. Wherefore he saith, God resisteth the proud, but giveth grace unto the humble.*

This suggests to me that our conscious submission and humility is a prerequisite of grace. I don't believe that humility is a learned skill or a Divine gift. It is an attitude of the heart that results from our conscious integration of our body, soul and spirit. We are responsible for our humility as an outcome for which we are predominantly responsible by the diligent application of the Golden Rule.

My inquisitors objected that in making this statement, I was diminishing God's sovereignty to dispense grace to whom he will, for his own reasons. However, I am not suggesting that God is limited in any of his capacities, other than to be consistent with himself. However, my experience and sense of scripture is that grace is not automatically given because of someone's good intentions or good behavior. Grace, it seems to me, is usually the result of an irregular and perhaps unconscious learning process where the outcome is that we make conscious progress intellectually, emotionally, relationally and experientially, rather than by new intellectual abstractions alone. This has always been a puzzle to me. There have been many instances in my life when I faced what seemed to be an obstacle to my faith in God, but as soon as I admitted to myself the possibility of seeing things differently, the obstacle seemed to vanish or at least, seem trivial once I accepted another view of which I had been ignorant or opposed to. This does not contradict what I have just said about intellectual abstractions, because the change of mind that I experienced, was the culmination of many factors. My instincts, experience and intellectual enquiry had led me to a place where my cognitive dissonance was resolved by new insights, enabled, dare I say, by the Holy Spirit.

I am aware that I am now treading on ground on which both literal and metaphorical religious wars have been fought and blood spilled over the issue of theology, Divine authority, faith, grace, righteousness and self-righteousness. Even as I write these words, I have been cautioned by friends and experts, whose counsel I have sought, that I am bordering on, if not transgressing into "works righteousness" or other controversial theological territory. I really do understand and appreciate their concerns but I am reassured by Dallas Willard that as far as faith and works are concerned, "effort" and "earning" are different matters. Earning is an attitude of self-righteous entitlement called "works". It is the belief that what I have accomplished has earned me credit with God. Effort, on the other hand, is an aspect of faith; hope expressed as "*hungering and thirsting for righteousness*" (Matt 5:6). Effort includes our fondest passions and desires plus the disciplines of prayer, study, meditation and other things that we might do to experience God's presence more intimately. It also allows the possibility of making many mistakes due to impetuosity and ignorance from which humility allows us to recover and see the error of our ways just before we start to feel too proud. As such, it walks the fine line between wishful thinking and faith, which in my view are often in a state of immature flux as we measure the difference between arrogance and humility. Furthermore, I believe that this is the uneven ground of *"working out our salvation in fear and trembling"* that Paul talks about in Phil 2:12, where fear is not dread, but the awareness of how easily we are seduced by our own self-importance.

I suspect that some of the lack of clarity around this important issue that is a hangover of Calvinism – the view that God, in his absolute sovereignty, determines everything, and that we, in our subjection to God, determine nothing, other than to discern and respond to his will for us. Several years ago, to understand the neo-Calvinist resurgence, I read a book by the acclaimed Calvinist teacher, Tullian Tchividjian, the grandson of Billy Graham. I found Tchividjian's book *Jesus + Nothing = Everything* and his podcasts quite disturbing. I thought that Tchividjian had taken the concept of God's dispensation of grace to its unbalanced logical conclusion with his suggestion that our contribution to our own spiritual growth was nil. Tchividjian seemed to have taken the principle of God's sovereignty too far by suggesting that our salvation and spiritual growth are wholly the work of God with no input from us. The give-away for me was that I could find no reference in his book or in his thinking to the Holy Spirit, who interacts with us in a gentle and comforting manner – something that I knew from my own experience to be a gross omission. However, I find his view to be quite common, particularly among the many American Christians that I met in my previous Baptist church. This leads me to think that this confusion about faith and works may be a reason why the Golden Rule is viewed with suspicion when it is presented to facilitate grace. My view is that our relationship to God is usually synergistic; that we are meant to become engaged and interwoven in a creative relationship with him, like Jacob wrestling with God, in that he lets us take the initiative from time to time. I believe that he certainly allows us to express our own desires and priorities, but it is always him leading and teaching us to recognize his absolute goodness and ultimate sovereignty, to which we eventually yield. This picture is almost farcical: that God would metaphorically wrestle with us. But that is what he does. He constantly restrains himself from the decisive killer blow, because he loves us and wants us to learn at our own rate.

My conclusion is that the purpose of the Golden Rule is to instigate the process where a person can enable God's grace in his or her own life by taking the initiative as the Golden Rule requires, but ultimately yielding to him in recognition of his overwhelming love for us. The alternative, in my view, is plain grey conformity where we all take cues from each other as to God's will and discover nothing of the scope of his grace and lovingkindness. This is after all, how a father likes to see his children behave; to keep within the boundaries they have set, but for the child to explore the possibilities of new discovery within them. From God's point of view, this use of freedom is vastly superior to the alternative of us using our freedom defiantly which we know he allows, to his dismay. While I do not intend to engage further in the

Calvinist/Arminian debate, I believe that Calvinism often leads to a misunderstanding regarding God's use of his sovereignty. My perhaps simplistic view is that while God can impose his irresistible will on every human situation, he does not. In so doing, God displays his greatest characteristic—that of self-restraint. God, who created the universe, gave up his power to become a little lower than the angels. God limits himself to the act of wooing us. While he could have commanded total compliance, he does not. Similarly, I propose that we are the recipients of his tolerance in that we are also sovereign, to a limited degree, regarding how we exercise our will. Even with a gun at our head, we can choose or refuse God's life-giving love for ourselves. However, that best possible use we can make of our sovereignty is to choose to recognize and accept God's sovereignty. We most clearly reflect the character of God not just by our faith and obedience, but also by our self-restraint, empowered and enabled by God's grace and his spirit within us. God's self-restraint is clearly demonstrated by the fact that even though he could cause us to accept his ultimate power, he never does. It is always up to us to accept the gift he offers.

School Days

Bill Puka, Professor of Moral-Political Philosophy at Rensselaer Poly Tech, condemns the Golden Rule with faint praise by pointing out that its most common use today is limited to teaching ethics to children, and that it has lost any other real purpose. As evidence, Puka mentions the Golden Rule in songs like Chuck Berry's "School Days" and Bill Haley's "ABC Boogie", both of which had also occurred to me as examples of the Golden Rule in popular culture. Although Puka's wide-ranging paper "The Golden Rule as Moral Philosophy" considers how although the Golden Rule has influenced many major thinkers throughout history, he argues that it has had its day. Despite the broad scope of Puka's work in which he also highlights many of the Golden Rule's features that I consider to be important, I get the impression that he thinks the value of its application to children's education is about the extent of its usefulness as a contemporary ethical principle, because the sovereignty of God is no longer considered seriously by most people. In an email to me, Puka revealed that he is sympathetic to Buddhist rather than Christian teaching, and this is, I suspect, the fatal flaw in his (and some other philosophers') arguments about the Golden Rule. Although Puka agrees that the Golden Rule was intended to be transformative, he has apparently not applied it to himself. In my experience, despite my high sense of commitment to the teachings of Jesus and the Bible as a whole, I would not have come to the same conclusions I have described in this book unless I had the experience of looking back over a lifetime and seeing the correlation between my conscious application of the Golden Rule and the outcomes of my life.

The decline of Christian consensus in the West

Western democracy is experiencing a crisis that I think is very clearly related to the loss of personal faith in God and the decline in the number of people engaged with the Christian church and its corresponding influence in society. Somehow, Christian faith is now seen as childish and anachronistic, disconnected from the important realities of life. Since the enlightenment, opposing forces have weakened Christian faith as the moral foundation and primary organizing principle of society. Christianity is now also on the wane within advanced Western democracies globally, due in part to apathy resulting from affluence, the rise of alternative ideologies including socialism, secular humanism and modern hedonistic Epicureanism. Total church attendance numbers in the mainstream churches of Europe, the United Kingdom, Ireland, America, Canada and Australia have been falling for many years in proportion to the rise of other religions and belief systems. The decline has been made worse by appalling sexual abuse of children by clergy within Christian communities, which seems now to be followed by radically changing social attitudes to religion generally, and more specifically, the acceptance of issues including abortion, homosexuality and transgender identification. The demise of the church is a crisis for democracy because the new influences, while often claiming to represent a "progressive" Christianity based upon love, equity and tolerance is often the polar-opposite of what it claims to be, as it gives ground to left-leaning politics rather than a vision of Jesus as the Lord of all creation from which personal renewal springs. While it may be true that this decline is due to a reduction in nominal or superficial Christianity as some commentators claim, the tide has changed against a Christian consensus, to one of increasing hostility.

Jesus. Lord and Savior

This is a crisis for the church first because many of the forces replacing the departing orthodoxies of Christian belief and practice are essentially deceptive, leading many unconsciously astray. Including me. This is an insidious problem as the invading forces are intolerant of any remaining opposition, seeking to assert themselves into every aspect of an already weakened culture. This is always the case, where those who held the previously oppressed view become the oppressor. In many cases, the true nature of the new order is not understood by many Christians or secularists until it is too late. As Christian influence declines, the Christian foundations upon which the West was based are undermined and weakened, causing the loss of relationships between people and God. Unless this is reversed, liberal democratic society as we have known it will not survive.[1] However, any corrective change must not be the "progressive universalism" of mainline protestant denominations, as they are already perishing in their attempt to remain relevant and compatible with current political and social ideologies. This decline can only be reversed by a making a return to a new understanding of Christian discipleship that includes obedience to Jesus as the highest priority. Only then can the ethics of justice, fairness, equity and social action take their proper place. The reason for this is that when accountability to God is lost, the resultant humility and servanthood of faith is replaced with the assertion of individual human rights, as we have seen, particularly since the end of the last war. The rise of secular values lacks the nuances and subtilties of Christian faith which is being replaced with ever increasing law and-not-so subtle political correctness.

I believe that this malaise among Western nations is evidenced by the lack of conversions to Jesus as Lord and Savior and the lack of baptisms in mainstream and progressive churches. This

---

1 https://en.wikipedia.org/wiki/Postchristianity

is substantially a result of the Christian church's failure to teach adherents to obey the explicit commands of Jesus Christ, upon whose teachings Western society emerged. According to the what Jesus claimed, the most important of these is his Great Command, summarized by the Golden Rule. My hope is that the church will urgently and wholeheartedly return to the first principle upon which the West became the most successful political and social system ever conceived. According to Jesus, the Golden Rule is the most succinct summary of His message as it contains "*the whole of the law and the prophets*" of the Judeo-Christian canon and tradition.

How the West was lost

2017 AD counts the years since the Christian era began with the birth of Jesus Christ. The name of this brief period in human history has recently changed from AD to CE, without much explanation. This change, however, reveals what is happening to us by stealth. AD means Anno Domini, "The year of the Lord," the years since the birth of Jesus. The term CE seeks to de-Christianize the calendar by referring to the Common Era. 1 AD immediately follows 1 BC or "Before Christ" which is now rendered as BCE,

Before the Common Era. This change suggests that a universal reference to Christ is no longer acceptable to the prevailing secular, multicultural mind. This change is made although the calendar remains the same, the point seems to be that the Christian ordering of history has been de-bunked, or so it appears. Since the enlightenment of the 18th century, Christianity has become increasingly seen as a superstitious, dogmatic and regressive religion belonging to a time now past and useful now only as a stepping stone as we progress toward a glorious future, without God.

    I have attempted to show that the advent of Christ was a pivotal event that divides the real metaphysical history of the Universe into two distinct halves, BC and AD. My evidence for this claim is not just arguments about religious history and theology, as important as they are. Rather, my evidence is that Christians worship Jesus because he has proved who he claimed to be: The Son of God and the Son of Man, who came to teach us about the reality of the Universe and how to live in relationship with God and with each other. He did this in many ways; he taught us the Golden Rule *of doing to others what we would have them to us.* I believe that this is a Divine Rule, and one that agrees with the discoverable natural laws upon which the Universe runs. My claim is not just that Christ's Golden Rule is an ethical foundation for life because it makes sense logically. Rather, I claim that we as individuals can prove the power of this rule for ourselves—not by reading this book or agreeing with the intellectual argument or any religious observance, but by applying the Golden Rule to ourselves and our relationships. My claim is that if you do accept this challenge wholeheartedly, your life will begin to change for the good immediately because of what you will learn about yourself and your relationships. However, some of what you learn will be very difficult to accept, and even harder to do. Christ's Golden Rule is easy to remember and to agree with instinctively, but almost impossible to do because it requires us to begin *"Being transformed by the renewal of our minds"*; to begin to think and act the way Jesus teaches us to think and act. If you apply this challenge wholeheartedly and persistently you will learn things about yourself and the Universe that you cannot possibly know or do any other way, other than *to have the mind of Christ* within you. If you do this, you may also come to the same conclusion (unless you have already done so) as countless millions have done before you—that Jesus Christ is Lord, Savior and Master; that he is God in the flesh who came to save all those who are willing to be saved by him.

Professor of sociology emeritus John Carroll charts the steady decline of the Church and now universities in his article "Disdain for the Best of the West". Carroll observes *"Here the university again followed the church, in compensating for a lack of belief in itself with political activism." "Activism was energised by a displacement of religious zeal into politics. With the death of God and the marginalization of the churches, salvation came to be sought in social crusades and highly charged moral causes, loosely guided by Marxist ideology."*[1]

John Carroll and many others believe that the Christian consensus upon which the democratic Western world was established has now been sufficiently undermined that it cannot be rescued, unless we return to our origins. The first pillar fell not just due the Enlightenment, which challenged the need for God, but the abuse of the authority and power by the church, seen most clearly in the Reformation, when the Roman Catholic church was challenged by Martin Luther's use of the Bible as his source of authority, rather than the church. The more frequently cited examples of abuse by the church such as the Crusades and Spanish Inquisition are insignificant and pale by comparison to the historical abuse of power, that we are now seeing manifest in sexual abuse and misbehavior. Against this background, even the

---

1 The Weekend Australian, June 9-10 2018.

reformation should be seen as just an adjustment and a salutary warning. Important as both the reformation and Martin Luther were, they had their problems from the beginning – especially when they attempted to standardize the improvements they made and impose them as the new orthodoxy.

First things first

A couple of years ago, I attended a Lutheran men's conference, which featured an elective presentation entitled *The most important doctrine: The assurance of our salvation*. In my Brethren experience, assurance of salvation was dogma that I had previously dismissed because I had seen it abused by my friends who, despite our hell-raising, pronounced the security of their salvation because they had "Made a decision for Christ." At least I knew I was on thin ice. The message of the conference discussion was that security of salvation was the bedrock of Christian faith, and that nothing was more important. When I naively questioned this assumption, I was sharply told that my question was out of bounds, and that no such "unhelpful" discussion was allowed. I am now aware of some of the Lutheran, Calvinist and other similar views about this subject, which are at least worth knowing, but they are not foundational and tend to divert us from the essence of Christian faith about our relationship to God and each other. Despite my concerns about denominational dogma, the important thing is not religious arguments about history, theology, biblical inerrancy or interpretation, the authority of the church or even the difference in truth claims or the emphasis on doctrine. Rather, the most important thing is the effect that our engagement with the resurrection of Christ has on us, and the extent to which our acceptance of the message transforms us into the image of Christ.

Back to the future

For those Westerners who have abandoned Christian faith, the alternative future seems to be destined to be atheistic Neo-Marxist socialistic humanism taken eventually to its awful logical conclusion. It is based upon our remarkable success of discovery and manipulation of the material world of science with some short-sighted humanistic ideology thrown in. However, we have confused our discovery of the principles of science by placing confidence in the notion that science and evolution produces endless progress. Foundational principles of life cannot be established by looking forward because we are only guessing about a future yet to happen. Only by looking back at what happened in the past do we see the re-occurring patterns that are the foundations upon which we can build the future. I suggest that we do not need new ideas about reality. What we need far more, is to be reminded again and again that the reality upon which we rise, or fall has already been discovered. Looking back, however, has come to be seen as anti-progressive, reactionary and conservative for its own sake. Religion is increasingly seen by many people as not only socially regressive, but also as superstitious belief in something that has no objective reality leading most modern people to think that religion does more harm than good.

My experience in discussing Christian faith with atheists, is that they have their own definition of what religious faith is, that usually reveals their prejudice before any discussion begins. It is therefore important to properly define faith as the basis of discussion according to scripture;

Faith is the substance of things hoped for, the evidence of things not yet seen (Heb 11:1)

This means that the outcome of faith is both our objective and the evidence of what we hope is true. Our hope a complex framework of what we believe to be real, good, true and beautiful.

In my experience, some of this belief will be an incorrect synthesis of uncritically acquired Christian dogmatism from my childhood mixed with other versions of wisdom, also uncritically acquired along the way. The problem with this is that unless I have been very well taught, it is very hard to sort the wheat from the chaff, until I have some hard evidence of personal experience to consider. Fortunately for me, my training in relationships by my parents, both in theory and practice, was excellent. So were some other principles about persistence and diligence, to which I wish I had paid more attention. Having a high view of relationships, though, was an excellent basis upon which to meet Elaine when she was 16 and I was 19. Beginning with the Golden Rule in mind, we resolved very early to tell each other the truth, as much as possible, which we have done to provide the foundation of a wonderful marriage and family life, most of which has been great fun. If only every other important experience in life was so clearly determined around an apparently simple principle. And if only I would have treated other issues with the same seriousness.

With the benefit of hindsight though, the real test of faith is having an unshakeable confidence and persistence in seeing how the Kingdom of God comes in us, as we seek to be obedient to Jesus, as he was to his father, God. The problem for us though, is that we have a mistaken view of the promises of scripture as we often try to read them through modern eyes, forgetting the principles of interpreting and understanding the language of the Bible. When we read the words of Jesus for example, we may want to make them totally literal and immediately effective, such as his promises for us to receive power for healing, prophecies, miracles and the like. Instead of reading his words as outcomes of faithfulness, we want them as proof or evidence for those of weak faith. Even if we have good motives, all we have accomplished, in fact, is to create a new dependency and delusions to replace the old non-religious ones we just got rid of. Or worse still, if the preachers are opportunists, they present these new illusions in place of the gospel of Jesus, the only miracles being their newly-obtained wealth.

To quote CS Lewis, we don't so much need new information, but to be reminded again and again, of the old principles taught by the Bible, and to see them through the lens of history; what works and what does not, so that we can spot false hopes and errors of belief, judgement and behavior before we harm ourselves too much.

The end of the best era in history

From my point of view, I reckon I have lived in the best period of human history. I know that this is not objectively true in any absolute sense, but it is for me. Born in Australia in 1946, I am officially among the first of the Baby Boomers. My cohort has experienced all the benefits of 2,000 years of the Christian era that has become Western Liberal Capitalistic Democracy: no major wars, relative peace, a Christian democratic egalitarian culture, free secular education, satisfying continuous work, steadily rising affluence, ability to buy property and invest in business. Religious and political freedom to learn and speak, freedom to travel globally, low cost medical treatment, low official corruption and many related benefits. With the recent availability of the Internet and smart phones, I can engage in almost unlimited learning with world-wide communication at my fingertips. Likewise, I have been free to express my opinion on almost any topic of my choosing. While I acknowledge that such democratic freedom must be properly balanced and maintained by eternal vigilance against extremes, Western Democracy has done reasonably well, with the help of its Christian foundations. However, the freedom that I have taken for granted which I believe to be so important to human flourishing, is under intense pressure because rising atheistic secularism is an idol that tolerates no competitors. To make matters worse, many of us have trashed our heritage and our personal place in it, and have begun to undermine the freedom that has given us so many good things.

Egalitarianism

Egalitarianism is a delightful word that helps to describe the Australian character. It means all people are more likely to be seen to be of equal value, and therefore deserve equal rights and opportunities characterized by the Auzzie "fair go'". Australia is considered an egalitarian society because we inherited a democratic Christian tradition. This caused our convict forbears to be rapidly emancipated by an early Governor of the colony, Lachlan Macquarie, until he was pilloried by an official inquisitor, Commissioner John Thomas Bigge. Macquarie had given convicts a free pardon called "tickets of leave", with a grant of land, tools and food to enable them to become responsible, productive individuals. His intention was not just to liberate the captives but to allow them to accumulate wealth. This, according to Bigge, undermined the British class system—to the horror of Macquarie's critics, who ruined him. Unfortunately, the meaning of egalitarianism has changed from equal opportunity to equality of outcome—a modern application of enforced Neo-Marxist socialism as a result of our misuse of freedom, where we have failed to properly value that which is most precious. Our rejection and mis-understanding of Christian values has led to the concept of equality and inclusiveness being given the highest place, to the extent that personal responsibility and accountability, as envisaged by Macquarie (and scripture) has been lost to entitlement and the assertion of human rights which seem to have no self-imposed limits. Tragically, I believe this amazing inheritance to now be at risk because of this distorted view of value and reality. I must confess to being of the Jordan Peterson school of equity, as when he says: Human beings are born with different capacities. *When they are free, they are not equal. When they are equal, they are not free.* As evidence, Peterson points to the natural hierarchies that form in every competitive area of life, where the very few accumulate the maximum benefit according to Pareto's law of distribution. This occurs in animal kingdoms, wealth concentration among people and nations and in many instances within plant, insect and animal life. His evidence to the contrary is the devastating effect of every socialist experiment to redistribute wealth and power, which has resulted in the deaths of 100 million people.[1] I am not against limited socialism or sharing of wealth for the common good, as long as there is an overarching organizing principle, such as Christian faith. I am concerned however, with the many forms of secular humanism which seem always to claim the "common good" as their objective. Socialism that is not accountable to God seems to be able to justify almost any atrocity in the name of the common good, because its leaders are usually accountable only to themselves.

An example of this socialism is the battle for equality in the recent discussion regarding the Australian gay marriage plebiscite, which reflects the global trend to change marriage laws to allow homosexual marriage in the interests of equity, liberty and progress. The pro LGBTIQ+ YES lobby objected to the plebiscite, claiming that the discussion involving NO voters would activate bigoted, religious hatred that would be offensive and harmful to already oppressed people of alternative sexualities. This harmful discussion, they said, would be the cause of increased rates of distress and suicide in the LGBTIQ+ community. In fact, in the lead up to the successful YES vote, the aggressive activity to curtail freedom of speech and opinion was from the "progressive" side of the argument with legal and social action being taken to silence the conservative point of view. For example, the Catholic Archbishop of Hobart, Julian Porteous, was prosecuted for distributing a pamphlet defending traditional marriage amongst his churches because, according to his opponents, it was discriminatory.

---

1 https://youtu.be/TcEWRykSgwE

Australian champion tennis player, Margret Court, also took the brunt of LGBTIQ+ vitriol when she expressed her opposition to gay marriage. Court, a multiple grand slam champion and Sport Australia Hall of Fame inductee, is also the founding pastor of a large Pentecostal Church in Perth, West Australia, and is well known for her work amongst single mothers and other disadvantaged people. Outrage resulting from her comment that she didn't support the YES vote for marriage equality was front page news in Australia, with calls for the Margret Court Arena (a tennis stadium in Melbourne) named in her honour, to be renamed. Although the phenomenon of the oppressed becoming the oppressor should not surprise us, I do not suggest that we attempt to regain lost ground by denigrating, abusing or mistreating those whose ideology or behavior we resist. On the contrary, the corrective in Christian faith is that Christ teaches us to love our enemies and to pray for those who curse us. This is a logical outcome of the Golden Rule applied with any rigor at all because it is clear in Jesus' teaching. Of course, many examples from history prove that Christians have not always followed Christ as we should, but there is an implacable corrective force, each time we read the Bible and insert ourselves into its narrative and find ourselves judged by the words of Jesus, or by another period of history when religious people have made the same mistakes we are now making.

My purpose is not to attack homosexuality per se, but the issue of sexuality has become a touchstone for religious freedom. It does seem that historically, rebellion against the established order and the concept of obedience to God's laws always includes transgression of biblical limits of sexual motivation and behavior. For evidence to support this claim, I point out that the opposite is also true. The phenomenal rise of Christianity within Roman culture was accompanied by a fall in predacious sexual behavior. Under the new Christian religion, women and children were immediately more valued than ever before, which made Christianity very attractive to women. This correlation is made clear by the Apostle Paul, who says:

> *Or do you not know that wrongdoers will not inherit the kingdom of God? Do not be deceived: Neither the sexually immoral nor idolaters nor adulterers nor men who have sex with men nor thieves nor the greedy nor drunkards nor slanderers nor swindlers will inherit the kingdom of God. And that is what some of you were. But you were washed, you were sanctified, you were justified in the name of the LORD Jesus Christ and by the Spirit of our God* (1Cor 6:9-11).

I believe that the uniform effect of the sexual revolution of the 1960s in Western culture, has been the rise in transgressive sexual behavior by comparison to the standards of the Judeo-Christian tradition. In the past 50 years, we have seen the normalization of pre-marital sex, divorce, abortion, "open" marriage, prostitution, group sex, homosexuality, transgenderism and now gay marriage. These changes have been made on the basis of "freedom from sexual oppression and personal repression", popularized by Sigmund Freud and adopted by Michel Foucault, one of the fathers of Postmodernism. Having gained these liberties, usually inspired by "equality" and pragmatic arguments about the harm caused by backyard abortions and similar arguments, advocates have now turned their attention to protecting their new liberties by attacking the conservative religious position regarding sexual propriety. This has given rise to a division within the Christian church, where the "progressive" faction has become "gay affirming" by welcoming practising homosexuals into full fellowship, including into leading roles within the clergy. On the other hand, the conservative church has condemned homosexuality. In the best case, conservative churches have become "gay welcoming, but not affirming", agreeing that while homosexuality has become normal in society, it is not to be encouraged, but rather, considered as sin from which Christ came to save us. I admit that I would not like a return to backyard abortions or criminalized homosexuality of yesteryear. I would rather hope for a transformation of all individual hearts by our acceptance of God's love and grace, which I know will not occur in time and space, so meanwhile, I must accept the tension of an imperfect world.

The rise of the "Nones"

Confirmation of this conflict in most, if not all, Western nations is that many people are abandoning their nominal religious affiliation to roughly the same extent that they have stopped attending church and have become the "nones". Nones are an ever-increasing group who declare no attachment to religion or decline to make a comment about religious affiliation in national polls.[1] This is partly motivated by increasing secular demands to separate church and state and to prevent religion from having a place in the public square of political debate and social commentary. I have experienced this personally in recent years as a participant in an academic media platform that encourages debate, called *The Conversation*, where I have maintained a stated position as a conservative Christian. (actually, I described myself as an ageing, contrarian Bible Basher) While I appreciate the opportunity to participate in a sophisticated level of discussion, many of my protagonists are adamant that my position is illegitimate not just because I am not an academic, but because I am a Christian in a forum where atheism is normal. I have been amusingly accused of being a "troll" paid by the church to be anti-progressive. While being attacked as a "reactionary" and reported for offensiveness, being personally demeaned, denied and dismissed of the possibility of having anything

---

1 https://en.wikipedia.org/wiki/Irreligion_in_Australia

valid to say, my opponents have not responded to my argument. I have since realized that such personal attacks indicate a lack of wit, imagination and substance among those who launch them. The good thing is that I have learned the rules of logical debate and the need to use evidence to support my point of view, rather than using opinion alone. In my experience, although a range of views are theoretically tolerated, the traditional Christian view is vilified as being irrelevant, intolerant, reactionary and patriarchal. Furthermore, considering the rise of provocatively "transgressive" alternative views, it seems now that as recognition of the Christian God declines, so other gods arise who demand to be worshipped. The difference is, however, that where the Christian God is tolerant and longsuffering to a fault, the new gods exercise no such restraint because they are false. My own unfortunate experience is that when I briefly mentioned the prospect of the loss of religious freedom while speaking in my church, I was reported to the senior pastor, who was absent on that day, for being "too political". As I found this attempt to silence discussion to prevent conflict to be intolerable, this was the first of several issues which resulted in me leaving my Baptist church after 17 years of service as Church Secretary.

Who cares?

The certainties of Christian consensus have been steadily eroded during the last three or four hundred years since the Enlightenment. On the surface, this is not a problem that most people worry about. Most people born since WWII have experienced growing affluence, and political and social freedom seemingly linked to the inexorable rise of science and technology. Today, despite the ever-increasing global population, there is a smaller percentage of people living in poverty than at any period in the previous 2,000 years. What should a Christian or a secular observer make of this? Are the atheists who protest the very existence of religion right?

Has the church lost its way? Certainly, if we read the scandalous headlines of the abuse of children by Christian clergy, we might think so. I believe that child abuse is an indication of the failure of the Church to fulfil its most basic role of obedience to the explicit commands of Christ to protect those who are vulnerable and innocent. Christendom's abuses of power needed to be challenged as they were with the protestant reformation, followed by the French enlightenment, the industrial revolution and the influence of Charles Darwin, Karl Marx and many others. These challenges combined to weaken the foundations of the church from within and to replace the certainties of faith with the scientific, philosophical and political optimism of the modern era. Following total failure of Marx's cultural and social revolution in which millions were killed, modernism became the postmodern era. I find it amazing that Marxist ideologies of utopia have now uncritically re-emerged under the new guise of progressive social justice and political correctness.

Love your enemies

To the world at large, the old notion that we should *fear God and keep His commands* is now as meaningless and as irrelevant as the notion of individuals being sinners in need of a savior. Similarly, the foundational idea that *fear of the Lord is the beginning of wisdom* has been confined to the dust of history as being a quaint superstition with no place in the modern contest of ideas. The failure of the Christian church is, I believe, that we have not done the most distinctive thing that Christ commanded of us: *to love your enemies, do good to those who curse you and to pray for those who persecute you* (Matt 5:44) This command, has been the sticking point of philosophers from Friedrich Nietzsche to Peter Singer, both of whom complain that it is impossible and unhelpful to love your enemies. To love our enemies is Christ's Golden Rule taken to its logical conclusion. It is this that we have failed to do because we didn't take our faith in Christ seriously enough, adding to the many failures of the Church in the modern era, whose chickens have now come home to roost. The decline of faith in God among Western Democracies is the result of our preferring to emphasize dogmatic religious abstractions and doctrinal innovations rather than obeying Christ. We therefore are responsible to correct this malaise, as it is the job of the church to take the good news of Christ's Kingdom to all nations—not just in word, but also in deed. Who will do this job if we don't?

Jesus' brother James says,

> "...judgment without mercy will be shown to anyone who has not been merciful. Mercy triumphs over judgment" (Jas 2:13).

Matthew, quoting Hosea, says,

> "But go and learn what this means: 'I desire mercy, not sacrifice.' For I have not come to call the righteous, but sinners" (to repentance) (Matt 9:13).

The two quotes above about mercy seem to be saying that if I don't make allowances for those that I disagree with, then I cannot expect allowances to be made for me. Not only is this consistent with The Lord's Prayer *(forgive us our debts as we forgive our debtors)*, but it is entirely consistent with the Golden Rule. An event in my own awakening began about ten years ago when my wife ran against an implacable enemy in a professional situation where she was constantly undermined and attacked by her boss. In response to my inept attempt to be friendly toward this person, I copped a barrage of foul language for my trouble. Considering the sensitivities of the situation, what was I to do? Feeling weak, defenceless and humiliated, I had little choice other than to take Jesus at His word and pray for this person, that she would find a better way of being for herself and those affected by her. To my surprise, the change was within me; and this was helped by the fact that my wife did not allow the toxic relationship to upset her.

In the face of the push-back that the church is now experiencing, we must take the initiative to do good at least as much as we try to defend ourselves. The normal human instinct for revenge or to at least to settle the score, is one of the most primal of human instincts according to Friedrich Nietzsche, who announced that *"God is dead"* and also said, *"Oh, that man should be delivered from revenge."* For as long as we believe that God is dead, there is no hope of delivery from our enemies. Christian churches are intended to be agents of the Kingdom of God by being exemplars of what who we represent and what we claim to preach. The gospel of which we are custodians is intended to be as attractive as a glass of cool water to a thirsty man in a hot desert. But we have poisoned the well. It is now time for us to correct the decline of faith, hope and love by returning to its source, and being obedient to Him as our priority. Even the attempt to love our enemies makes a difference, because it requires a change of attitude to begin. The challenge is to persist, as this is where real change starts to emerge as we realize our personal shortcomings and begin to seek help to make the change now required. For a man, these changes are to do with character that are often contrary to conventional wisdom as increasingly, we draw our ideals of character from sports stars, business of political heroes, or most disastrously, celebrities. The elements of real character are to do with honesty, accountability, responsibility, patience and self-control. As I will discuss in Chapter 10, these ideals are often confused with competing ideas about competitiveness, autonomy, and the "rugged individual Marlboro Cowboy" type. Jordan Peterson partially concurs with this ultra-male image of independence based upon male advantage of superior strength, size and attitude of protector of women and children as an initial male instinct. However, Peterson then says that a man, feeling his strength and capacity for violence, should then immediately restrain himself and offer what seems to be the opposite of quiet, confident gentleness that typifies a Christian man who is prepared to give his life for his love of his wife and family.

As I have mentioned, this current era is inspired by the notion that equal value of each individual person is the highest good. This is an implication of the Judeo-Christian teaching from Genesis that we are made in the image of God. However, equal value and the freedom implied by it cannot be measured by equal outcomes, especially such crude measures as the gender pay gap and the role of women in business, to say nothing of men's roles in families. To value each person highly (as God does) demands that we are free to express our differences within the boundaries proscribed in scripture and endorsed by society based on treating others as you would want to be treated. Freedom related to equality has come to be considered as the most basic human right; but freedom can never be imposed, as this is a contradiction in terms.

Justice and love

The Christian writer Robert Royal observes that the compilation of the Golden Rule from the Old Testament, as retold by Jesus, resulted in charitable behavior towards all people throughout the Roman Empire. *"Christianity was doing something out of love for God, largely unprecedented"*. Additionally, Royal credits Augustine with attributing God's love to the pagan cardinal virtues of temperance, fortitude, justice and prudence plus his focus on the human mind and will as the basis of inwardness, prefiguring Luther, Calvin, Descartes, Pascal, Kant and Hegel.[1]

The lapsed Marxist and atheist Jurgen Habermas, a German sociologist and philosopher considered to be among the "world's leading thinkers", goes a bit further than Royal. Habermas maintains that ordinary people, and Christians in particular, must be free to add their voice to discussion about values in the public sphere. The basis of his argument is that there is no alternative to the Judaic ethic of justice and the Christian ethic of love:

> *For the normative self-understanding of modernity, Christianity has functioned as more than just a precursor or catalyst. Universalistic egalitarianism, from which sprang the ideals of freedom and a collective life in solidarity, the autonomous conduct of life and emancipation, the individual morality of conscience, human rights and democracy, is the direct legacy of the Judaic ethic of justice and the Christian ethic of love. This legacy, substantially unchanged, has been the object of continual critical appropriation and reinterpretation. To this day, there is no alternative to it. And in light of the current challenges of a*

---

1 Robert Royal, *The God who did not fail*, Encounter Books.

post-national constellation, we continue to draw on the substance of this heritage. Everything else is just idle postmodern talk. [2]

In addition to recognizing the beneficial Judeo-Christian influence on history, Habermas continues to insist that the ordinary experience of everyday life must be compared to Christian theory as a source of evidence of the benefits of Divine revelation to human life. I wish that some of the Christian Social Justice Warriors would take note and see that it is the plain reading of scripture (as against a literalistic fundamentalist reading) that is the most valid source of morality for society rather than re-hashed Marxism. Both neo-Marxism and post-modern humanism, if you have experienced their cold hand, have become manifest as a diatribe against others about the use and abuse of power and oppression without considering their own abuse of power. They claim to be motivated by compassion, but the reality of what they do in the name of compassion is plain by contrast with what they claim. They constantly pitch the oppressed against the oppressor, and foster jealousy and resentment against anyone who has something that they don't have. The answer to the carping of post-modernism is not to engage in an endless debate about rights or wrongs, about history or the future, about abstractions or ideologies, and certainly not to point the finger of accusation. Rather, a proper response to post-modern neo-Marxist atheism is to point out the inconsistencies in their argument, and to materialize rather than merely make claims about what you think is good and worthwhile in your own life by taking whatever small steps of faith, hope and love are possible for you. The inevitability of a godless death compared to the goodness, hope and vitality of a faithful life is a stark comparison. So choose life. Do whatever is truly life-giving.

---

2 (Jürgen Habermas - "Time of Transitions", Polity Press, 2006, pp. 150-151, translation of an interview from 1999).

Do whatever real actual thing you can do today that will enhance your life, the life of your loved ones and the common good.

Most people acknowledge the existence of good and evil. However, they will define it differently depending upon their world view because when traditional values are tipped on their head, good becomes evil and evil becomes good. Regardless of your agreement or disagreement with this statement, I am sure you will have your own ideas about good and evil. The Bible says that humans are fatally flawed by sin in the fall of Adam and Eve in the garden of Eden.

> *For all have sinned and fall short of the Glory of God* (Rom 3:23).

Despite all objections to this claim, this is one area where evidence for the Christian point of view is overwhelming as evil abounds all around us. Many people now ironically claim, "I am spiritual, not religious", suggesting that spirituality is above good and evil. This view demonstrates a lack of understanding of the nature of both good and evil and spirituality. The spiritual entity (the Devil) who tempted Eve in Eden is the same as the Devil who tempted Jesus in the wilderness. His greatest skill, perhaps his only real skill, is deception. He is the father of lies (Jn 8:44). When we say we have no evil in us, this is evidence of evil deception on a grand scale (1 Jn 1:8).

Redemption and repentance

Redemption is a biblical concept about being "bought back, reclaimed or re-purchased" into a relationship that was previously fractured. Repentance is a Judeo-Christian response to becoming aware of having the fatal flaw called sin which is common to all humanity. Russian author Aleksander Solzhenitsyn said; "*The battle line between good and evil runs through the heart of every man (and woman)*."[1] This reality of evil indicates that we have fallen short of God's standard of activity of belief or practice, which is required for relationship with Him. Repentance demonstrates that the penitent is sorry for their sins and does something about them, both now and into the future. Repentance is not a one-time event, it is an attitude of the heart that continues for a lifetime as we gain more insight into our situation and have more resources to deal with our sin as we are increasingly transformed by the renewal of our minds. Nor is it repentance to feel guilty for the sins of the world and to want someone else to do something about it. Certainly, you may be able to influence people by what you say about the need for change but what you do will always send a far stronger message. This book, therefore, is a call to Christians and the Church to repentance, and for anyone else who hears the message of these pages. My challenge to you is to take some immediate positive personal action to correct this malaise, by deciding to be obedient to the teachings of Jesus Christ. This challenge will be re-issued throughout the text, but there is no reason to delay. Redemption means to restore the status or the value of a thing or a person such as you. Begin now to desire the best life that is possible for a human being to live. I hope that reading this book, you will become redeemed by seeing your intrinsic value, not just to yourself, but to your friends, family and society at large and ultimately, to God, who desires that you take your place as an elected or chosen son or daughter, to be elected or adopted into his family, to fulfil the good works he predestined for you to do before the creation of the universe began.

Choose life

To begin requires a conscious decision to want to improve some aspect of your life, regardless of your circumstances. Your

---

1 https://www.brainyquote.com/quotes/aleksandr_solzhenitsyn_405286

motivation can be for yourself, your family, friends, neighbors, religion, humanity, or eternal salvation for any good reason. Francis Schaffer says that the *"True spirituality, is to believe in Him one moment at a time."*[1] The advantage in choosing life is that you will have something that cannot be taken away, not even by the threat of death. This is the secret of life—to invest yourself in the highest good, one small step at a time. Just do it, now. If, on the other hand, you want to wait a while longer, I will try to give you further reasons, encouragement and guidance as to how to take these steps of faith, by implementing Christ's Golden Rule in your life. For some of us, just to acknowledge that such a change is necessary, desirable and possible will be a change by itself as you may never have contemplated this step of repentance before. For others, this will be something they wish they had done earlier and not put off until now. Or perhaps, it will be a turn back to the faith of your childhood, a returning to the familiar rhythms and comforts of home. All comers are welcome.

Summary

Who needs a Golden Rule? I do. I think a more valid question would be to ask has there ever been anybody ever, who did not need to be transformed into the image of the perfect man, Jesus?

---

1 Francis Schaffer, *True Spirituality.*

Interlude 1

Progress on the road

Spirituality grows in autonomous individuals by them being accountable to themselves by referencing themselves to another who transcends them.

— Soren Kierkegaard.

Early in 2018, when I introduced myself to a couple at church who I hadn't seen before, I met Professor C Stephen Evans, an American philosopher who with his wife was visiting Melbourne to speak at an Australian Catholic University conference. To my delight, I discovered that he was a world authority in his specialty, known as Divine Command theory. According to the theory, it is essential for us to obey Divine commands to be morally good, which I believe to be true as I have yet to encounter anything that even remotely resembles "good" that does not derive from God's pre-existing biblical commands. Stephen is also a specialist in the work of the Danish Theologian Soren Kierkegaard, from whom he draws inspiration and an approach to understanding Christianity, including the historical role the Bible has played in shaping modern Western culture. Although I have tried vainly to read Kierkegaard's book *Works of Love* which Stephen recommended to me, I have had much greater success in watching Stephen on YouTube, as he speaks clearly in his punchy rapid-fire, densely packed style in which almost every word is memorable. According to one of Stephen's videos, *Kierkegaard on Human Spirituality*, Kierkegaard says that all humans have spirits with the capacity and duty of being accountable to the Creator God and the potential to grow into his image, in which we are made.[1] But first, we must grow as "*individual persons*" as we respond to the small voice inside us which seeks to "*practice the presence of God.*" Spirituality, then, is the state into which we grow as autonomous individuals by making ourselves accountable to another person or entity external to us. Therefore, we must become accountable to God for our spirituality to grow in what I have called the "*inward journey.*"

Previously, I have used Dallas Willard's definition of "spirit," which he defines as personal power. Both definitions are right in my understanding. I think Evans is describing what spirit *is* relationally. Willard is describing what spirit *does* relationally. Spirituality, therefore, involves making myself accountable to a power higher than myself so I can exercise that power. This definition acknowledges that this "higher power" does not have to be God as there are other entities to whom we may give our devotion. In any case, my accountability to any entity might vary from very low to very high. This is an important insight that has many resonances in this book that I would like to explain using Evans' Kierkegaardian terms, rather than my own simpler and less well-developed ideas. My reason is to have a very high point of reference and framework for my thoughts to avoid the most obvious traps of ignorance and self-delusion. I do not attempt to explain Stephen's view verbatim, as I have added some of my own words and examples so that I can at least convince myself that I understand what I am saying.

I have attempted to roughly follow Evan's approach to spirituality in the Prelude, Interludes and Postlude of this book, combined with my own experience to show how I have encountered God and have learned as a Christian. I hope that this is an imaginative

---

1 https://www.youtube.com/watch?v=uP9576Wna5w&t=1199s

picture of how the ideas, concepts, details and power of Christian faith became manifest in my thinking, behavior and relationships aided by Brett Cardwell's illustrations as metaphors to explain the Arc of the Universe to visualize what I see as progress toward the Kingdom of God. As always, I accept that my concepts are only representations of reality. They are not truth in any absolute sense other than as they align with my experience of the Logos as it exists in scripture and in the minds of others fellow travelers.

Spiritual consciousness

Stephen Evans explains that we become self-conscious beings through childhood, beginning with an inherent consciousness of God because we are made in his image. All humans initially encounter God via the wonders of nature and awareness of God's most basic moral requirements through our conscience to form a natural state called *Generic Spirituality*. This can be enhanced by many life experiences, including religion and self-discipline, but it is only when we accept the possibility of becoming more fully conscious of God incarnate by the exercise of faith in Jesus Christ that our full spiritual potential, called *Christian Spirituality*, is realized. Growth toward this state is a relationship that is enhanced by our trust in God and obedience to his commands combined with the disciplines of prayer, meditation, reflection, worship, fellowship and Bible study, plus putting all that is learned into practice in service of others, in what I call the "outward journey", which I will develop more in Chapter 8.

If we are unaware of the story of Christ's incarnation, or if we otherwise refuse to take the path of Christian spirituality, we can make some progress, but we cannot fulfil our Divine spiritual potential. Kierkegaard argues that the solution is not just the provision of more certain knowledge of God, because to try and create a proof of God's existence from evidence elevates it to become a "criterion" of belief. Rather, as the problem of unbelief is still in us, we should simply challenge ourselves to investigate faith by taking the necessary steps toward believing in God, by "actualizing" what we hope to be true by our actions, rather than as an intellectual exercise of religious apologetics. I know that this is a disputable claim in some circles because it elevates experience over the authority of scripture. However, the Christian claim of the incarnation of God in Christ is either objectively true and valid, or it is not, as there can only be one God, one Lord and one Savior. If God is incarnate in Christ, then I claim I can witness to Christ being incarnate in me, more or less. We have previously discussed the important question as to whether a person must know about Christ to be "saved" to which we will return later.

Which spirit?

As I mentioned, according to the Evans-Kierkegaardian view, all humans have either a generic spirituality or Christian spirituality. The difference is that Christian spirituality always recognizes Jesus as Lord and Savior as the basis of admission to the Kingdom of God. Evans points out that it is possible to be a member of a Christian church without this declaration of Lordship. Although a person has access to relevant information, they may ignore it and thus not recognize or pursue what they don't want or cannot recognize as they have lost the skills required for the search. Spirituality in

either form involves growing as autonomous individuals by being accountable to ourselves by referencing what we do in relation to another person or entity, external to us. This view adds insight to the question regarding the modern claim of many that they are "spiritual, but not religious," since it explains how spirituality can be both secular and Christian, as they both describe the same thing each through a different lens.

Stephen Evans' Kierkegaardian explanation is that if we have a small consciousness of reality, we are like a primitive man who looks after cattle and, as the master of his small domain, "defines" himself by reference to his herd since he can exercise control (and power) over them. This would also be true of a slave master, whose self-consciousness is established by his authority and power over his slaves, and who also may have a very limited ability to describe reality because of their status as captives. It is similarly true of a person who sees himself as subject to the state or any other external entity. The state is a much bigger external point of comparison than cattle, slaves or the state, as it controls many aspects men's lives and experiences of reality. But the state is still not a very big entity by comparison to other alternatives, such as a continent, the world, the cosmos, or God. As an infant child develops, their self-consciousness changes as they become more aware of the new reality that they discover each day as they are increasingly socialized and educated. As they grow, so their view of reality grows, even if it is still shaped by their parents' worldview and presence, until they begin to experience a greater degree of autonomy as a teenager and become conscious of a much bigger reality. Young adults become more autonomous as they are socialized into the relationships of respect for the power of the state according to the many "*scripts*" embedded in each culture. This facilitates a transition from the parents to the state as the external reference that defines their self-consciousness – a change to which they conform since they desire to be like others who share the same view. However, a Christian parent might hope that their child will see that the state, or perhaps the common Western democratic *"zeitgeist"* (or the spirit of the age) with its many imperfections, as an inadequate false ultimate ideal. Rather, we hope that they see the limitations of the state or conventional wisdom as only an acceptable expedient for social cohesion and the production of wealth and wisdom for the common good in relative freedom and peace. They may then attach themselves to another ideal, such as a relationship, career, politics, technology or personal wealth and power or ultimately, to the highest external entity we can identify and attach ourselves to, which is God, the creator and the source of life and love. Christian spirituality, then, is to *"practise the presence of God"* according to what we understand and have experienced of Jesus Christ, as the incarnate Son. To become conscious of God in this sense is not to pretend to be God, but to become like him by a process of self-discipline and Divine empowerment because he is our highest ideal of accountability. On the other hand, the secular version of spirituality is to ignore God as he is presented in this way, and to replace him with consciousness of some lesser entity as the object of highest regard, whether it is the state, science, politics, wealth, power, ideology, the self or whatever. In any case, we are choosing one spirit over another to be the object of our highest regard, and in the practical sense, to be the object of our worship (worth-ship) even if this is unconscious. According to the Christian view, the Bible is a mirror in which we see ourselves in relationship to God reflected in the stories of the Old and New Testaments about the patriarchs, prophets, Israelites, disciples and apostles of Jesus Christ. This story is incarnated and perpetuated in us as we apply it to ourselves as an act of obedience to God's commands. Unfortunately, many people use the complexity of the Bible stories as an obstacle by allowing their understanding to remain obscure and a sticking point to the possibility of faith, which limits our knowledge of or conscious acceptance of Christ.

We face the frightening prospect that the choices we think of as entirely our own, are not, as they are influenced by an external power that we choose, consciously or unconsciously as a matter of faith, by the exercise of what we hope is true. It is also worth remembering that while we cannot change the past, we can, to some extent, choose our future as an outcome of who we believe in that secures the future for us. Let's just add that up. We cannot change the past other people, or ourselves, but we can choose the power by which we change and prepare for the future. That makes my choice simple. I'm going with Jesus who said he is the source of life because so far, I have proven his claim to be true in my own life.

Binary baloney

The notion that we are susceptible to malevolent spirits has lost much of its currency because many people no longer believe spiritual good and evil, let alone the likelihood that we are subject to the influence of evil spirits that might possess us. But let me assure you that any person, power, force or entity that does not have my best interests at heart has the potential to become evil if they are not already. We already know that there are forces for good or ill in the sense that an idea or a belief may control how we behave, especially in our relationships. When we abandon belief in a good God, then, as we are reminded by GK Chesterton, it is not that we believe in nothing. Rather, we are likely to believe in anything. This reality, in my view, renders the concept of "secular spirituality" hazardous for the unwary to say the least because it is a gateway to forces, we don't understand, and that's the way they like it. By the way, it is important to remember that there are not binary equal and opposite "dualistic" forces in the Judeo-Christian view, rendering the popular Taoist Ying Yang motif to be misleading, despite what Jordan Peterson says to the contrary as his explanation of the ultimate forces of reality that are opposed to each other.[1]

There is only one God. All other gods who claim ultimacy are imposters.

Toward the Kingdom

According to Francis Schaffer and Brother Lawrence, a 17th-century Carmelite monk, Christian worship requires that we *practice?? the presence of God* with our whole lives. *Practice the Presence of God*, compiled by Father Joseph de Beaufort. To me, this is what is meant by faith, hope and love, which I will later explain in more detail. Martin Luther King's vision of faith of the Promised Land flowing with milk and honey is a metaphor for something far greater than the abundance of food and drink in Canaan's fertile valleys. King's vision of mountains being made low and valleys being made high, were both a literal and a metaphorical hope that his children would experience the Day of the Lord themselves, because justice has been done now, and because his children had accepted the Lord's

---

1 https://youtu.be/EfPLHx6jELc

invitation to enter his Kingdom which also applies both now and in a time yet to come.

But we have seen even more deeply into the Ultra Deep Field of the Cosmos with Hubble's telescope, extending our vision into what was previously the blackness of space. Now we have a new vision of countless trillions more galaxies than we knew of, many of them far bigger than our own. So now we must reconfigure our understanding of the scope of God's Kingdom, which is vast beyond all comprehension. As we glimpse the apparent infinitude of the Universe, no longer limited to just the naked eye, our faith must once again be magnified beyond what we can see with our eyes. It is up to us to use our imagination, led by the spirit, to visualize our place in a future eternity which we are being prepared to manage as responsible agents of the Most-High God and executive partners in the family business.

I have seen the promised land, I have seen the Glory of God!

Martin Luther King

Here be dragons

Evans encourages us to remove the barriers to spirituality for each other as much as possible while admitting that there is a limit to what we can do, as it is always up to us individually to see the opportunities God is offering us, and to accept them. As I mentioned, the barrier is not so much the need for more evidence of God, than we already have. Rather, it is our lack of imagination or ability to begin to see the unfathomable scope of God's admittedly unfathomable Kingdom and his identity in Christ, plus his equally unfathomable love, which reaches far beyond the limits of Earthly time, space and matter.

In the same way that our galactic maps of the Cosmos have areas of unknown blackness, so the ancient mariners had maps of uncharted areas of the seas in which dragons lived. I think of dragons as metaphorical barriers of our personal and societal sins, as they are inventions of fear built on deceptions put in our way to keep us from God. However, the effect of sin is real enough, as it keeps us from anticipating the reality and substance of God's Kingdom while we remain in bondage to an impoverished concept of reality with chains of arrogance, complacency, fear and unbelief.

Since our perception of God's Kingdom is limited to what we can conceptualize in our imagination, just as we can see further with the aid of telescopes, so too we can dream of a greater Kingdom. However, regardless of how much of reality we can see, it is essential that we see the barrier of sin for what it really is. Rather than our sins fulfilling our desires as they promise to do, in fact they keep us from realizing the purpose for which we were designed and made. Our modern age has created the illusion that we are insulated from sin by our being "enlightened" to believe that they do not exist, or if they do, that we are protected from their worst effects by medicine or the Internet, which allows us to transgress into dragon territory without being harmed – or so we think. But we have not counted on the terrible harm they do to our fragile souls, to say nothing of our stunted spiritual growth that we see manifest in the despair and emotional disorders around us resulting from the host of different ways of ignoring God's love.

Spiritual competence

God's invites us into his Kingdom now. Not to have to wait until we are sinless before we become his adopted children and co-workers in his Kingdom. He invites us to come to him as we are and to begin the inward journey of transformation into his image by trusting him and being obedient to his commands, not by being perfect. Our acceptance of the impoverished state of our relationships due to our fear, sin and incompetence is evidence of the need for us to start to become spiritually competent by treating each other as we would like to be treated. Then we have a path to follow where the outcome of faith and obedience is reconciliation with God, and with each other. I encourage you to take this small step of faith in the hope that Kierkegaard, Evans and I are right that God is love, and that his love is his greatest gift to us. He is waiting on our simple acceptance and willingness to do the easiest things first and establish a foundation and a framework upon which we build our lives and see what happens next.

5

HOW DOES THE GOLDEN RULE WORK?

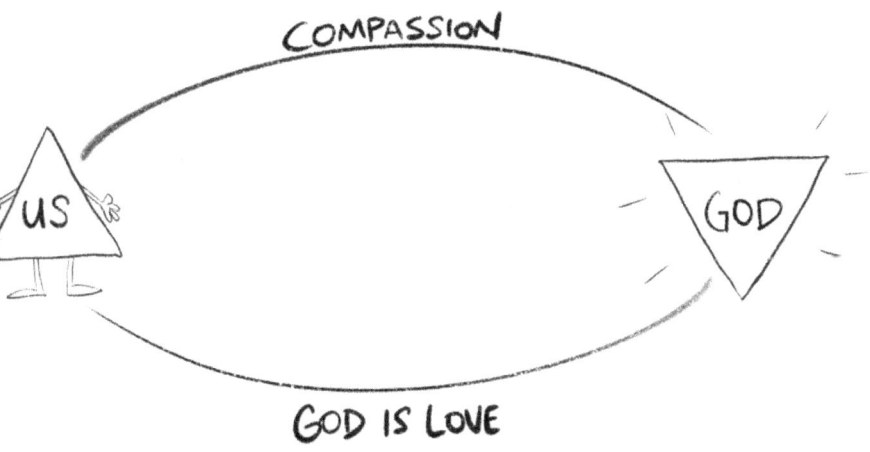

God's love for us is fundamental to our lives as it raises questions about who God is and who we are.

DEUS CARITAS EST Pope Benedict XVI.

The Golden Rule is a double universal. Everybody says they believe it, but nobody practices it.

Noam Chomsky. *The Golden Rule* YouTube. https://youtu.be/6Jq0q6fTKo4

Impossible to ignore, impossible to do

I hope I have presented a convincing case that the Golden Rule reached its optimum within the teachings of Jesus Christ, and that its purpose is to teach us how to love, by become aware of our blind spots and overcoming them with grace so that we can achieve our goal of reconciliation with God: justifies by faith in and obedience to Jesus. But before we look more carefully at how this works, we need to acknowledge what Noam Chomsky (in the quote above) says of our commitment to the Golden Rule – that while we all say we agree with it, as a rule, we don't tend to follow it. According to the Bible, although we are wonderfully intelligent and capable of being wise, we are also desperately wicked in that we don't do the very thing that we think is important for our own human thriving, let alone what might be beneficial for others. At the same moment that we latch onto an intelligent and beautiful truth that we know has the potential to liberate humanity, we immediately begin to look for ways of avoiding being personally responsible for playing a role in saving humanity. Usually, we do this by deflecting the need for change away from ourselves and towards other people. I am ashamed to admit that I have had many episodes where my hypocrisy was on display. One that sticks in my memory was when I criticized my younger brother for smoking cigarettes at a party at my house. I deserved his stunning reversal of my sanctimonious judgement that still stings 40 years later – not because of the seriousness of the offence or his words, but because of my hypocrisy, which he pointed out to me in very clear terms. The human condition is described in scripture with these words:

> *The heart is deceitful above all things, and desperately wicked: who can know it?* (Jer 17:9).

While most of us will automatically reject this charge, if we were to have an honest look, the case is proven by our behavior. Indeed, as a later passage goes on to say:

How does the Golden Rule work?

> *There is no one righteous, not even one; there is no one who understands, there is no one who seeks God. All have turned away, they have together become worthless; there is no one who does good, not even one.* (Rom 3:10-12)

Although I think that some of these texts use hyperbole to make essentially the same point made in Genesis about Adam and Eve's (and therefore humanities') fall into sin. When we are left to our own devices, chaos and anarchy results.

In practical terms, part of our lives is an elaborate hoax – one that we weave to show ourselves in a better light than we deserve. As an aside, this is possibly another reason why the Golden Rule is ignored by so many. We avoid the risk being exposed by our charade of our apparent goodness, while behaving like demons in the dark recesses of our minds. For example, I recently watched a TV documentary hosted by Louis Theroux as he reflected on the life of Sir Jimmy Saville, an English kids' TV entertainer. Thoreau had previously made a documentary about Sir Jimmy, who was knighted for his work as an entertainer and charity fundraiser, who for many years was rumored to be a pedophile. Following Saville's death in 2011, it was revealed that he had diabolically molested, and in some cases raped, up to 500 vulnerable females from the age of 2 to 75 years old, often targeting those who were psychologically or physically impaired to whom he gained access by his charitable work. However, the scandal exposed by the documentary was not just Saville's reprehensible behavior, in my view. As a celebrity fundraiser for hospitals, he used his fame and wealth to control people, including, by his own admission, Louis Thoreau, who had become one of Saville's friends. It was amazing to see how people who had worked with Saville for 20 or more years could not accept that he was a pedophile, despite overwhelming evidence. In one sequence, Theroux interviewed a hospital administrator with whom Saville had raised millions of pounds. Asked what she thought Theroux had missed in his earlier documentary, she laughed and said, "He lied to you," going on to say that Saville lied to everyone about mundane subjects as a matter of course. By this statement, she implied that Theroux himself, an experienced and disarming interviewer, had been seduced by Saville and silenced by his charm, as well as the unspoken threat of public opprobrium if Theroux, or anyone else would dare to say anything against him. My point is that evil exists on a continuum on which we all have a place. Most of us are at the lower end of the spectrum because we don't have the opportunity or social license to get away with too much. Saville, with his calculated strategy to molest vulnerable females, was at the high end of the spectrum because of the opportunities he had and because hundreds of others including his powerless victims who knew about his behavior, were afraid to say what they knew to be true because of trauma, fear and, in some cases, outright cowardice.

Repentance that requires change

Perversely, we often project our guilt about our dark side onto another person, unconsciously thinking that this will somehow save us from guilt. Appallingly, this happens between parents playing the child off against each other until they realize how harmful it is and decide to work on their child rearing project together. It also happens in prisons when some classes of criminals, including pedophiles, must be isolated from those inmates who would try to kill them, if they could, for the same reason—to relieve their own guilt by finding someone worse than themselves. Jesus, on the other hand, with his penetrating insight into human behavior, addresses this universal impediment with an accusation;

> *Hypocrite! First get rid of the log in your own eye; then you will see well enough to deal with the speck in your friend's eye* (Matt 7:5).

How does the Golden Rule work?

This statement in Matthew comes at the end of the Sermon on the Mount where Jesus began with the Beatitudes by declaring to his audience that they can be the blessed ones he has just described as the salt of the earth and a light on a hill, provided their righteousness is greater than the Pharisees. They are confounded by this statement because they believe it to be impossible, because the Pharisees pretend that *they* are especially favored by God, and that ordinary people cannot be special. But suddenly, the atmosphere seems to have changed. I imagine that the air may have been tingling with excitement because Jesus is now saying something that ordinary people can become righteous. If only they could stop accusing and blaming others for their sin and repent, (which is also a process) they too could become transformed to become a "blessed ones." Jesus has given them a glimmer of hope because his audience sense the irony in his words. Everybody knows that the Pharisees abuse their power and keep people in subjection. Maybe Jesus has a solution... But then reality strikes home. Jesus' warning about diverting responsibility from yourself by blaming another is where they know they constantly fail. It is all very well to see that the Pharisees are hypocrites, but so are they. What are they to do as just when they have seen a tantalizing glimmer of hope, now they seem to be stuck between a rock and a hard place for which Jesus has the solution.

While they are wondering silently about their predicament, Jesus summarizes the Golden Rule by saying,

> *...so in everything, do to others what you would have them do to you, for this sums up the law and the prophets* (Matt 7:12).

Jesus' challenge to them is to take the Golden Rule seriously, which implies that their repentance requires not just an admission of guilt, but a resolve to change by:

1. Having a high moral standard to which they can aspire by saying that we love God with our whole being, or at least, we should love him as much as we can and be accountable to him.
2. Making ourselves the point of reference in how we judge another's moral standing.
3. Being prepared to review our relationships based on this moral principle.
4. Subjecting our review to the common laws of logic and non-contradiction.
5. Being prepared to admit our hypocrisy when we have no choice.
6. Repenting of our contradiction by admitting we were wrong and resolving to change our ways.
7. When we fail to change, being prepared to admit that we cannot make the changes required of our repentance without some Divine assistance.
8. Being prepared to accept that it is God who changes us, rather than us pulling ourselves up by our bootstraps.
9. Being humble in view of the need for this process of transformation.
10. Accepting God's gift of grace as the ultimate solution.

The new law of love

The full version of the Golden Rule requires us to love God, unconditionally, unreservedly and without limit— with a sublime love expressed through our total trust and obedience toward him, to which we might readily agree, in principle at least. But when we are required to love our neighbor as ourselves, as we must, we know that we are not so good at doing it because our love for neighbors is at best limited, and conditional. While sometimes we might be thoughtful and kind towards others, we usually have an ulterior motive because we expect something in return and are not altruistic, as much as we might think. This is also true in intimate relationships that depend upon quid pro quo: *I'll scratch your back if you will scratch mine.* Certainly, there is a distance we are prepared to go, but it has its limits.

Even though we might say that we love God, we hold our relationships with neighbors at a distance. Then we justify ourselves by holding God at arm's length, waiting for him to provide things for us because of our sense of entitlement, while we hope to get an advantage from him.

The solution to this confusion and the key to applying the Golden Rule ultimately lies not in our own hearts or minds, but in the contradiction between our values and our faith in God. When we learn to trust him in small issues by comparing our love for him to our love for neighbors, we find that we are inconsistent. When we have a sufficiently clear picture of what God requires and how valuable he is to us, then we invest more trust in him, both out of obedience and to see what happens. As we take small steps of faith toward God and see them rewarded first hand, we begin to trust his commands more, which in turn, enables us to make further good decisions about our relationships with people. Jesus presents the Golden Rule as a relational dilemma to wrestle with, not as an abstract intellectual exercise. It is presented as a high ethical principle that requires the details of reality to be written into it by me, not by some ethical authority external to me. As I will explain later, I think this is both why the Golden Rule works, and why ethicists and some philosophers don't like it. They reject it for the same reason as legend has for philosopher, Bertrand Russell, who when confronted with the moral dilemma of his philandering, went and played backgammon to take his mind off his hypocrisy.

The Golden Rule as dialogue

From one point of view, the Golden Rule is democratized ethics where the individual applies an ethical principle to themselves and others, with a high regard for personal accountability to God and the laws of logic, human intelligence and emotions, that are hard to refute. Rather than a single grand theory that cures all ills, the Golden Rule is very much like the rest of the Bible; it asks us to create our own stories about relationships with people and with God, from which our principles may be observed and compared to the Divine standard. I believe it is fair to say that the Golden Rule itself is derived from complicated sets of laws, some given by God and some developed by experience, which Jesus summarized as the "Law and the prophets," when he combined two of them. We should remember that God's laws began with only one law in the Garden of Eden, to not eat the fruit of the Tree of Knowledge of Good and Evil. Other laws were added as a remedy for this original sin and to prevent further sin, which we know did not work.

When Jesus says that the Golden Rule supersedes the law and the prophets, he states his case clearly by quoting Old Testament scriptures from which the principles are derived. However, rather than make the same mistake that was made previously, where the laws multiplied to satisfy every situation, Jesus says that this one law will suffice as a maxim into which you will have to insert the details and think the process through, based on the highest possible principle; the universal principle of love. This suggests to me, that the Golden Rule is intended as dialogue between God, me and you, where I must take the initiative to respond to an invitation that God has given to all humankind. It is important to realize that if I am going to improve my relationships, that I must take the first step in the hope that this principle will work, not just for my benefit. To begin, though, I must acknowledge my hope that God will reward my faith as I make myself accountable to him because I believe that he loves me, so I will try to love him in return. So I commit myself to the task in faith, hoping that God and his love for me is real and that my obedience will be rewarded by him. This first step is most important because otherwise, I might hedge my bets and defer any risk that I must take now, by asking more increasingly irrelevant questions, that cannot be answered intellectually as atheists and sceptics always try to do. This is because my questions simply beg more questions rather than to produce answers, based on actual events in my life. If there is a leap of faith, this is it, but I don't think of it that way. I think it is as one small step.

There are always at least three people involved in this conversation; ME because I have a sense of consciousness of my identity and the value of my being in relation to GOD in whom I trust as being the ultimate authority and power. YOU and perhaps some others because the Golden Rule requires that I begin to work out my sense of values by reference to God and You.

Although I may not even tell you that I have involved you in this discussion, I believe that God knows and will reward my seeking him and my accountability to him, such as it is. My hope is that as I proceed, I will see evidence of God's involvement as he rewards me and manifests his presence in this relationship, thus fulfilling the definition of faith that it is the *"substance of things hoped for, the evidence of things (as yet) unseen"* (Heb 11:1). As I engage, and God replies, so the evidence of His existence increases and rewards me. Although I have included you out of obedience and faith rather than out of altruism, a secondary effect of my involving you, is that I begin to realize that you have the same potential for relationship with God as I do. Now I have begun a transition from individualistic, perhaps even selfish reasons for my relationships, to begin to discover that there is a far bigger game in play than I first thought possible as I see that my relationship with God depends upon my relationship with you. This fulfills Alfred North Whitehead's suggestion that our spiritual journey toward God must first be an individual inward journey, then it must immediately become an outward social adventure. This is the beginning of many such events of inward and outward movement toward God.

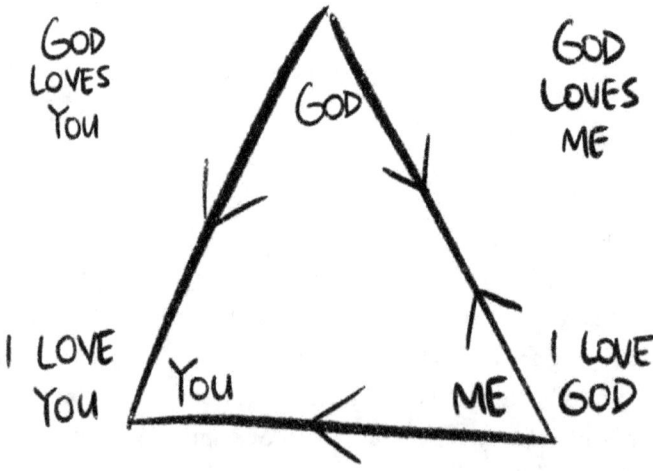

If I have made progress in expressing love toward you, then

you may become aware of it and reciprocate my love. If I can explain what I have done, I would tell you that I love you because God loves you because my relationship with God depends upon my relationship with you. If you find this to be attractive, you may see your relationship with me and God in a new light. If, on the other hand, you reject what I say to you, then I continue to have the problem of deciding what to do next. If I realize that what I thought was love for you was not, then I can confront this realization and to ask for God's help.

Get wise

A favorite line from the Blues Brothers movie is where Curtis, the janitor of the orphanage in which Jake and Elwood Blues grew up, says to them: "*You boys could use a little churchin' up. Slide on down to the Triple Rock Church and catch Reverend Cleophas the preacher there. You boys listen to what he's got to say*". Jake replies, "*I don't want to listen to no jive-ass preacher taklin' to me about heaven and hell,*" to which Curtis responds decisively, "*Jake, you get wise, you get to church."* Jesus warns us to be *"as wise as serpents and as harmless as a dove,"* as distinct from the chaotic instincts of Jake and Elwood as he makes many counter-intuitive statements suggesting that his view of wisdom contrasts strongly with ours because like the Blues Brothers, we are being invited to see greater depths of reality. One important example of *getting wise* questions the value we place in scripture as a source of truth. Jesus charged the Pharisees with being superficial in their use of scripture:

> *You study the Scriptures diligently because you think that in them you have eternal life. These are the very Scriptures that testify about me, yet you refuse to come to me to have life* (Jn 5:39-40).

This is a restatement of what Jesus says about himself. *"I am the way and the truth and the life. No one comes to the Father except through me."* (John 14:6.) It is also what Paul says; *He has made us competent as ministers of a new covenant* (of Love) —*not of the letter* (the literal letter of the law) *but of the Spirit; for the letter kills, but the Spirit gives life.* (2 Cor 3:6) These passages warn us that biblical literalism is dangerous. Being wise in this case requires us to accept a difficult concept against our instincts to rely on our own interpretation of scripture that we dogmatically assert as infallible. Wisdom requires that we accept Jesus as the Logos, the living embodiment of the Word of God. Although we call the Bible the word of God, it is not the Living Word, as this title is reserved for Jesus. This is an ironic intellectual challenge to our notion of conventional wisdom that if we don't grasp, then we cannot proceed with being *transformed by the renewal of our minds* which I claim is the purpose of our salvation. If our minds are not renewed, then we cannot become *transformed into the image of Jesus Christ.* The thing that is most difficult for us to accept and by which we are often embarrassed, is our identification and encounter with Jesus himself, who sends us his spirit to teach, comfort and guide us through the difficulties and opportunities of life. This essential and fundamental acceptance of reality for Christians is an easy target for ridicule in comedy, popular media and movies that make fun of *being born again by trusting Jesus to take my sins away.* My answer to the charge of being naive and childish is to say yes, because to deny this relationship is the slippery slope of trusting in our own understanding as against the command to;

> *Trust in the Lord with all your heart, and do not lean on your own understanding. In all your ways acknowledge him, and he will make straight your paths.* (Prov 3:5-6)

Furthermore, our simple trust in Jesus as the Living Word, requires that we also accept our reliance on the Holy Spirit, who Jesus has sent for our empowerment, teaching and comfort, who is numinous. This means that he is awe inspiring, elusive, and hard to capture or pin down. This is not intended to make our encounter with the spirit obscure, but to teach us that the Word of Jesus is unlike anything else that we are familiar with, and that we have to learn a new language and behavior directly from him, via his spirit who is never subject to our idea of wisdom, as his wisdom is directly from God. This irony is reinforced many times by Jesus and Paul who make equally confusing statements which warn us of the dangers of such precious emblems of Christian faith as:

> Prayer. *And when you pray, do not be like the hypocrites, for they love to pray standing in the synagogues and on the street corners to be seen by others* (Matt 6:5).
>
> Giving. *But when you give to the needy, do not let your left hand know what your right hand is doing...* (Matt 6:3).
>
> Preaching. *Woe to you, teachers of the law and Pharisees, you hypocrites! You travel over land and sea to win a single convert, and when you have succeeded, you make them twice as much a child of hell as you are* (Matt 23:15).

Another clue to the numinous nature of our encounter with the Holy Spirit, is the warning that the unforgivable sin is to blaspheme or to slander the Holy Spirit. (Mk 3:29) In my view, our proper attitude toward an encounter with God's Spirit is to be very cautious before we wholeheartedly approve or condemn a manifestation attributed to him. The test we should apply before we approve or condemn, is to check on the outcome or the "fruit" of such an encounter, as we will see later in this chapter. Paul goes to great lengths in Acts 5:1-11 to explain the story of Ananias and his wife Sapphira who are killed for lying about the proceeds of the sale of a property they gave to the Apostles. These and other hair-raising stories are the reason that we should literally fear God, and not just accept our own or another person's literal understanding of scripture without testing them in our hearts and in our relationships and with Jesus. The problem we all face is that we don't truly know what our own motives are until we humbly allow Jesus to send his spirit to test us. I believe that this can be characterized as the need to try to tell ourselves the truth. It is a further irony that people who claim to be committed to telling the truth as a self-proclaimed high ethical principle are often profoundly self-deluded. To tell the truth requires a diligent process of becoming conscious of our attitudes and motives, which as I have mentioned, is a difficult but essential first step. Of these, true humility is the most difficult because it is so easy to contrive. Humility is a totally honest response to a situation where we say, *I trust in Jesus because I am at my wits end and I don't know what else to do.* As we will see later, our genuine humility is the precondition of God's grace being made available to us through his spirit.

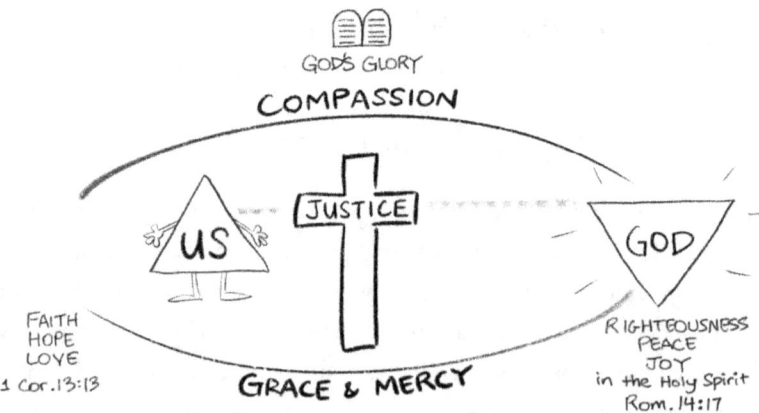

This illustration suggests that we have made some progress toward God. I believe that we are responsible for initiating our response to the process of transformation by the renewal of our minds, because we are responsible for the input of *faith, hope and love* (1 Cor. 13:13) which in turn, facilitates our *transformation by the renewal of our minds*. (Rom 12:2). Transformation results in evidence that we experience as righteousness, peace and joy "*in the Holy Spirit*", for which we are not responsible, because it is an outcome of transformation. Just before I am accused of "Works righteousness" as I have been, implying that I believe we are responsible to earn our own salvation by what we do, I would like to defend myself by saying that the faith, hope and love which I say we must invest, are themselves gifts of God, but they are under the control of our will, for us to invest as acts of faith, which please God. Alternatively, we may choose not to invest ourselves in trusting that Jesus will save us from our sins in which case God allows us to suffer the consequences of our decision. Having started this discussion about the difficulties involved in loving our neighbors as ourselves, we are still faced with further difficulties in Jesus' teaching. Such as loving our enemies and going the extra mile and not resisting the evil one. To do this, we are required to make reasoned judgements which allow us to make decisions that demonstrate our complete trust in Jesus as Lord rather than seeing ourselves as victims, or worse, that we think we are earning a righteous relationship with God.

Why is the Golden Rule so hard to do?

The Golden Rule is necessary for our continued participation in the story of Jesus through which we become one of his "Blessed Ones." As such, it is tangible, concrete and practical and part of the everyday struggle to let the good overcome the evil within us as individuals. The Golden Rule is a maxim for living; it is an orientation towards life, a process of discovering yourself and your place in the world. And in addition to all these good things, it is a guaranteed method for improving our relationship, including with God. If this is true, why would I not want to do it? Among the many reasons people avoid the implications of the Golden Rule is because it is painful. To implement the Golden Rule requires telling truth that I instinctively know requires the death of my ego. It is also a fatal to the delusion of self-sufficiency. As we will see in Chapter 8, to avoid the pain of ego death is cowardice. Rather than make myself accountable to God and face my own indolence and malevolence, I deflect this necessary self-discipline to become more and more entrenched in self-indulgent gratification or blame shifting, to the extent that it becomes almost impossible for me to change to become responsive to God, like Jesus. Blame-shifting is when I project my personal need to "fix myself up" to blame someone else for my condition or to find someone worse than me, implying that if I am not as bad as another person, then I don't have to take any action. For example, by pretending to fix the problems of society, Social Justice Warriors' contribution to society is to find fault with others, or with "the system." Similarly, I am bemused by some environmentalists' effort to save the planet while giving no consideration to saving the individual lives of men and women, to say nothing of saving their eternal souls as this seems to me to be a classic case of blame shifting and wrong priorities.

Fear God

I propose that the Golden Rule is a totally practical and tangible way of exercising our duty to get ourselves in the right relationship to God. Ironically, this is accomplished by dealing with our sin obliquely with a mixture of self-interest, altruism and fear which I suggest is an essential source of motivation. According to Psalm 111: 10;

> *The fear of the* LORD *is the beginning of wisdom; all who follow his precepts have good understanding.*

Similarly, Ecclesiastes 12:13 says;

> *Now all has been heard; here is the conclusion of the matter: Fear God and keep his commandments, for this is the duty of all mankind.*

Finally, Luke 12:5 says;

> *But I will show you whom you should fear: Fear him who, after your body has been killed, has authority to throw you into hell. Yes, I tell you, fear him.*

The point is that sin is heavy stuff, and we need to treat this matter seriously by fearfully accepting our accountability to God.

Some Christian teachers and pastors have said to me that they teach the Golden Rule incidentally. They say it is implied by other teachings and themes such as discipleship and faith. This might be so. But I find this an inadequate response to an explicit instruction of Jesus that we should take very seriously with a combination of fear, faith, hope and love. If Jesus meant what He said, then Christians need to take Him at His word. In my view, there is nothing more important than the realization that God loves us so much that He sent His only Son to be our teacher and our savior. In the same way that he was obedient to his Father, so we need to be obedient to him. Because we are all made in God's image, and because each of us stands in the same potential relationship to God, none of us is more valuable to him than another. When we become conscious of our status as a much-loved child of the Most-

High God, then our fear is replaced with love as we place ourselves under God's scrutiny, because we want to be accountable to Him and receive everything that He gives us for our benefit. In any case, if preachers do prioritize the Golden Rule in their teaching and if it is effective, then their teaching will be manifest in their own lives and in the life of their church as there are no subjects to which the Golden Rule does not apply.

Love casts out fear

The need for self-love remains a major conundrum, to which I shall return. Briefly, however, to love ourselves does not mean what the modern "self-esteem" movement says it means—that we are okay just as we are, and because God loves us so much, he will overlook our shortcomings because no-one is perfect, after all. This is a serious misunderstanding. According to 1 Peter 1:15-16, God requires us to be holy because he is holy; but this does not mean we have to reach God's standard of holiness before we are acceptable to him. According to Paul, the word "holy" in this context means being set apart for God's purposes.

> *He has saved us and called us to a holy life—not because of anything we have done but because of his own purpose and grace. This grace was given us in Christ Jesus before the beginning of time* (2 Tim 1:19).

I understand this to mean a person who is chosen by God in the sense that they are elect and predestined to fulfil God's purposes by being transformed and becoming holy as any one of us are free to do. As I have mentioned in Chapter 3, I can only make sense of this concept if I accept N.T. Wright's view of the meanings of "elect" and "predestined". Wright revises traditional Calvinist doctrine, which says that the elect are the only ones who can accept God's grace, and therefore his holiness, and thus go on to fulfil roles for which they were individually chosen and predestined before time began. Rather, I understand Wright to say that the "elect" and those who make themselves available to fulfill roles that are "predestined" to bring about God's purposes for His creation by their obedience and transformation into the image of Jesus.

To my mind, it is a logical contradiction to pretend that you as an individual are more valuable than your neighbor. If you think you are more valuable, you do not love yourself by seeking your highest good. You are narcissistic—you love a false image of yourself in a way that always leads to emotional harm for you and your neighbor. If you do value yourself very highly and always choose the highest good for yourself, then you will want to make the same reasonable choice and value your neighbor highly. Jesus does not allow you to choose one standard for yourself, and another standard for others, including your enemies. To extend the logic of the Golden Rule from *to treat others as you would want to be treated* to taking the initiative to *Love your neighbor as you love yourself,* then to *Love your enemies* makes the need for reasonable non-contradictory fairness all the more compelling, plus, it is the basis for truth telling about our sinful motives and our humble need for God's grace.

Getting in the zone

Both my wife and daughter are educators who have talked about the zone of proximal development for many years. This concept was first articulated by a Russian psychologist, Lev Vygotsky, and later rediscovered by many educators, and has since become a popular teaching method for optimal learning. The zone of proximal development is the difference between what a learner can do without help and what they can do with help from a teacher who senses the optimal time, information and steps required for a student to learn. This reminds me of Rom 10:14, which says, "*How shall I learn without a preacher?"* as this is how I understand the Golden Rule to work. My conscious obedience the Golden Rule is a response to Jesus's command, which creates a relationship between me and the Holy Spirit, who teaches me by the renewal of my mind at the exact moment when I am ready to learn. This, to me, is an example of the zone of proximal development, whereby I learn in conditions and at a rate to which I may respond optimally. If I am willing, these conditions combine to make me ready to learn by applying the Golden Rule, which then enables me to make further discoveries by myself. But here is the real secret. While it is very good to have good teacher, as the French Philosopher Blaise Pascal reminds us: *"We are generally better persuaded by the reasons we discover ourselves than by those given to us by others."*[1] As we set out purposefully to be obedient to Jesus, we begin to make discoveries about ourselves. If we are fortunate, we will find someone to guide and encourage us. If we are truly blessed, we will discover that the Holy Spirit is hovering nearby, waiting to teach us when we are ready.

Warts and all

A very common misunderstanding about the Golden Rule and a faithful life in general, is that we have somehow to become perfect before we begin the process of transformation. But this is impossible. To begin to apply the Golden Rule, we need only to have a desire to improve or to be obedient to Christ. Actually, it is likely that the more I try to solve all my problems at once, the more I will become stuck. The best I can do is to be honest in what I say, and at least have good intentions toward the other and towards myself. Another way of looking at this is to say that I must be willing to see myself as God sees me: both as a sinner in need of a savior and as a favored child of the Most-High God,

---

1 Blaise Pascal, *Pensées*.

both at the same time. The process of transformation by the renewal of your mind is, as I have mentioned, slow and painful. This requires solutions in proportion to our individual situations, including, as Jesus says, prayer and fasting which are necessary in some cases, to overcome some evil spirits, according to Matt 17:21. Although we may not see our evil in terms of indwelling spirits, that is what evil is. The spirits don't control us, but if we allow them to remain, they will continue to deceive us and tell us lies about ourselves. Prayer and fasting is an intensely solitary self-discipline for which I may or may not be ready. Confessing my sins, however—either to a respected authority such as a priest, pastor or professional counselor, or to a group of friends such as we suggest in our BunchOBlokes groups—is a very normal and essential social experience.

The Golden Rule algorithm

I recently read an article in *The Conversation* by Geoffrey Robinson of Deakin University in which he coined the expression "Technology of self-governance" to describe how Christians *"reflect on their conduct and thoughts and try to live according to a moral code."* My reply to his article was: *"If only it was true to the extent that is required by Jesus who issued the Golden Rule to his disciples as the great command, not just a great idea."*[2] Regardless of my disagreement with his overly-simple characterization of Christian motivation, I do think that his use of the term *technology of self-governance* provides an insight into what the Golden Rule is intended to be. As I mentioned earlier, it was the prospect of a technological connection to the Golden Rule that led me to ask my computer scientist son Brock for some help writing an algorithm to express the Golden Rule, he said sagely, like his childhood Star

---

2 https://theconversation.com/why-the-australian-christian-right-has-weak-political-appeal-93735

Wars hero, Yoda, "Just use words, Dad!" Although I have devised what I think is a useful process diagram to show the basics of the Golden Rule, I have taken his advice. However, I can't resist the temptation to use some symbols and tables as I have below.

Based on my understanding of the Golden Rule, the following diagram illustrates my desire to have a satisfying and fulfilling life.

This requires me to love God with the resources of my heart, mind, soul and strength, not because I already do necessarily or because I am already conscious of what I am doing, but because I see the benefit of the progress I am making and seek to improve on my current situation as much as I can. This suggests a first step toward my awareness that God loves me and wants what is good for me. However, I may not have distinguished between his point of view and my own, still thinking that they are the same thing. If I have chosen to be obedient to Jesus' command, then I invest *faith, hope and love*, meagre though they may be, toward initiatives that I alone can take to prepare me to:

- Accept responsibility for myself to be the best that I can be, initially for my own benefit
- Want the share with others the benefits of faith, hope and love that I enjoy
- Acknowledge my constant accountability to God, who is the giver of all good things
- Trust and obey God
- Be prepared to learn from him

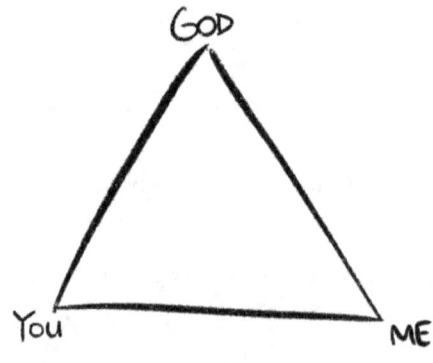

Given these conditions, I can proceed on the basis that:

1. I believe that God is love and that he loves me. My experience of his love will enhance my life because he is the source of all good things and has made me for his good pleasure
2. I want to love God and to return his love as an expression of my gratitude
3. I see that you have the same potential for relationship with God as I do

Therefore, I must love you as a precondition to my loving God. The outcome of this process is that my investments of faith, hope and love will grow. I will begin to be transformed so my behavior is more clearly aligned to the principle of treating others as I would want to be treated. This means that I will experience a shifting balance of my own interests and the interests of the other person, which, although they are now more aligned with serving God, are still very human passions, needs, wants, doubts and fears. My conscious thoughts will tend toward asking what does God want of me, and what is the highest good for me and for the other person, not just momentarily, but for the longest possible time? As such, I will share the mind of Jesus, who said, "*I seek only to do the will of him who sent me,*" as he sought the mind of God. The big difference, of course, is that Jesus was sinless, and we are not.

In practice, the Golden Rule is a set of conscious thinking about my thoughts in steps conducted in the privacy of my mind that support what I do and how I reflect on the resulting experience. The thoughts and actions required of me to implement the Golden Rule occur under many and varied conditions with perhaps thousands of possible outcomes, so I acknowledge that this dialogue is simplistic. I propose, however, based on my understanding and experience and the discussions that I have had that the process may go something like the following table where I chart the process of learning by the Golden Rule, which I believe is always a combination of inward and outward growth:

Table A. Inward Growth

Table A attempts to track my thoughts and self-talk as I prepare to commit to the Golden Rule. Initially, I may not be conscious of it being a process, or even as an obedient act or duty. Rather, I may think of it as just a good idea—a way of being "fair", "kind", "good" or even of obtaining selfish benefit. This process may take many more steps forward and slips backward over many years. The big challenge and the most important lesson, though, is how I deal with the likelihood that I am imposing my selfish view onto you in contradiction to the Golden Rule.

#	Table A. Inward growth. Thinking and emotional steps required by the Golden Rule.	Self-talk.
1	I am in awe of God and fearful of not keeping his commands or I may be motivated by my awareness of his love.	This is a pre-condition.
2	I have a high view of myself and want to be accountable to God. I will try to do what the Golden Rule suggests is good for you by treating you as if I were in your position.	I love myself and seek the highest good for myself.
3	I am becoming aware that my relationship with God is dependent upon my relationship with you.	I will test this idea.
4	I will at least attempt to do the right thing to treat you as I would want you to treat me.	I am motivated by high idealism.
5	There is a risk that you may not respond favorably to my attempt.	I will take a risk with you.

How does the Golden Rule work?

5	If I am rebuffed by you, I may take offence or become angry because I may think you have misinterpreted my attempt to do what I think is right.	**My self-righteous anger is a contradiction**
6	My anger creates a problem for me which I must recognize and deal with.	**I am ashamed of my anger.**
7	I may realize that I am still trying to get you to *treat me as I would like to be treated*.	**I am becoming aware of my manipulation of you.**
8	As I learn about myself, I begin to see the limitations of my instincts and the corrupting effect of my ego upon both my thoughts and my behavior.	**I am becoming aware of my limitations.**
9	As I become more self-aware and conscious in my accountability to God, I think more about myself and my relationship with you.	**I want to improve myself.**
10	When I see my unreasonableness and limitations (that is, my sin) clearly, I cry out to God, in humility, and perhaps to others asking for forgiveness.	**I humble myself and say, help me Father!**
11	God responds through his Spirit by giving me insight or some corrective, because God gives grace to the humble.	**God gives his grace to the humble.**
12	God's grace gives me insight into my sinfulness and what I can do in my relationship with you to overcome it.	**I am grateful to God.**
13	As I try to treat you with some new insight, you may begin to respond.	**In my gratitude, I say thank, you Lord.**
14	If we become more conscious of our relationship, you may begin to get a glimpse of what God wants for both of us.	**This is reciprocal love which I find very attractive.**

15	I begin to see the potential for both of us to improve our relationship with each other and with God. This is what we are called to do if we see ourselves as part of God's family.	**I experience God's righteous love as a source of peace and joy.**

Table B. Outward Growth

Assuming I have made some progress with the Golden Rule, I will be aware that I am too proud, selfish, blame placing and manipulating to take credit for the changes that have occurred in me. The transformation always has distinctively different qualities known as "fruits" or outcomes of the influence of the Holy Spirit. They are characterized in me by growing humility in my thoughts and actions toward you. Even if I have not developed this self-awareness yet, I hope I might persist with a clearer picture of the process in mind where I am conscious of the potential for a relationship to be deeply fulfilling, not just of my emotional immaturity, but of my deepest needs of my body, soul and spirit. In the transition from being bound by my human frailty to becoming a more attentive to God's Spirit, I become aware that my growth is not just good fortune, but a result of the conscious of the renewal of my mind and transformation into the image of Jesus that I want to share with you. However, I am aware that I cannot impose my view on you, nor can I manipulate you. The best I can do, however, is to tell you what I think is the truth. This means that I will continue to make many mistakes which I hope you will forgive me for, because I will try to admit them, as I am able.

I am beginning to see a vision of the Kingdom of God as the object of faith. When what we hoped for is seen, faith is no longer required for that thing, so I can now focus my attention on something greater.

How does the Golden Rule work?

Table B. Outward Growth.
Further steps in the Golden Rule process.

ME	PROCESS	YOU
When I obey Jesus' command, a vision of my transformation and the Kingdom of God forms in my mind.	A vision is formed in me of what is possible by simply being obedient to Jesus Christ. I recognize that you and I are different, but it would be a contradiction for me to place a high value on myself, without applying the same value to you. Because I have a high view of my own value, if I want good things for myself, I will also want good things for you.	**You may still not know what I am thinking, but you are glad I am at least friendly.**
I am beginning to feel well disposed toward you.	Because I don't want bad things to happen to me, I will not do bad things to you. By working together, we can both improve our lives with altruistic reciprocity.	**You may feel the difference, more than understand it.**
Becoming conscious.	I have begun to learn about myself in my relationship with you. This is becoming a bit painful because I realize that there is a price to pay— one which my ego resists strongly.	**You may experience a growing feeling of goodwill towards me.**
God's Holy Spirit is more active within me as I allow it. I am becoming aware that you do good things for me.	I act in good faith to take the initiative to do good to you. I may or may not get something good back from you, but I am making some progress with self-discovery. I am experiencing some pain as my ego is required to take the back seat. I realize that I cannot do this by myself and happily accept help from the still small voice that encourages me. I have experienced the power of love. God's Spirit is now engaging with me more	

I am still sometimes confused by you. I love my enemies	because I have become responsive to his presence. The Golden Rule is taken closer to its logical conclusion. I am going to do good to you despite knowing that you may be hostile toward me. I know that I benefit from loving you, even if you don't at this stage. I have begun to realize the benefits of self-sacrifice.	
Self-transcendence	These steps have made me more aware of who God is, and what he wants for me and you together. I can now say truthfully that I love God.	**Maybe you are starting to see a glimmer of good things between us. If you ask, I will explain that they are from God.**
United purpose	You and I are beginning to see the great potential in having a shared goal and purpose.	**United purpose**
United existence under God's creative purpose	We have both realized that we have become engaged in God's creative process.	**United existence**
Fully-fledged member of God's family	We are both engaged in God's Kingdom. We see the benefits to ourselves, family, friends and the common good. The price we pay for the loss of ego is nothing by comparison to the benefits.	**You see yourself as a member of God's family and begin to experience united purpose**

I love God with my whole being.	I now see that I have been in a symbiotic relationship with you and God for a long time. As I have engaged with you, so I have learned about myself and seen my need to accept God's grace.	**We experience God's love and God together.**

Small steps

What is not so obvious is that when we start to apply some of these steps and relational values to ourselves, we are acting in faith, because we don't know what the result will be. If we take the initiative in a relationship as we are required to do, believing that the result will be good because we hope that God's purposes for his creation are good. As we make progress, we begin to change to resemble Jesus, who is the object of our desire, in ways that we could not have predicted or otherwise achieved. This is not blind faith. It is taking small steps into the unknown on the basis of what we have discovered to be true, or what we hope is true.

Putting aside Christ's version of the Golden Rule, the other historical versions of it listed in Chapter 2 all bear some of the same features, including an objective ideal of universal justice and fairness, if they are applied seriously to any personal relationship. None of them, however, are identical to Christ's Golden Rule, because they lack the same assumptions, such as man being made in God's image, the possibility of becoming like God with the help of God's Spirit and, most of all, the direct command of Jesus Christ, who claimed to be God's Son, and therefore God incarnate.

Easy to say. Hard to do

There are many implications of Christ's Golden Rule, some of which take time to emerge. To begin, we can see that the Golden Rule is derived from the Old Testament law. Jesus demonstrates this in his discussion with the lawyer in Luke 10: 25-28, where he quotes directly from the law which He claimed He was here to fulfill. He further fleshes out what He means when He later says in John, Chapters 13 and 15 that if we are to be His disciples, we must love one another as evidence of our transformation. Jesus then makes perhaps one of His most memorable statements: We are not just to love our family, friends and fellow believers, but also our enemies. John follows this up by saying that if we claim to love God, but hate our brother, then we are liars (1 Jn 4:20). To leave no uncertainty as to whom we should love, or to what extent we are to love others, Jesus followed His most comprehensive account of the Great Command in Luke 10 by telling the story of the Good Samaritan to drive home the idea that we cannot be selective as to whom we consider our neighbors.

The Good Samaritan story, which Jesus tells after he commands the Golden Rule, is one of the great accounts of human decency, to the extent that has become enshrined in everyday language and in the law of many cultures, where citizens are required to help those in desperate need. The story, as Jesus tells it to His Jewish audience, is about a Jewish man travelling on the road between towns who is attacked and robbed by thieves. As he is lying there, stripped of clothing, beaten, and half dead alongside the road, a Jewish priest and then a Levite comes by, but both avoid the man. Finally, a Samaritan happens upon the traveller. Samaritans and Jews generally despised each other, but the Samaritan helps the injured man. Jesus is described as telling the parable in response to the question from a lawyer, "And who is my neighbor?" whom Leviticus 19:18 says should be loved. In response, Jesus recounts this parable, the conclusion of which is that the neighbor who figures in the parable is the man who shows mercy to the injured man—that is, the Samaritan. As He often does, Jesus overturns conventional wisdom by making the good guy in the story a Samaritan who was despised as an unbeliever by Jesus' audience of religious Jews.

What kind of love?

I believe that Jesus' mission to extend God's love to his disciples is summarized by John 3:16. They in turn, are to extend God's love to all men and women without reservation. It is essential that we carefully define words that are key to our understanding of what the written words are intended to mean. Love is defined in the New Testament, by two Greek words: agapē and philia. However, there are several Greek words for love. Erring on the side of simplicity, those of interest to me are:

Agapē. In the New Testament, *agapē* is charitable, selfless, altruistic, and unconditional. It is parental love seen as creating goodness in the world, it is the way God is seen to love humanity, and it is seen as the kind of love that Christians aspire to have for others.

Philia. Also used in the New Testament, philia is a human response to something that is found to be delightful. Also known as "brotherly love".

Eros (sexual love) is to do with impulsive desire. It is not used in the New Testament but is implied by Paul in several references to marriage, where *eros* is fulfilled within the definition of agape.

Storge (needy child-to-parent love) only appears in the compound word philostorgos, meaning kindly affection. For example: *Be devoted to one another in love. Honor one another above yourselves* (Rom, 12:10).

The only situation in which the Bible applies all four types of love, is in the ideal of an extended family of a married man and woman and their child and relatives, which in my opinion, defines what human beings are generally designed to experience. Obviously, not every person will experience this, as it is a description of human potential and a command. If you would like a more complete and graphic rendering of the way the Bible describes erotic love, I invite you to read the Song of Songs, to appreciate its beautiful and deeply erotic poetry describing the sexual desire of a young man, the Lover, as he pursues a young woman, his Beloved. Not only is this a beautifully comprehensive account of the man's experience of human desire with its descriptions of the delightful features of the woman, it implies the context of delightful integrity and wholeness where physical characteristics are described and employed in fulfilled pleasure in sublime ecstasy. The Lover anticipates the satiation of his desire complete with food and wine in a bucolic countryside as he prepares himself and invites her to be his beloved. She responds by giving him her neck, mouth, teeth, breasts and her "secret garden" without restraint because this is what she and he were made for; to enjoy the fruits of humanity at the right time, in the proper setting for which a man and a woman are so delightfully made. There are many further allusions to this union throughout the Bible, with Paul talking about sexual relationships being motivated by the "man's desire" and marriage being a metaphor for the "mystical union" between God and his church. As this is not the time or the place for any further investigation of this wonderful topic, I invite you to read the Song of Songs and study with the help of the following guide:

https://www.biblicaltraining.org/library/mystical-union/systematic-theology/louis-berkhof.

As with all such definitions and descriptions of truth, there are many corruptions and counterfeits of the meaning of love such as saying that a person loves their cat, that I am going to ignore because they will do nothing to clarify our understanding. To understand the application of love, I prefer the definition attributed to Thomas Aquinas. *Love is to will the highest good for another.* This implies an act resulting from the will (rather than an emotion) applied beneficially, reasonably and purposefully on behalf of another person (or persons, including one's self). This is not to say that there are no alternative definitions, but for our purposes, I accept that this definition is accurate, comprehensive and easy to remember. Similarly, we must also define the word good. This word normally opens a Pandora's Box of philosophical and religious meanings, most of which add more confusion than clarity. I prefer: good (or the common good) meaning *anything that is life giving or life enhancing* that we would properly (as against perversely or corruptly) desire. More generally, good, means anything that is always naturally beneficial to the desires, motivations and lives of all people, rather than the desires of one person.

Jesus completes His discourse on the mountain by summarizing what He has said with the statement, *Be perfect, therefore, as your heavenly Father is perfect.* This summary is the law of love, which is impossible for us unless we are transformed by the Spirit of God. Matthew 5:43-48. In his book, *Works of Love* (1847), Søren Kierkegaard claimed that Christianity is unique because love is a requirement. The early Christian apologist Tertullian wrote regarding love for enemies:

> *"Our individual, extraordinary, and perfect goodness consists in loving our enemies."*

To love one's friends is common practice, to love one's enemies is required only among Christians. It is very instructive that the biblical test of love is not a strict behavioral prescription of do this, or don't do that. According to the Apostle Paul, love is indicated by its relational outcome of consideration for each other in a powerful, beneficial and dynamic way.

> Love is patient; love is kind. It does not envy, it does not boast, it is not proud. It is not rude, it is not self-seeking, it is not easily angered, it keeps no record of wrongs. Love does not delight in evil but rejoices with the truth. It always protects, always trusts, always hopes, always perseveres. (1 Cor 13:4–7)

Proof of love

Proof, we are told, is a mathematical concept that does not really apply in areas such as religious faith or human emotions, because they lack the objective and logical rigor. However, an alternative definition of proof is "persuasive evidence" that a case or an argument has been satisfied. Regardless of which definition we prefer, I propose that there is proof of love, where the definition of love is "*to seek the highest good*" for yourself or another. Love, in my view, is fulfilled by tangible evidence that was predicted as a goal and is objectively observable and measurable in behavioral, qualitative and statistical terms. For example, I would claim that the outcomes of love are deeply satisfying and fulfilling of human needs and desires which can be measured on a scale of 1-10, with 10 being the highest good. This does not mean that we or our situation are perfect, because nothing in human experience is. Rather, our experience, as in a relationship between a husband and wife, father and son or son-in-law, father and daughter or daughter-in-law, the person next door, the lady at the supermarket, the mechanic who services my car or anyone else, is as good as I can reasonably expect it to be.

Paul writes:

> *Therefore, do not let what is for you a good thing be spoken of as evil; for the kingdom of God is not*

> *eating and drinking, but righteousness and peace and joy in the Holy Spirit. For he who in this way serves Christ is acceptable to God and approved by men* (Rom 14:16-18).

This text is a discussion about the difference between good and evil in relationships, where while one person may consider eating or not eating certain foods may be good, another person may consider it to be evil. Paul is not saying food is good or evil. He is saying that what we consciously do or do not do to one another could be evil depending upon our motive and if it offends or harms them.

> *You, my brothers and sisters, were called to be free. But do not use your freedom to indulge the flesh; rather, serve one another humbly in love. For the entire law is fulfilled in keeping this one command: "Love your neighbor as yourself." If you bite and devour each other, watch out or you will be destroyed by each other.*
>
> *So I say, walk by the Spirit, and you will not gratify the desires of the flesh. For the flesh desires what is contrary to the Spirit, and the Spirit what is contrary to the flesh. They are in conflict with each other, so that you are not to do whatever you want. But if you are led by the Spirit, you are not under the law.*
>
> *The acts of the flesh are obvious: sexual immorality, impurity and debauchery; idolatry and witchcraft; hatred, discord, jealousy, fits of rage, selfish ambition, dissensions, factions and envy; drunkenness, orgies, and the like. I warn you, as I did before, that those who live like this will not inherit the kingdom of God.*

> But the fruit of the Spirit is love, joy, peace, forbearance, kindness, goodness, faithfulness, gentleness and self-control. Against such things there is no law. Those who belong to Christ Jesus have crucified the flesh with its passions and desires. Since we live by the Spirit, let us keep in step with the Spirit. Let us not become conceited, provoking and envying each other (Gal 5).

I have summarized the term *"fruit of the Spirit"* as righteousness, peace and joy in the Holy Spirit. By this I mean the outcome of our transformation into the image of Christ, where as far as possible, we are on good terms with other people with no unresolved hostility to the extent that our relationship is peaceful and productive. This is experienced as enjoyment because two (or more) people enjoy each other within the proper limits of the particular relationship, with no impediment. However, while we would recognize this as an ideal state, it is not something for which we can claim credit or moral superiority, as it is the result of our transformation by the Holy Spirit acting within us.

Software for the soul

At the risk of overplaying the algorithm metaphor, I would like to propose that we can create a software for the soul. By this I mean a way of thinking about ourselves and regulating our relationships with others—those to whom we relate daily, such as family, neighbors, workmates, teammates and others—and a way of making our words and actions as consistent and positively encouraging as possible both to ourselves and others. Historically, this has been a problem for the church as it has often come to be seen as the moral guardian of society with an endless list of "Thou shalt, thou shalt not" decrees by which the church judged the heathen.

How does the Golden Rule work?

First, let me repeat that the biblical laws are essential guidelines for society that must be retained. However, the law is never the means by which we are transformed. Laws are the guidelines that allow us to know what a good standard is to aim for and when we have fallen short of the mark. We now need to see the fulfillment of laws differently: as the outcomes of a faithful life, not as rigid rules which govern behavior as they were misused by the Pharisees and by some quarters of the church today. Jesus says he intends to fulfil the law, not to dispense with it. I think he means to show what the law was intended to do as an outcome of transformation when people's hearts are changed as a result of them being spiritually "born again" and progressively transformed into the image of Jesus. Software for the soul would include a lot of things that we already regard as wisdom. So much of what we recognize as the basics of good ethics, relationships, business, education, medical practice, science, engineering, politics and international diplomacy are the laws and guidelines we should recognize in each different context. It may be also known as "Best Practice", although this is often far too optimistic for my liking as it too easily becomes an unachievable goal, or an unworkable legalistic imposition, closely aligned to political correctness. It is helpful to think of sin as the absence of love, according to the very comprehensive description of 1 John 4. Just as darkness is the absence of light, and cold the absence of heat, sin displaces love.

There is another way of thinking about what our souls need to function as they were designed (as we will discuss later in Chapters 6 and 10): namely, to feed our minds, emotions and wills with things that are good for our whole beings, body, soul and spirit. I understand our human spirit to be the distilled and aggregated essence of who we are—body, soul and spirit combined. They include things needed for our survival and comfort like shelter and clothing. Then they include our social need for relationships, and what Maslow called self-actualization, including the following things usually considered to be high culture. Things of beauty in human form, nature, architecture, and all of the sciences, which according to Paul includes;

> *...whatever is true, whatever is noble, whatever is right, whatever is pure, whatever is lovely, whatever is admirable-if anything is excellent or praiseworthy-think about such things.*
> (Philippians 4:8)

Notice that the first thing on Paul's list is truthfulness, which in this age of "fake news" is getting a bad reputation not assisted by the Postmodern concept that there are no absolute truths. I have for a long time been conscious of William Shakespeare's words, *"To thine own self be true"*. Another version of this is Paul's injunction to *"Speak the truth in love"*. Jordan Peterson reminds us that we are given the Logos, God's words to speak, which have creative power. Our words, which we should consider as our Logos also have potential to create or to destroy. Truth is always creative because it is from God. If it is not creative, it is not from God, but from Satan, the father of lies who, when he speaks, seeks only to deceive. In summary, we can say that love in Jesus' Golden rule is the basis of an ethical framework applied to relationships where there are recognized standards of behavior (or law). The Anglo-Canadian pastor Barney Coombs tells a good story about a strip joint bar operator who was converted in his church in Basingstoke, UK. His first small step of transformation was to stop watering down the beer. Although we may smile patronizingly, we are actually the same; there will always be someone ahead of us in their development and someone behind. Therefore, we should be patient with others as we also should be with ourselves.

The fact that love is not just simple compliance with the law in some dogmatic sense ensures that it is more than just intellectual assent to an abstract ideal. Love requires a relational context in which a person is engaged in a process of learning about another for the individual and mutual benefit of the parties of the relationship. This is a complex process because even the instigator of the action does not know where this relationship will end up. Each person who initiates an act of intentional love, such as the Golden Rule requires, is engaging in an act of faith because they are trusting a process that they hope is reliable, but for which they have no guarantee. When they engage with another person, they are taking a guess as to what will be good for the other based on their own view of reality. This, of course, is fraught with difficulty because most of us don't even fully understand our own motives, let alone those of another. Regardless of this ignorance or uncertainty, we begin by taking an action of faith that we hope will be beneficial to the other. If it is recognized as beneficial by both parties, we have made progress. If, on the other hand, our well-intentioned action is rejected, then we may have a problem in which the initiator should learn something about themselves. Keeping in mind that the Golden Rule is conducted under the scrutiny of God, it can only be hoped that what is learned is beneficial. However, we know from bitter experience that this is not always the case, as with religious abuse, which is the ongoing outcome of religious manipulation by a narcissist.

As I have mentioned before, the Golden Rule in its simplest form is not a statement about what we normally think of as religious behavior, but rather practical advice about relationships. Even in its full version, accountability to God is not the complex acceptance of extensive religious dogma. Nor am I saying that religion accounts for nothing, or that all religions are the same, as even from the point of view of the Golden Rule, they clearly are not. What I am saying is that it is the commencement of a learning process that inexorably and mysteriously leads us to God, via his Son, Jesus. This is indeed mysterious because of the dynamic relationship produced by this process, which is best described as an algorithm that brings us to learn to understand while we commit ourselves to obedient and faithful relationships. It is important to note that we don't need to know anything to begin to implement the Golden Rule, apart from the realization that God gives good gifts to his children.

The deep mystery behind the Golden Rule

A couple of years ago, while attending a men's conference, I overheard a conversation next to me in which a guy, Peter Stone, who turned out to be an ex-medical doctor, said to the person sitting opposite:

> *We have accepted that we cannot make another person change to suit us, but we have not accepted that we cannot change ourselves. All we can ever do, is to choose the power by which we change.* [1]

This glance into the deep mystery behind the Golden Rule suggests that our obedience to God begins when we understand that human nature is fatally flawed by sin. Only when we make the free decision to become disciples of Jesus by doing what he commanded us to do can we begin to become conscious about the scope and purpose of our mission: to be transformed to resemble the one that we worship. We are now involved in a symbiotic relationship where the offer of God's grace and power is available for our acceptance. I have developed this theme more fully in Chapter 10, but this is a key to understanding not only the Golden Rule, but the reasons why it is essential for us to engage in a conscious process of learning about how difficult our ego is to overcome, and the amount of external power required to do the job. It is important to remember this when we are talking about "spirituality", or more correctly, "self-transcendence" because herein lies a trap: not all the forces and influences external to us

---

1 Verbatim conversation with Peter Stone.

that we might think of as "spiritual," are good or even benign. On the contrary, they are on a spectrum that extends from being very good, and therefore from God, to very bad from God's evil adversary, Satan.

First, do your best

It is true, of course, that in a symbiotic relationship we can and must be the best we can be by drawing upon our own inner resources. This is the normal stuff about recognizing the good by honouring the law, our parents, being self-disciplined, hard work, becoming educated and accomplishing all kinds of moral, ethical and personal goals to the limit of the fatal flaw within. Each of us needs to choose a master to guide our apprenticeship with the warning that *The student is not above the teacher, but everyone who is fully trained will be like their teacher.* (Lk 6:4). Paul urges us to be competent ministers of the new covenant of love, by the spirit, suggesting that when we in humility, exhaust our human resources, then the spirit is waiting to encourage and teach us more about how to become like Jesus. In any case, it is us who initiates the attempt at self-transformation. God's offer of grace is always waiting for our acceptance, but only when we realize that we need God's help to do what we cannot do alone. It is the same when we pray, as it is we who utter the first word to God because he never imposes himself upon us. This is a reason why prayer is so important. God does not usually drive us to our knees to pray. He may invite us, but it is we who must always take this first step in obedience to him.

Traditional tosh

But the obstacles in our path are subtle and deceptive because at just the moment when we think we have made some progress, our religious instinct pops up to defend our self-righteousness, as Jesus points out:

> Then some Pharisees and teachers of the law came to Jesus from Jerusalem and asked, "Why do your disciples break the tradition of the elders? They don't wash their hands before they eat!" Jesus replied, "And why do you break the command of God for the sake of your tradition?

Notice that Jesus insists that we should be obedient to his commands, rather than to the impulse of our self-righteous religious traditions. There are some modern sacred cows that Jesus might equally condemn if they are seen as an end in themselves such as:

- Denominationalism
- Four spiritual laws
- Signs following
- Giving to the poor
- Being born again
- The Golden Rule
- Venial vs. mortal sins
- Liturgy
- Separation from the world

How does the Golden Rule work?

I don't intend to analyze any of these traditions in detail other than to say that I think I understand that each of them have become traditions because they have had something important to say at some time. But the greater problem is that when we adopt traditions, they lose their meaning because we make assumptions that we are not entitled to make. Plus, we misunderstand the need for personal effort when we imagine that God will save us from ourselves.

You will note that I have included the Golden Rule as a tradition. I believe it is a profound maxim, principle, truth, law or key foundation of faithfulness, capable of transforming us powerfully. Except that while I thought I did a reasonable job of applying it to my marriage, I took it for granted in my relationships with my kids. This is such a huge problem that, in my opinion, if I give myself religious credit in this way, I must counter it by looking at myself through another set of eyes, to see my pretentious self-deception for what it is. This, I think may be the meaning of the words from the Lord's Prayer: *lead us not into temptation but deliver us from evil.*

Tosh, by the way, is the right word for self-deception to remind ourselves of the deception we encounter when we take something profound for granted, having lost our sense of mystery, awe and fear for God. My point is that because of our tendency toward tosh, we need to have some remedy from this fatal flaw. I propose that a version of the Golden Rule kicks in when we consciously engage with people who have an opposite view to us. If we can do this by listening to them rather than making them listen to us, we create an opportunity to see ourselves from their point of view helping us see what our delusions are. In some cases, this religious delusion can be very serious indeed. The Roman Catholic church insulated itself from tosh so well, that it must now suffer public humiliation while their sins of sexual abuse are exposed in forensic detail. If I have such serious delusions to overcome, such as an unconfessed crime or a deep-rooted psychological or moral problem, I must get the best help available to avoid my deliberate legal and moral culpability because there are some sins that can only be dealt with by applying the highest possible remedy, including confession with prayer and fasting (Mk 9:29). Similarly, if I find myself stuck in repetitive low-order sins, then I probably need to confess to someone who I trust and who can help me. Things such as professional Rational Emotive Therapy or being a member of a support group, both of which I have done, to my lasting benefit. The ideal outcome of our use of the Golden Rule is that each person experiences a degree of shared purpose, enjoyment, pleasure, happiness, peacefulness and productivity providing us with footholds on the road to the Kingdom of God. Herein lies an important difference between the Golden Rule and other more explicit forms of remedy. It would be ridiculous for me to announce to wife, for instance, that I am going to do some Golden Rule work on her. Rather, I must make this decision in the privacy of my mind and hope that she sees the outcome in my behavior over the long haul, rather than my self-righteous words.

Can the Golden Rule work universally?

As I have mentioned earlier, critics often assume that the Golden Rule is a rigid religious formula whereby one person imposes their view on another. Of course, if this is true, then such an abuse of relationship should be condemned because it lacks any understanding of love and the good. By comparison to the way in which Christians practise Christ's Golden Rule in its fullness, this view is reductionism; an attempt to describe something in overly simplistic terms, by leaving out some of its most important parts. This is why atheists often cannot understand the Golden Rule, let alone apply it. If they exclude the possibility of God and his love from their reasoning, they cannot accept that anyone else could have a sense of conscious accountability to him. Therefore, they cannot even begin the process required by the Golden Rule, unless they have a very strong rational framework based on the Law of Non-Contradiction. Soren Kierkegaard's idea of common grace is helpful in understanding how the Golden Rule is limited by our concept of accountability to God as it explains how they will never have the imperative of love and obedience to Christ that Christians have.

Perhaps it is possible to get people to see that we owe our neighbor whatever we would wish for ourselves based on logical reciprocity which views morality as a sort of a balanced equation, in which a person who receives the benefit of a moral action has a responsibility to respond in kind. Such moral treatment of others requires things like being fair, equitable or even-handed. It means 'I'm-OK-if-you're-OK', or 'you-scratch-my-back-and-I'll-scratch-yours'. Although reciprocal responsibility between citizens sounds like a pretty good way to run a society, there are good reasons to suspect it will not work on its own. Many aspects of society require more than an equitable give-and-take basis: something higher and much more morally demanding is involved in maintaining a society. Societies require the often unmentioned principle of *sacrifice* which is implied, but not mentioned in the most common renderings of the Golden Rule.

The idea of sacrifice will come as no surprise to anyone who has been happily married, or who has had children. Marriages simply do not function unless the partners are prepared to make sacrifices without expectation of return, and children certainly cannot be expected to repay the sacrifices parents find it necessary to make in raising them, other than by having their own children. Those who are in a serving profession – a teacher, a pastor, a doctor, a charity worker, a counselor, or even a politician (sometimes) – know that their profession could not continue without what they contribute to the public welfare without expectation of reciprocity. A society cannot survive without people going beyond the call of duty or reward. Even if we agree that reciprocity is not enough of a foundation for society, we can hardly argue that it represents the essential core of human morality as no principle of equity will ever be enough for us to see the value of sacrifice. Rather, we need a reason to accept *inequity*. We must be content to render, for the good of others, things that cannot be returned. The very optimum of this behavior is the one who, like a soldier in a good cause, lays down his life in order that others may live freely. This is the basis of Christianity, represented by the ironic symbol of the cross on which Jesus willingly gave his own life in obedience to his father.

Despite all of this fine rhetoric about the universal nature of idealism, respect, equity, mutuality, moral principles, intelligence and so on, there is one thing still missing. None of the advocates of the universal Golden Rule, gave their lives for it, no-one, except Jesus.

Treat others as you would have them treat you. Jesus.

Christ's Golden Rule always begins with the initiator's point of view. By consciously or unconsciously referring to themselves and their own values, they commence trying to do good to others, as their concept of God's goodness requires. This, of course, could be an entirely wrong view, which the initiator will soon discover if their attempt is sincere. If they already have a reasonably developed moral sense based on their understanding of God's law of love, then they will know that God's justice is an interplay with His mercy and compassion, with scripture and the law as a guide with the Holy Spirit as teacher and coach. The tension that separates us from God is always overarched by compassion, which is God's love applied sympathetically toward us. As we look to our understanding of first principles to figure out what love demands in a situation, we either come down on the side of compliance with the law as we understand it, or if the circumstances allow it, we might be merciful, perhaps to the extent that we have experienced God's grace and mercy ourselves.

An interesting example of this dichotomy is Bishop Robert Barron's explanation of what appear to be inconsistencies in Pope Francis' recent encyclical, *Amoris Laetitia*, "...*the Roman Catholic church always makes many great demands, but it is always greatly merciful.*" https://www.youtube.com/watch?v=-5ruTwxiLqs

The Crown

Another unexpected demonstration of the complex interplay between justice, mercy and compassion was portrayed brilliantly in the Netflix TV series, The Crown. Episode six of series two portrays Queen Elizabeth becoming increasingly interested in the American Evangelist, Billy Graham, during his 1954 UK visit. She is so impressed with him that she arranges for Graham to speak in Westminster Cathedral, followed by a private audience. The Queen discusses with Graham her dilemma regarding a request from her uncle. Edward VIII, the Duke of Windsor, had previously abdicated his throne in favor of the divorcee, Wallis Simpson. His request was that the Queen should allow him to return to the UK. The law was very clear, however. Only the Queen can allow it. Edward's friends in high places had organized a powerful lobby to gloss over his abdication to get him back in. In her encounter with Graham, the Queen reveals her love for her uncle, but is concerned about the law and her personal accountability to God. Graham speaks passionately about God's mercy, but Elizabeth is ahead of him by recounting that there were two thieves on crosses at Calvary, only one of whom receives forgiveness by repenting his sins as he begs for Christ's mercy, which he memorably gave by saying, "today you will be with me in Paradise." As she applies this reasoning to her uncle, she is aware that Edward has committed treason by conspiring with Adolf Hitler during WWII, which Graham does not know. She is portrayed brilliantly drawing a parallel with the unrepentant Edward and the unrepentant thief, and so resolves to disallow his return based on her magnificent understanding of the conditions required for God's grace and mercy to be received. This is the position that a diligent Christian may hope to eventually emulate, after years of struggling with the Golden Rule, based upon their knowledge of God.

The Golden Rule is not another abstract theory, vague notion, fad, good idea, psycho-babble or wishful thinking. Nor is it an end. Rather, it is a beginning that never ends, at least in this life. It is, though, in modern terms a self-help process which enables us to make the changes required to enable us to experience the Kingdom of God in our lives. It is also an antidote to pathetic repeated pleading and begging God and others for forgiveness for repeating the same habitual sins because we cannot break the cycle by ourselves. When we begin to see our inheritance as adopted sons and daughters of the Most High God and commence transformation into the image of Christ, the baggage and sins that hold us back can be dealt with by our reception of the offer of grace—not as a cover for sins, as this has been accomplished by Jesus, but as a result of a new sense of dignity, self-worth, and a new potential to see reality for what it is and to humble ourselves and pray for God's grace.

Contrary to the views of progressive Christians, it is not possible to conscientiously read Christ's Golden Rule as key to universal salvation without doing violence to the text. The claim that God's love never discriminates between one person and another has no support from the overall scope or the details of the biblical view. Universalism has more to do with postmodernism, dividing society into power categories of victimhood where people are either on the side of the oppressed who can never be blamed or the oppressor, who is always blamed. The narrative from Genesis to Revelation is one of human rebellion against God beginning in the Garden of Eden and the struggle to heal this fractured relationship, culminating in the advent of Jesus, where each person has an opportunity to choose reconciliation with God for themselves. The idea that God imposes himself upon anyone is unsupported in scripture. Contrary to the victimhood view and classical Calvinism, for that matter, God is portrayed as a grieving parent, patiently waiting, hoping for our return like the good father of the Prodigal son story. In my opinion, scripture constantly asserts the absolute sovereignty of God. He is the incarnate creator, law giver, ruler, judge and coming king. His omniscience, omnipresence and omnipotence are limited only by his own laws. However, God's "omni" qualities are dwarfed by his willingness to become incarnate and to share the experience of humanity with us. We too are sovereign, though in a vastly more limited way, in which our ultimate power relates to our ability to choose our own attitudes—even when there is a gun to our head. Our role in the act of reconciliation with God is to use our sovereignty to choose God's vastly greater power rather than complain that we have been victimized in the struggle of life. As the Golden Rule is dependent upon the law of non-contradiction, it requires that if I define a good for myself, it must be equally good for another. The Golden Rule suffers from misidentification to the extent that many "experts" declare that the many versions of the Golden Rule should all be called by the same name. This misnomer is so well entrenched that when we use the words "the Golden Rule", it is often necessary to add or imply the qualifier, "Christ's Golden Rule". This is because, as we have seen, no one in history was as uniquely qualified to give meaning to this expression as Jesus Christ, based only on the historical impact that his use of this expression has had. While we could say that all versions of the Golden Rule are designed to facilitate good relationships, the qualitative scale of the many versions extends from the sublime to the ridiculous. If we qualify reciprocity by calling it altruistic reciprocity, it moves up a few notches, though this only adds to the confusion as the words reciprocity and altruism have different meanings.

Just as a loving parent treats a child for the child's benefit, the Golden Rule cannot ever be predominantly manipulative, coercive, exploitive, abusive or violent. But as we know, because some parents are less than ideal, their poor motives become manifest in their relationship with the child. Therefore, the usual outcome of a bad relationship is dysfunction in both the parent and child, manifested as anger, violence and mistrust. The opposite of an experience of peace, enjoyment, satisfaction and fulfillment is banal chaos. Uncontrollable anger, despair, hatred, violence and death. We are properly horrified when we see examples of the extreme opposite of loving family relationships, such as when children are abused, typically by a de facto father, with the contrivance of the child's mother. We are shocked because a child's safety in the care of parents is assumed.

Conclusion

I would like to return to my theme of being transformed into the image of Jesus, who is good for my soul and the soul of others to whom I relate. Tragically, the opposite is also true, as this sad tale of fractured relationships demonstrates. The Golden Rule, according to Jesus, is the summary of the whole of the Old Testament law. It is in fact, an application of God's Law of Love. Increasing secularism, boasting its great success has dispensed with the need to worship God by worshipping scientific materialism and the narcissistic cult of self. Instead of fulfilling Christ's command to *treat others as you would be treated,* many Christians have also adopted the anti-religious reductionist-materialistic view and have preferred to argue about religious differences and abstractions, rather than to be obedient to Christs' Great command. Christians can have no hope of addressing the decline in religious and other freedoms and the many benefits we have taken for granted until we, as the universal church, decide to become the example of God's Kingdom, by becoming consciously and purposefully reconciled to the King Himself.

This apparently simple command is in fact extremely difficult because it requires that we submit to learning about our deeply imperfect selves and suffer the pain of the death of our selfish and deceptive egos.

6

TREAT OTHERS AS YOU WOULD HAVE THEM TREAT YOU

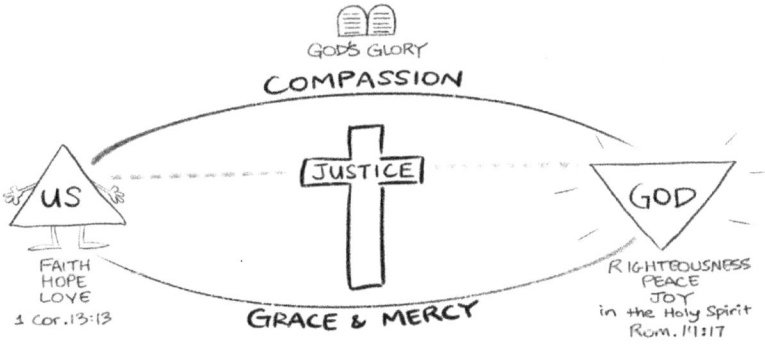

I am the way, the truth and the life. *Jesus of Nazareth.*
John 14:6

Although the Golden Rule is an ethical principle simple enough to teach children the basics of fairness and cooperation, the same rule enables our transformation to become children of God. Each application is a process of aggregation, principle upon principle, proven by experience as complex as life itself. Often, the most difficult relationships are the most intimate, especially with siblings and family members where our expectations may be unreasonably high. Therefore, understanding how to apply the Golden Rule will be important to you for the rest of your life. It is also the curriculum for teaching ourselves the most important and most difficult principle in life – how we learn to love others, including God. It describes the learning process, the objective, the conditions and limits of learning, the measures of success, the outcome and assessment methods that can be learned no other way than by us becoming our own masters. My inspiration here comes from the French philosopher, mathematician and theologian, Blaise Pascal, whose words I displayed over my desk 30 years ago when I was the national training manager for an automotive tire retailer.

> *We are generally better persuaded by the reasons we discover ourselves than by those given to us by others* Blaise Pascal.

The reason we need the Golden Rule is that we instinctively resist learning about our failings whenever anyone *tells us* what we have done wrong. The Golden Rule puts us in the position of consciously taking responsibility for our own learning by observing our contradictory view of how we value others as compared to how we value ourselves. Ironically, this self-assessment of our failings happens only when I value of myself highly and I want to grow, or alternatively, when I know I have faults which I want to overcome. The Golden Rule makes us realize, to quote the Johnny Cash song, Belshazzar: *You have been weighed in the balance and found wanting.* This discovery is foundational to our relationship with God, whose standards we can never satisfy by our own efforts other than to accept Divine assistance. This level of intentional self-awareness of our impoverished state and self-criticism is very unusual and difficult, to say the least. It is unusual because, by definition, it is an exercise in humility, for which we cannot take credit. This approach to *life* is unusual, in that it also requires that we have a person to whom we are accountable and an objective for our lives that is greater than ourselves. This reminds me of another Burl Ives song from my childhood; *Watch the donut, not the hole,* which means that when we focus on the actual substance of what we hope to achieve rather than thinking wishfully about something that is really not there, we are on a path to success where the outcome may be much greater and more satisfying than we imagined. This means that to flourish, we must have a life-goal to gain something tangible, greater than what we are and already have and could otherwise be. This is a view that many sages have learned from human history, including Arnold Toynbee, who observed that nation states (and individuals) flourish when they have a goal greater then themselves.[1] It is possible now to be side-tracked into a philosophical discussion about God's sovereignty and our free-will, which I will refrain from at present. I will say again, however, that I am sure that we humans do have a limited range of free choices to make that lead us into a truly symbiotic relationship of interdependence with God in which he engages with us by limiting his power to do otherwise.

The cure to all ills?

I am reminded again, that the Golden Rule is not the cure to all ills. Nor is it as though when faced with a problem of any kind, that we should whip out our Golden Rule Ready Reckoner to find an immediate answer to our problem as this chapter may appear to recommend. Nor am I suggesting that we should always just recite John 3:16, or John 14:6 as I have done at the beginning of this chapter. Rather, I am proposing that the Golden Rule should be an attitude to life as to how to think about ourselves in relationship to others that will lead us to different conclusions than we might have otherwise. Then we can discover and apply all sorts of solutions to the array of relational challenges we must face, from the whole range of legitimate human treatments and solutions including biblical, spiritual, social, religious, medical, psychological, legal, political and so on. My criticism of some Christian groups such as Biblical literalists, Fundamentalists, Sacramentalists, Evangelicals, Legalists, Pentecostals and others is that they appear to have a one-

---

[1] Arnold Toynbee, *A Study of History*, Thames and Hudson

size-fits-all approach to the complexity of life when we know for sure that life does not work that way. It is full of complexity and specialization in every area, including the religious sector and there is no over-arching principle to be applied, other than our admission that God is love and that Jesus is Lord, of which the Golden Rule reminds us.

My hope is that Christians would see themselves as different members of the Body of Christ, under one Lord, Jesus, whose banner is love. However, I realize that in this competitive world where we look for assurance that our way is right and others wrong, we ignore the possibility that we are all wrong, unless we attempt to treat each other as we would like to be treated.

Love, manifest in me

If there is a single thing that convinces me that Jesus is God and that the Bible is the word of God, it is this aspect of the Golden Rule: When we come to Jesus willing to obey him and receive from him, his first instruction to us is to attempt the one thing that we cannot do alone, and that no one else can require of us or teach us with any authority. If we are obedient, Jesus immediately becomes manifest within us as we begin to be transformed into his image. Jesus is the one with no mixed motives and at whom no finger of accusation can be pointed, because he is love personified whose love is proven within us. God's love is made real in Jesus, who was prepared to give up his own life in order that we can live. We begin to experience the actuality of God's love as we obey Jesus' command to love one another as we love ourselves. Under these conditions, we learn about ourselves, not because an authority figure – a teacher, our parents or even God – tells us what is right, but because we create the conditions in which we learn by being obedient to Jesus, who claims to be the way, the truth and the life. We become aware of who he is because when we relate to him in obedience and as the object of our worship and adoration, he sends us his Spirit to gently convict, correct, guide, comfort and teach us things that we can learn no other way. My first-hand experience provides me with evidence for the claim that God's love is manifest in Jesus. His love is demonstrated in the transformation I have experienced and in the lives of others I know who are willing to learn from God and receive his grace. This becomes the yardstick against which I must now measure myself and begin to see that I am stuck in my prejudice and self-righteousness, unless I take this initiative to trust and obey him.

Jesus, take me as I am

As the song goes; Jesus take me as I am, I can come no other way. This is profoundly true. We cannot come to Jesus other than as we are. In fact, if we try to make ourselves righteous before him, we will fail and continue to fail unless we go back to the point of departure, trusting only in God's grace and mercy, made available by Jesus. According to my understanding of the Golden Rule, we begin to love others and God with self-love because if we have the good fortune to be emotionally healthy, this must always be our starting point. The prerequisite of self-love is the result of being well nurtured as a child to believe that your life is precious to your family, yourself and increasingly, your community and to God. Self-love is demonstrated by our natural seeking for what we think is necessary for self-preservation. However, as we diligently apply the Golden Rule, we soon discover that our concept of self-love is often limited to selfishness. Ironically, self-love is pointless and ultimately unsatisfying unless it is love shared with others because then we discover that shared love gives us the satisfaction we crave. To experience this, we should not just suppress or sublimate self-love. Rather, we test and redirect it toward mutually beneficial relationships—eventually towards all people and God himself. Not just to those who are already obliged to help us, but to all comers, including our neighbors and those who we are able to help in the ordinary course of our lives. When we begin to redirect self-love toward others, we begin to apply what we think would be good for us, to *another*. If our guess is right and our attempt is well received by them, then we have made progress toward the next point of learning. If, on the other hand, our well-intentioned attempt is rejected by the other, we might project blame onto them, only to find we have made our situation worse. So then, if we really are well intentioned, we might further reflect on our motives and review how we have presented ourselves to the other. If we conclude that we could have done better, we will try again. When we find ourselves making the same mistake over and over, then, in resigned frustration, we ask for help and help comes. This is a moment that requires special awareness, because we can easily attribute an inspiration from God's spirit, to many other sources, such as good luck, our own wisdom or a sense of entitlement that good things always happen to me because I am already so important or good as to deserve it. The reason I know this is because I have done it myself, by blaming my wife for a situation involving one of our children, that caused us great anxiety. It was only when I realized that my blaming her was making things worse, that I was deeply convicted of my narcissism and repented in bitter tears. This was the break-through that resulted in the final solution of allowing God's grace to intervene.

Humility and grace

If I am aware of this process of humility and grace in a moment of inspiration, so begins a cycle of reflection upon my relationships with God, as his Spirit assists me to discover that my relationship with *others*, helps me to learn about the thing that is missing from my relationship with God. Love of this kind should normally be encountered in a marriage where both people have made a vow to help and to please each other and to always defer to each other's best interests, come whatever. If they do this persistently, they lead each other toward God. Jesus, I believe, establishes this principle as a universal maxim as an outcome of the Golden Rule and explains it in the context of resolving differences between two people.

> *Truly I tell you, whatever you bind on earth will be bound in heaven, and whatever you loose on earth will be loosed in heaven. Again, truly I tell you that if two of you on earth agree about anything they ask for, it will be done for them by my Father in heaven. For where two or three gathers in my name, there am I with them* (Matt 18: 18-19).

I have heard many explanations for this quotation over the years, most of which are meant to confirm a religious authority of some kind. But the point of the story, in my view, is that when a couple's goals are so closely aligned that even though there may have been potential for disagreement, they both defer to each other because of the high regard they have for each other. The result is that when they commit to a shared goal, it will be regarded as a godly contract, even if it is imperfect, because they are in it together with good will. Under ideal conditions, they will both learn from the experience and come to the same conclusion to continue or to change course, because the attitudes of their hearts are aligned. So it is in our relationship with God. If we regard him highly and take him into consideration in our plans, he will allow us to proceed even though our path may not be ideal, because he knows that we will adjust our path when we realize that we have gone astray from his ideal. Not to say that no harm will be done by misadventure, but there will be no harm done to the relationship as we learn the error of or ways together, which is of far higher importance than any other setback. There is, however, a necessary tension in this relationship that we must recognize—one that is also designed into the Golden Rule. This phenomenon, which I call loving indifference toward the detail of outcomes, prevents us from becoming over-zealous in our attempts to do the right thing, thereby deluding ourselves with self-righteousness or the idea that good things happen because we deserve them.

Love others, but don't watch their eyes too carefully

Have you noticed that as a pedestrian, if you make involuntary eye contact with a person walking in the opposite direction, that you tend to crash into each other? A far more dangerous version of this is when learning to ride a motorcycle on a bush track or race track. If you stare at an obstacle in your path such as a rock, a tree or a hole in the road or a wall, you will crash into it. This phenomenon is called target fixation which applies in many situations where there is a fear of collision. If two pedestrians focus on the other excessively, they will be inexorably drawn together and will crash. As we become competent at the task of walking amongst other people, we become unconscious of this risk as we avoid target fixation by not making eye contact. As an aside, motor cyclists are at risk of very serious injury until they develop a technique called Hand Follows Eye. The rider intentionally looks to the middle distance, choosing where to go to avoid fixating on hazards in the immediate foreground. The rider knows the hazards are there because they have seen them earlier as they scanned the path ahead, but they do not focus on them so that your hands follow the path that your eyes have chosen. This is an essential skill that must be gained to be able to ride safely, even at low speed. Paradoxically, once the fear that causes fixation is overcome by gaining a new skill, it can then be used to have the opposite effect, where a rider picks out a target on a race track and misses it by a tiny margin lap after lap with amazing concentration and pin-point accuracy. It is also a useful accident avoidance technique, whereby a rider deliberately engages eye contact with another driver to ensure that they are entirely aware of each other. Anyone learning the exhilarating art of high-speed riding or driving must master this is as a key step in the process of gaining competence. A learner passes through several stages of gaining discrete new knowledge, skills and attitudes which must be consciously learned, until they become a smooth blend of abilities of which they are no longer conscious.

There is a similar phenomenon at play when learning about the dangerous art of relationships. If people have expectations that are too high or if they are too concerned for their own safety or for the safety of another, they concentrate too much on the outcome of an exchange to the extent that they founder on the rocks they are trying to avoid. Rather, they need to focus on the input they are bringing to the situation. The Golden Rule is an antidote to obsessively focused relationships as it provides a process by which we see the rocks in the road in our mind's eye and learn an effective avoidance technique while we are becoming competent. We gain these otherwise obscure techniques by simply obeying a command to treat others as you would want to be treated yourself. Provided we have the grit and wisdom to persist, then we begin to gain new skills through experience and becoming increasingly conscious of anything that holds us back.

Consequently, I am proposing a Golden Rule technique that I have called loving indifference—a version of tough love. Not that this idea is new. It is how parents allow babies to fall over and crash into obstacles for them to learn how to move independently. Loving relationships should not usually be too intense because when they are, the parent imposes not their *love*, but rather, their *anxieties* onto the child. The Golden Rule proposes that once you have targeted a person as the object of your loving attention, you should turn down the temperature and treat them with confidence that could be interpreted as slight indifference, to ensure that your expectations are not unreasonably fixated. For this reason, loving your enemies is such an important aspect of learning the Golden Rule. If you do set out to love your enemy, it is unlikely that you will overcook the relationship by loving them too much, more out of your own anxiety than out of willing the best outcome for them. Rather, you will be more inclined to love them from a distance and wait to see if there is any change in them or, more likely, in you.

With rhythm and E...

If we are to apply the Golden Rule over all relationships, then we need to begin at the beginning. If you were in Chuck Berry's class of 1957 to learn the Golden Rule, how would the curriculum have been? I suspect that Bill Haley and His Comets' hit song *ABC Boogie* from the same era has a clue, especially as this tune also insists on the Golden Rule being part of the foundations for learning the lessons of life:

> *Down around the corner in a little school*
> *Children learn their lessons and the golden rule*
> *'Cause they got a teacher up from Basin Street*
> *And she does her teaching with a boogie beat*
> *Teachin' the abc with rhythm and E*

Treat others as you would have them treat you

Every single morning, it's the same old thing
All the kids are waiting for the bell to ring
When they hear it ringing, they all jump in line
Walking to the classroom, feeling mighty fine
They learn their abc with rhythm and E

Well, a-reading, writing, arithmetic
Taught to the tune of a liquorice stick
No education is ever complete
Without a boogie-woogie-woogie beat, well all reet

When the day is over and it's time to go
The children get their books and stand right at the door
Teacher is so happy, because she's done her bit
To educate the kids and make 'em really fit
To say their abc with rhythm and E

Well, a-reading, writing, arithmetic
Taught to the tune of a liquorice stick
No education is ever complete
Without a boogie-woogie-woogie beat, well all reet

When the day is over and it's time to go
The children get their books and stand right at the door
Teacher is so happy, because she's done her bit
To educate the kids and make 'em really fit
To say their abc with rhythm and E...[1]

Notice the "*...because she's done her bit; To educate the kids and make 'em really fit...*" I'm not sure what E is; maybe Ease or what I think of as loving indifference which at the end of the day, means to leave the rest to God.

---

1 ABC BOOGIE (A. Russell / M. Spickel) Bill Haley & His Comets.

Combining the wisdom of both Bill Haley's and Chuck Berry's school-days hits, learning the Golden Rule is intended *to make us really fit*. But I wonder if this is what we actually learned. Nothing against rock and roll, mind you, as it was one of the influences in my life; but I think the rock and roll message needs to balanced against other more enduring points of view about making us really fit. By *fit*, I mean, *fit for purpose*. To fulfill our designed purpose of being truly human, to be remade into the image of God, to love and worship him, and to enjoy him forever. Nevertheless, the teacher with the boogie beat is happy because by teaching the Golden Rule, she played an important part in developing a child's ability to learn how to make them fit for the complex challenges of life.

Speaking for myself, my childhood left me with a deposit of Christ's teachings, including the Golden Rule, but my teenaged response was usually to raise objections as to the practicality of what Jesus was saying. I remember clearly a discussion I had with my mother about not retaliating against a bully with verbal offence and physical threat—a lesson that, I must confess, I have not fully resolved today. For instance: If my grandchild were being bullied at school, would I say, "Turn the other cheek", "Run-away", "Kick them in the shins" or "Tell the teacher"? Of course, I would try to choose something appropriate for them and their situation; but the answer is not always easy, even for myself. I suppose if I were smart, I would say, "What do you think you should do?" because to some degree, we must be free to make our own mistakes.

On one hand, I know enough about the need for good family relationships and the principle of Golden Rule to apply it to my relationship with my wife with some success, given that we are still married after 48 years, and enjoying each other more today than ever. As to how well I applied the Golden Rule in my relationships with my three children, that is more a matter for them to say. I think the reality is that I learnt more about it from them, the hard way, by making mistakes. Although I had a very good foundation to discover what Chuck Berry and Bill Haley were talking about, I was confused for a long time by mixed messages. Do I believe in love? Or do I believe more in rock and roll? Regrettably, it was not until about 15 years ago that I finally began to understand the difference and began to think through the Golden Rule and how it applied to my beliefs, experience and behavior over a wide range of applications to discover its real meaning. These are important lessons for which we may not discover perfect answers, other than a sense of making progress within ourselves, with others and with God which eventually results in us keeping the whole of God's law. Not because we are good, but because we have become more like him.

As we have seen, the origins of the Golden Rule are lost in prehistory. But there is enough of a remnant throughout the records of humanity to know that it has been recognized as a universal principle for thousands of years, at least. We will see that there is good reason to agree with Pope Benedict that the Golden Rule, in its various forms, is arguably the most universal of all principles of human relationships and ultimately, cannot be separated from faith in Jesus Christ. There are many universal elements in human behavior that make us human, despite differences in history, culture, education, wealth and status. The simple reality that all humans speak in languages that can be translated, suggests that there are universal patterns of thought and belief and behavior, that translate into universal rules to some degree. I believe, then, that the Golden Rule should be recognized as the most universal of all principles for ethical relationships.

Whose rules rule?

It does appear that humans, as rulemaking social animals, are free to choose which rules (admittedly from a limited range) we will abide by, and which we will not. I once had this same conversation on a bus in Los Angeles with a young, powerfully built but slightly hostile African American construction worker. His complaint was that society was essentially lawless and unfair at every level. I reminded him that he was free to have a job, live in his own home, wear nice clothes, travel on a bus and to have a conversation with an unknown bus passenger from a foreign land without being at all fearful. The bus was free to travel its route provided it obeyed the traffic laws while the driver and passengers observed the normally unspoken laws about paying fares and cooperating with one another with reasonable courtesy. Whether or not he was convinced by my argument, we parted on good terms after about an hour of interesting discussion with a potentially mad Australian.

Most rules of society are unspoken natural laws such as those of gravity and mobility, which then creates the friction between our feet and the road that enables us to move from place to place without falling over. Most of the rules of human movement and social interaction are equally unspoken, so we take them for granted too. From the time a child is born, they learn most of these rules by themselves without gravity, friction or movement being explained at all. Just watch as a new-born baby discovers that they can roll over, using the effect of gravity on their own body weight to move across the room to grab the dog or to escape out the back door. Babies continue to learn at an astounding rate long before their formal education begins. So much of our childhood learning is unquestioned until, as adults, we experience the need to relearn many of the things we assumed as infants to gain a more useful understanding of our world.

Tell the truth

One of Jordan Peterson's 12 Rules for life is to; Tell the truth, or at least don't lie. Becoming conscious of the higher relational rules of nature and society is an essential step toward responsibility, essential for productive independence where we discover the need and sufficient confidence to tell the truth. As usual though, there is a trap for the unwary where "truth telling", particularly in a relationship or group situation, can become a deceptive performance, as it may be used for other purposes than to relay actual events and real points of view. Truth telling in social situations is encouraged by having a wise guide who can keep the discussion and relationships on track by allowing truth to be told objectively in difficult conditions, thus helping us and others to grow. While we all look to authority figures for leadership, we are also quick to see their limitations and shortcomings. What we need is a guide and a teacher who is above reproach and can lead us into the transcendent unknown because we don't need more opinions or ideas, rather than factual explanations as to the purpose and meaning of life and whether what we are doing now will help or hinder us to get where we really want to go, especially when we know we are on the wrong path.

Failing Forward

Management writer John Maxwell wrote a book called *Failing Forward: Turning Mistakes into Stepping Stones for Success*.[1] This book contains seriously good advice that we learn by our mistakes,

---

1 John Maxwell, *Failing Forward: Turning Mistakes into Stepping Stones for Success*, Thomas Nelson Inc.

as hard as that may be. This is not to say that we should deliberately make mistakes so that we can learn, but for many of us there is no alternative as we will discover in Chapter 9. It is too much to say that the Golden Rule alone is the cure to all ills and the single path toward transformation into the image of Christ, which I believe to be our ultimate destiny, but it is a major element. The Golden Rule requires a unique type of truth telling where we have a confessor who already knows what we have done wrong, but who is prepared to forgive us, provided we tell ourselves the truth. This is because God's grace is not available without our humility, which allows the other elements of growth to make themselves known and become more likely and possible if our relationships help, rather than hinder us on this path. Furthermore, it is not just us who benefit from change, one mis-step at a time. It is those we love, with whom we share life who feel the impact of our success and failures.

It is likely that when we do begin to treat the Golden Rule seriously, we suddenly expect that others will see our new motivation and will immediately understand our motives and agree with us. In fact, we are inclined to make things even worse by announcing our new-found enlightenment, which our friends will in turn be inclined to use as a stick to beat us with. This is the first lesson. Spiritual growth, which is what this is, is in the first instance a deeply personal and solitary matter as we begin an inward journey, wrestling with ourselves. Even if we are being supported by another person or a group, our great moments of initial insight will most likely be dark moments of the soul rather than moments of great enlightenment.

An important misapplication of our learning occurs when we take the initiative to apply what we think is a good idea to our friends without having worked it out in our own experience, or without allowing them to work it out in their own time and space. In either case, we are likely to get it wrong and cause the opposite effect to what we were hoping for. Certainly, we can guide and encourage others, but when we take an uninvited patronizing role, we have overstepped the boundaries of relationship. This is important because we need to resist the impulse to be the source of all wisdom, which we freely dispense to others. I know this because I am an expert. The lesson in this instance is that while the learning process involves others, it is us as individuals who must face the challenges of being taken out of our comfort zone. While the important lessons of life will always involve other people, it is important to remain conscious as to how we reflect on this interaction, because we are all engaged in a continuous process of learning that it will last a lifetime. When we look back over our lives, we will see that some decisions that we make determine the path that our lives will follow. Some decisions are far more important than others. For instance:

- Am I realistic about what I expect?
- Have I made the most of my situation?
- Have I treated others as equals?
- Have I continued to learn?
- Do I always tell the truth?
- Do I admit my mistakes?
- How do I deal with disappointment?
- Do I blame others?
- Am I jealous of others' success?
- Do I seek help when I need it?
- Am I prepared to humble myself before other people and before God?

Self-control

To begin to treat others as we would like to be treated requires significant self-control even to *pretend* that we are doing it. This is a primary objective of personal growth. Perhaps we cannot always control our circumstances as much as we would like, but we can control our reactions, or responses, to our circumstances. I believe that self-restraint is a God-like characteristic that we should emulate. If we conduct a search for God's attributes, we will find a long list relating to His immutability, omniscience, omnipotence and omnipresence and other characteristics that require many books to explain. Some experts say that God's grace toward us is His greatest characteristic, but even behind this lies God's self-restraint. If God is God, then he is unlimited in his power (except to contradict himself). Despite this, there are many instances in scripture and in our experience in which God is merciful toward us although we don't deserve mercy—especially when he gives up his supreme position and becomes a man, allowing himself to be crucified as a sacrifice for our salvation. Our self-control and transformation are not automatic or things that can happen overnight or by fulfilling a simple obligation. They are like other forms of discipline and exercise that usually require training and daily practice. But this exercise is not like pumping iron. It is our intentional and growing awareness of our need of God's goodness toward us and our acceptance of his offer of grace which makes us

strong. True freedom is also dependent upon self-control. Although it is tempting to imagine that freedom is the ability to do whatever we want, it is the opposite. Freedom is the ability to not act compulsively, but to be discerning and selective in what we do, particularly to others. When we have acted toward another person with full consideration for their independence and best interests, then we will have made a step toward freedom that benefits us and them as love requires.

Honesty begins with "I"

Treating others as we would like to be treated requires that we become aware of our inclination toward selfish entitlement and self-importance, self-pity and other forms of low-level manipulation of others. This is a difficult lesson to learn, but there are several well-established techniques that enable us to be truthful by being candid about our expectations. One of these involves learning to make "I" statements, that is used by therapists in training clients to be more self-aware and more assertive. It is ironic that to gain self-awareness and humility we must get used to being honest about our motives and desires, including all our religious and philosophical ideas and about what we want from relationships. This is because when we feel powerless, we try to get people to do what we want by manipulation and coercion, by which we de-personalize and dis-empower them. By learning to say *I think, I hope, and I want* as reasonably and as honestly as possible, we reduce our stress and increase the likelihood of the other understanding what we are saying and feeling more secure to speak truthfully to us in return. This is not to say that our wants are always valid or good, but we are discussing where to begin to learn to treat others well, not where we will end up.

Golden Rule 101

I do think children should be taught the Golden Rule, because that is what good mothers already do. If a child is provoking or teasing their sibling, then the mother says, "How would you like it if they did that to you?" This is the negative version of the Golden Rule, but the parent chooses the teaching method that is best suited to the situation at hand which only they can know. To the Boogie beat if appropriate. As much as we might want say to a child or a classroom of children, "Do to others what you would have them do to you", in the absence of a live interaction with other kids, this approach to education is still too abstract and theoretical, and therefore not ideal if we want a child to become self-reliant and resilient, which they must become. My wife's primary school teaches the Golden Rule in a contextualized set of values along with the preferred culture of the school that they call the Albert Park Way. They also practice "Restorative Justice", which might sound an even more abstract concept than the Golden Rule, but they use it to resolve school yard skirmishes. The protagonists are required to face each other and say how they feel, and what should be done to remedy the situation. This very sophisticated method was employed by Bishop Desmond Tutu in his leadership of the South Africa Truth and Reconciliation Commission, to which he was appointed by Nelson Mandela to resolve outstanding differences at the end of apartheid in South Africa. A similar process was later used to heal deep divisions between Tutsis and Hutus of Rwanda, who had engaged in a genocidal civil war. The civil courts allowed for some participants to be discharged by a process of confession and mercy.

Who teaches the teacher?

A truism about learning is that if we want to really learn about a subject, we should try to teach it to someone else. If we try to teach others when we don't know enough about the subject ourselves, we will be very embarrassed. Rather, if we do the thinking, research and personal learning required, we will make great discoveries about our topic from our own experience, both positive or negative, that will inspire and inform our teaching of others. How much of this formative training in the Golden Rule carries through into adulthood is difficult to say. I suspect that not much makes it through to become a useful tool in adulthood unless it continues to be practised. A serious problem, in my view, is the lack of consistency in many of our religious teachers personally believing the Golden Rule to be effective, let alone secular instructors, so it succumbs as other cultural influences creep in during the teenage years and adulthood.

Nevertheless, I am greatly encouraged at the other end of the spectrum, by three examples of training adults in applying Golden Rule as a high principle for business management that stand out in my experience: (and why they may be a bit out of date)

- Max de Pree, who wrote *Leadership Jazz: Leadership as an Art.* De Pree emphasized the foundations of character that determine how we behave toward others, arguing that "Leadership is much more an art, a belief, a condition of the heart, than a set of things to do. The visible signs of artful leadership are expressed, ultimately, in its practice."
- Robert Greenleaf, who wrote the classic management book, *Servant Leadership,* based his writing and leadership on his experience as a trainer of AT&T linesmen with the Golden Rule.[1]
- Peter Drucker was a very influential management theorist and a prolific writer of 39 books over more than 50 years with titles including *The Practice of Management* and *Post Capitalist Society.* He based his life's work on what he called the practical wisdom of Christianity.

---

1 https://www.greenleaf.org/winning-workplaces/workplace-resources/features/workplace-perspectives/the-golden-rule/.

All three authors avoid simplistic statements about successful management. At the heart of their work is the message of the gospel of Jesus emphasizing the dignity of each person and the need for deep inner learning about their craft, themselves and their influence upon others. This is the point of learning from the Golden Rule: to learn about ourselves in purposeful relationships under God's scrutiny.

Trust and obey

I think we can say that people need to be taught the Golden Rule over their lifetime, beginning in childhood. The message of the Golden Rule needs to be re-applied to every important stage of development, especially in times of major change such as beginning school, becoming an independent teenager, becoming an adult, forming intimate relationships, commencing work and taking leadership responsibility and becoming a parent. If the Golden Rule is well established during childhood, then these further applications become a simple extension of the foundation upon which to build a life. If there is no childhood foundation, then adulthood learning is far more difficult and prone to - more serious mistakes. Even so, we may often need to be reminded to apply the Golden Rule to a new situation, that we may think requires a different approach.

Tragically, however, many people including Christians begin the many stages of life without this key foundation in place. Although this lack of understanding is disastrous for marriages, families and careers, it is utterly devastating when evangelical Christians begin proselytizing without this foundation, because they are at risk of becoming self-righteous hypocrites. My view is that the Golden Rule should be a key ethical maxim for teaching Christian discipleship during the late teenage years and adulthood. It should be presented as an explicit objective response to Jesus' command, which is the basis for lifelong discipleship as a process of growth by which we are *"transformed into the image of Jesus, by the renewal of our minds."* If the question is ever asked of me by a Christian struggling to understand how they should relate to the Golden Rule, or any of Jesus' teachings for that matter, I would say that they must rely upon faith to *"Trust and obey for there is no other way."*

A stitch in time saves nine

To be practical about the Golden Rule curriculum, it is a lesson that must be learnt and relearned repeatedly throughout life. My ideal approach to teaching the Golden Rule is to apply it as a maxim when it will be most easily remembered and applied by the learner. Certainly, I don't think it is something that can be presented once only in childhood and relied upon to be re applied intuitively throughout a long and varied life of challenges. The following table illustrates events and life phases that create a need and a learning opportunity to take the initiative to re-apply what we have learned to rely upon in other situations.

Golden Rule Applicability Table	
Item	Why the Golden Rule applies?
Early childhood	Sharing toys, games and food.
Pre-school	Truth telling, relationship to parents, siblings, friends
Primary school	Relationships with classmates, teachers, friends and enemies
Secondary school	Relationships to opposite sex, general education, life skills
Educational, social aspirations	Self-love as the basis of making good choices
Emotional self-management	Stress management, anxiety reduction strategy
Sport	Competitive relationships, winning, losing, fair play, motivation
University, life values	Ethics, philosophy, non-contradiction, alternative world views, tolerance, ideology

Religious faith	Faith, hope, love, obedience to Jesus' teachings, accountability to God
Romantic relationships	Impact of personal behavior on other, family, children, social responsibility, community
Politics, social questions	Benefits for the other and the common good.
Learning to drive	Consideration of other drivers, defensive techniques
Career ambitions, aspirations	Role in society, providing for family, passion, sense of calling
Marriage, sexual relationships	Intimacy, realistic expectations, disappointment, shared enjoyment and pleasure
Child rearing	Agreement of priorities and strategies with spouse, extended family relationships
Household duties	Fairness, equity, sharing
Finances, wealth	Fairness, equity, sharing, responsibility, accountability
Conflict resolution	Honesty, tolerance and understanding other views, forgiveness
Adultery, divorce	Maintaining self-love, truth-telling, forgiveness, accountability, future orientation
Community service	The common good, reconciliation beginning with the self, peace-making, altruism
Generosity, hospitality	Self-giving without the promise of reward.
Relational crisis	Self-love as a basis for loving another and reciprocal love.

I have noticed recently that there have been many suggestions for primary and secondary school students to be taught ethics, rather than religion which has become increasingly problematic in secular schools. I am in full support of this idea, provided that the ethics are based on the first principles of Christ's Golden Rule, including the extent to which it has influenced Western cultures and its distinctiveness from other similar religious principles. This, however, is becoming less likely as opposition to Christian teaching increases. Ideally, an individual, parent, teacher, pastor or mentor should choose the right moment to refer to first principles of the Golden Rule as a solution to a current problem and then approach the topic as an interactive discussion or a "case study" rather than as dogma. This topic is covered in more detail in the following chapter, but the rule of thumb is for the individual to work it through themselves verbally and experientially, with some guidance. Of these important life-events listed above, a most important one is when a person is considering the issues in the context of religion and Christian faith. If obedience to Jesus is not the basis of faith, then one risks struggling with undisclosed and unresolved ideologies, doctrine and behavioral issues all one's life, because nothing will make complete sense unless it can be integrated and sustained case by case with Jesus' teaching of the Golden Rule. If, however, a young person does learn the Golden Rule as an embedded and consistently reinforced principle, then it becomes much easier to apply it to all subsequent situations.

Competencies of the new covenant

I am always slightly puzzled by well-meaning Christians who say that they are *"Waiting on the Lord to discover what he wants them to do"*. I don't deny that God does indeed inspire some of us to commit to incredible unanticipated undertakings, *"...far beyond what we could dream or hope for because His Spirit works within us'"* according to my interpretation of Eph 3:20. To me, this waiting is more like the Buddhist expression *"sitting under a banyan tree, waiting for inspiration"*. In my view, Christian inspiration is usually relying on taking an initiative to do what we already know is right, or at least, think is right rather than sitting around waiting for inspiration. This is always accompanied with a risk of presumption in my experience of which there is plenty in Christianity, especially among those who say that prophecy is an exclusive right which cannot be criticized. In my experience, if someone claims to be a prophet, they are probably not. However, the risk of a counterfeit inspiration is small by comparison with the possibility of each believer being free to make their own progress and mistakes. I suggest that we are intended to have the mind of Jesus within us in a genuinely mutually beneficial, interdependent, cooperative relationship, as against a parasitic relationship suggested by the Banyan tree metaphor. We should all accept that most of what we do, will initially be imperfect because we are imperfect. The point of the Golden Rule is that it provides us with a framework for learning by reflecting on our experience, rather than always finding perfect answers to every problem.

Paul—the Apostle who told us that we should be transformed into the image of Jesus by the renewal of our minds—gave us a far more objective model to emulate, not by sublimation of human desire, but by taking a risk of fulfilment of our intended design purpose of glorifying God, then constraining and amending our application by studying both the inputs and the outputs for evidence of God's grace:

> *He has made us competent as ministers of a new covenant—not of the letter*
> *but of the Spirit; for the letter kills, but the Spirit gives life* (2 Cor 3:6).

Paul contrasts the *letter* and *Spirit* to illustrate the contrast between an controlling master/slave relationship and a less controlled creative relationship over which neither party has ultimate control. This is because the fruit of the Spirit or the outcomes of a creative relationship, is based on the combination of human enterprise and the enabling presence of God's Spirit rather than compliance to a preconceived set of rules. Later in this same text, Paul talks about the freedom we experience when we begin to be transformed:

> *Now the Lord is the Spirit, and where the Spirit of the Lord is, there is freedom...(we) are being transformed into his image with ever-increasing glory, which comes from the Lord, who is the Spirit* (2 Cor 3:17-18).

The practical role of the Spirit is sometimes missing in contemporary Christian dialogue, other than having become the specialty of the Pentecostal and Charismatic churches. However, a distinction is required. Spirit-filled Pentecostal believers have a high expectation of ongoing supernatural empowerment by which Jesus and the Apostles demonstrated the coming of God's Kingdom (Matt 11: 4-6). As important as this is today, it is not the same as the "fruit of the Spirit" that Paul says is an outcome, not of Divine endowment, but of the conscious mind and Spirit renewal of our minds to transform us into the image of Jesus.

> *But the fruit of the Spirit is love, joy, peace, forbearance, kindness, goodness, faithfulness, gentleness and self-control. Against such things there is no law* (Gal 5:22-23).

I think that the two references to the spirit are talking about difference in the degree of the same thing rather than different things. The apostolic demonstration of the gift of miracles was an inauguration of a new role for the Holy Spirit, now available to all who were willing to receive it, as the spirit so desires. I don't think the outcome of this outpouring should be any different from the development of the real presence of the spirit mentioned in the text above. Nor should we think that the demonstration of spiritual power has ceased, but it has changed from being a spectacular phenomenon of inauguration of the Kingdom of God, limited to the few "gifted" ones, to a spiritual gift who desire to exercise this gift.

The modern use of the term 'competency' is very helpful in understanding the above text from Galatians. It implies a person who meets a standard or passes a test that reflects the integrated ability to perform tasks or a role without being supervised. In HR terms, it means that a person has acquired the knowledge, skills and attitudes required to fulfill a task or role to a specified standard.

This concept derives from Peter Drucker's 1954 invention of performance management: achieving results in a manner that is consistent with organizational expectations. As Drucker explained, it refers not only to what is expected, but also how a task is performed in observable terms. Drucker further explained how this requirement, which became known as "Behavioral Objectives", can be achieved through the implementation of a purposeful, systematic feedback loop that designed to enable an individual to contribute to the accomplishment of evolving organizational goals.[1] As a workplace trainer and training manager and as an autodidact (a self-taught person who learns informally) I very much like this concept but to some it implies a disconnect between theory and practice because a person could learn to perform a task without the supporting theoretical knowledge. One of my professional roles was as a formal competency assessor, where my judgement would recommend someone for a certificate of competence based on "recognition of prior learning." There are many benefits from this approach to learning including the possibility of gaining a qualification without doing an expensive and time-consuming formal course to which a student may not have had access. I have done this myself, both as a motor mechanic and as workplace training manager because it suits my preference for self-paced learning. I did the motor mechanics certificate assessment for fun to see what score I would get from a very comprehensive questionnaire that examined my theoretical knowledge and my knowledge of how to perform a series of skilled activities, such as tuning an engine. In fact, I got a very high score without having ever been an apprentice or completed a course, because of a lifetime of self-motivated learning both the theory and practice.

I think my preference for self-learning has been very important to my development and crucial to my interest in the Golden Rule.

---

1 Peter Drucker, *The Practice of Management*.

It is not that I reject formal training and qualifications as I have done some of that also. Although my learning is always a bit disorganized, I have usually followed one theme or another, a bit like pulling a strand from a tangled ball of wool. If I believe that a topic has value and I  want to explore it, I begin at any point where I can find a lose end and start to pull on the loose stand from my ball of wool analogy. This is possibly a result of my non-conformist religious training in the Brethren church, where most of the men who taught and preached, were untrained. It may also be a result of my being a stubborn know-all. The result is that it may take longer to learn, but what I do learn sticks pretty well, especially as l as I have also developed the habit of arguing my position for my entertainment. This often results in my getting out of my depth with someone who does know what they are talking about, but even so, this has the additional benefit of filling in the gaps in my knowledge. These quirks have enabled me to make steady progress in my journey of faith. The "ball of wool" has always been clear in my mind, even if it was as simple as the childhood hope of going to heaven when I die, or more honestly, the fear of not going to heaven. Rather than try to understand the whole subject of faith in God all at once, I have studied various parts of the puzzle when they seemed relevant. Even then, when I have gotten too far ahead of myself with theory, I have often made the conscious decision to back off, and to wait and see the effect that new belief has had on me. I now know from experience that to try to get the theory of faith in God figured out perfectly before I embark on the journey of faith, is impossible, because it is far too complex a subject, at least for me. The result is that I try to learn only what I can confirm in my experience, which I think is the way that the Golden Rule works.

The paradox of freedom

It is for freedom Christ has set us free. Gal 5:1

When we become Christian believers, we are faced with a plethora of religious dogma, doctrine, sects and emerging trends competing for our allegiance. We must then ask ourselves "*What is the purpose of my relationship to Christ?* Great care must be taken because it is possible to leave the spiritual bondage of one kind only to become ensnared in another kind of religious slavery. Paul uses extreme hyperbole wishing that teachers advocating religious circumcision would castrate themselves,

> *You, my brothers and sisters, were called to be free (from religious law). But do not use your freedom*

> to indulge the flesh; rather, serve one another humbly in love. For the entire law is fulfilled in keeping this one command: "Love your neighbor as yourself" (Gal 5:12-14).
>
> ...I say, walk by the Spirit, and you will not gratify the desires of the flesh (Gal 5:16).

Paul lists the corrupted desires of humanity that we already know can enslave us if we do not constrain them, or rather, if we don't put ourselves to some better use, some higher purpose.

> The acts of the flesh are obvious: sexual immorality, impurity and debauchery; idolatry and witchcraft; hatred, discord, jealousy, fits of rage, selfish ambition, dissensions, factions and envy; drunkenness, orgies, and the like. I warn you, as I did before, that those who live like this will not inherit the kingdom of God (Gal 5:19-21).

Paul then contrasts the flesh with the spirit by listing the outcomes of the Golden Rule:

> But the fruit of the Spirit is love, joy, peace, forbearance, kindness, goodness, faithfulness, gentleness and self-control. Against such things there is no law (Gal 5:22).

The reality of freedom

I would like to present what I think is at once the most ironic, powerful, difficult and important of all Jesus' teachings on love and the Golden Rule. It is important because if we do not grasp it then we will not understand the concept of how agape love applies to us as the means by which God reveals himself to us. We all desire freedom, but we often go looking for it in all the wrong places. Generally, we think of freedom in negative terms, as *freedom from* such things as pain, poverty and hunger, because fear is a very strong source of motivation to avoid pain and discomfort. The opposite is the *freedom to do* a range of activities that used to be considered as the preserve of the rich who can indulge themselves in luxuries related to food, power, comfort, security and travel. However, there is nothing more pathetic than a person who has grasped at freedom from pain and suffering by taking what they thought was a cure, which had the opposite effect to what they were expecting.

Despite the pit-falls, I suggest that our quest for freedom is right because according to the gospel, Jesus *came to set the captives free and give sight to the blind* (Lk 4:18). We could say that this type of freedom is a metaphor for spiritual freedom that is, according to some, unmeasurable and therefore illusory. But research confirms that real quality of life measures, such as life span, health, wealth and happiness, seem to accrue to people of religious faith (https://en.wikipedia.org/wiki/Quality_of_life).

Enforcing equality?

The modern notion of freedom requires social equity, where there should be no discrimination toward anyone within an equal society. This idea has the same biblical origins as the Golden Rule, as it is implicit in the command to "love your neighbor." This is meant to include anybody with whom we have day-to-day contact, especially family members. Jesus' brother James makes this command into a serious duty by elevating what we understand as an obligation of equity based on love, to the extreme of an ultimate accountability to God. James opens his argument by saying:

> *My brothers and sisters, believers in our glorious Lord Jesus Christ must not show favoritism.*

James presents the case that improper belief in Jesus' teaching of the Golden Rule may result in our becoming guilty of evil:

> *Suppose a man comes into your meeting wearing a gold ring and fine clothes, and a poor man in filthy old clothes also comes in. If you show special attention to the man wearing fine clothes and say, "Here's a good seat for you," but say to the poor man, "You stand there" or "Sit on the floor by my feet," have you not discriminated among yourselves and become judges with evil thoughts?* (Jas 2:1-12)

Although the Gospel of Jesus and the Golden Rule are characterized as the law of love, James is giving yet another meaning to the word "law" in contrast to what Paul said, James is referring to Jesus' statement that the Golden Rule is a *summary of the law and prophets*. Then he agrees with Paul by saying that there are severe consequences for those who ignore its demands. In my view, this suggests that all of the law is fulfilled not by our self-disciplined compliance with it, but by our being transformed by love. To add to this puzzle, Jesus said: *"I did not come to bring peace, but a sword* (Matt 10:34). This is a metaphorical "sword" by which Jesus (who is also known as the Prince of Peace) means that his love will not to bring peace on earth to make everybody happy, but as a weapon to wage war against sin and evil where a man's enemies may be his family because of his allegiance to Jesus. Jesus drives this point home with the paradoxical statement, "*Let the dead bury the dead*" (Lk 9:60), where he rejects the excuse of family obligation to avoid the duty of Christian discipleship and re-emphasizes the serious consequences of neglecting the law of love.

> *Listen, my dear brothers and sisters: Has not God chosen those who are poor in the eyes of the world to be rich in faith and to inherit the*

> kingdom he promised those who love him? But you have dishonored the poor. Is it not the rich who are exploiting you? Are they not the ones who are dragging you into court? Are they not the ones who are blaspheming the noble name of him to whom you belong?
>
> If you really keep the royal law found in Scripture, "Love your neighbor as yourself," you are doing right. But if you show favoritism, you sin and are convicted by the law as lawbreakers. For whoever keeps the whole law and yet stumbles at just one point is guilty of breaking all of it.
>
> For he who said, "You shall not commit adultery," also said, "You shall not murder." If you do not commit adultery but do commit murder, you have become a lawbreaker. Speak and act as those who are going to be judged by the law that gives freedom, because judgment without mercy will be shown to anyone who has not been merciful. Mercy triumphs over judgment (Jas 2:13).

This final sentence reflects the end of the Lord's prayer where it says: *and forgive us our trespasses as we forgive those who trespass against us.* The seriousness of this statement cannot be over emphasized. It means that if we are not obedient in being merciful to others, then we should not expect God's mercy when we face the Judgement Seat of Christ. Rather, we will face judgement. Will it threaten our place in the Kingdom of God? According to Paul, *So, if you think you are standing firm, be careful that you don't fall!* (1 Cor 10:12).

My point is two-fold. First, the Golden Rule is the non-negotiable requirement of obedience for Christians who claim to follow the teachings of Jesus. I am not saying it is the basis of justification, as that is by faith alone. I am saying, however, that is it the basis of sanctification or transformation into the image of Jesus, by the renewal of our minds, which I can't see as anything other than a conscious act of obedience to Jesus.

Second, The requirement of obedience to the Golden Rule is so stringent and utterly dependent upon our transformation by the spirit of Christ, that it is ludicrous to pretend that equity can be established by any means other than by the salvation and transformation of souls, by the power of God's love, manifest in Jesus.

Course prerequisites

The only prerequisite of the Golden Rule training course is that you must be willing to take it. This may come as a surprise to many, who might believe that this is too simple—that there must at least be some entry criteria, such as being born of good parents, being religious or baptized, belonging to a church and so on. I believe that none of these is required to begin this journey. Furthermore, I don't believe that you have to be a Christian for it to work, at least at the beginning. For many, this makes the course too easy, so they pass on the Golden Rule 101, and go straight to one of the following existing courses, including: How well do you know your Bible? How well do you fit into your youth group? or, How well do you conceal your sins and many others?

One aspect of the Golden Rule that is often misunderstood is that it does not preclude one making mistakes despite one's bestintentions. To *"love yourself"* suggests to me that I have a natural degree of self-preservation and self-importance, which tends to make me think of myself first. To expect otherwise is unrealistic. It is also unrealistic to expect a learner to come emotionally and intellectually prepared for their adventure, as that is what most of us have yet to learn. In my experience, usually, we are most inclined to learn by our mistakes more than our successes. Success usually suggests that we have done something right where as failure suggests a necessity to learn.

In my mind, the Golden Rule requires obedience to a godly command—a command that we have no hope of understanding when we begin. That is the point of obedience. It requires us to act as if we will eventually understand, because the point of our obedience is to learn things about ourselves that we cannot learn theoretically. Behavioral Objectives should be stated as affirmations of faith: a first person, present tense description of what a person would be able to do when they are competent. They should describe learning outcomes as a process designed to help students reach an outcome, but not the details of what the teacher will do to help the student to become competent. They should state an explicitly clear and understandable learning goal using observable verbs such as: The learner will be able to demonstrate knowledge or skill that contribute to the goal of their behaving in a certain way. I would like to present the Beatitudes as the learning objectives of the law of Moses, the Ten Commandments. The Golden Rule is the learning method and the conditions under which we should learn.

Course assessment

The Beatitudes, for example, describe the competency outcomes of a blessed one when you demonstrate the following attitude assessment: when you are poor in spirit, when you mourn, when you are meek, when you hunger and thirst for righteousness, when you are merciful, when you are pure of heart, when you are a peacemaker, when you are persecuted for the sake of righteousness. The competency outcomes of training qualify those who meet the requirements to enter the Kingdom of God, and inherit its full value of the Kingdom of God. Then, you will be satisfied, you shall be comforted, you shall inherit the earth, you shall obtain mercy, you shall see God face to face, you shall be called children of God for your is the kingdom of heaven (Matt 5:3-10).

Repentance means that you no longer behave as you did previously, or no longer display the same attitudes. Repentance means turning aside for your old ways and demonstrating new ways of being.

Notice that none of these are prerequisites to begin training. Nor are they training inputs. They are certainly training goals and outcomes to be achieved when the training is complete—outcomes that fulfil the requirements of the Ten Commandments. This fulfilment is a result of the transformation that takes place within the trainee, who is taught by the Spirit as their mind is renewed. Nor is the training specified or limited by time or training inputs. It is considered to be complete only when the trainee consistently demonstrates the behaviors and the attitudes required, which for most of us, will be never in this life, at least. Notice also that a demonstration of knowledge by itself is not enough, because knowledge can easily be a superficial display. This, in my view is the Golden Rule fully manifest in us. It is not the result of our compliance with the law although compliance with the law is achieved. It is not the result of our wisdom or effort, although both wisdom and effort are engaged in the process. It is the result of our trust in and obedience to Jesus Christ's command by which we are truly transformed by God's love, renewing our minds with our cooperation. This is truly, a self-directed, self-paced learning system because we control it by the exercise of our will, to engage or to not engage and to persist or not.

Even though we are engaged in the process of having our minds are renewed, we cannot take credit because our transformation is God's gift of grace to us as his reward for our faithful obedience. As Paul suggests; ...*We know that We all possess knowledge. But knowledge puffs up while love builds up* (1 Cor 8:1).

The competency assessor, by the way, is Jesus.

Patterns of failure

Throughout my business life, I have had my share of success, but I have also made some repeated mistakes. Usually, this has to do with my sense of responsibility for my own ideas and decisions. Given my over-active imagination, I can often come up with elegant ideas and solutions to problems. This, coupled with my tendency to be an enthusiast who embraces new ideas readily, provided me with many work-related opportunities, to my great advantage. My problem came with implementation, when my lack of confidence would sometimes result in me trying to offload responsibility to other people. Similarly, if someone came to me with a request for assistance, I would usually take the bait, hook, line and sinker. These immature characteristics tended to make me prone to promising more than I could deliver, especially if I lacked emotional support from my boss. These characteristics also tend to make me a sucker for a good story from someone more senior or more intelligent than me. I also tend to project my optimism onto others about whom I also have unrealistic expectations.

Having observed this repeated pattern over a long period, it becomes possible to see myself doing the same stupid things that I know won't work. Alternatively, in my enthusiasm, I might accept a business proposition that I am not able to deliver. This has cost me a great deal of money in several ways, including the failure of a major project that was perfectly successful until I started meddling with it. It took me about three years to recover from that adventure while I paid back a debt to my major creditor. In other cases, I invested in a project on a handshake, did all the preparatory work myself and took the financial loss when the project didn't go ahead because my business partner didn't deliver his side of the bargain. More recently, in the church of which Elaine and I were members for 17 years, the senior pastor silenced me, because as the Church Secretary, I disagreed with her on some unresolved major policy issues. The fault was mine because I had not addressed the growing divide between us with complete honesty, allowing minor disagreements to accumulate. Each of these events should be salutary as we learn more about ourselves with each incident. However, the wasted large amounts of time, money and energy can be substantially avoided if we learn these lessons about ourselves with a conscious application of the Golden Rule, since it requires us to consistently tell the truth and to confront issues with others, as we would want them to confront issues with us.

The Big Ten sins

It is true, I think, that God regards most sins as equally bad. However, not all sins have the same adverse effect upon us or on others. Some are harmful but socially acceptable, such being rich and loving money more than anything else. Or being powerful, and using your power for your own advantage, rather than to benefit others. Then there are sins that feel good, often of a sexual nature, where instant gratification or sexual conquests are the payoff. Drug and alcohol use also fit this category. According to scripture, there are some sins that lead to death and some that do not. Whether this is physical death or spiritual death does not matter at this moment. I think the Big Ten align with the Ten Commandments, which makes the first few about loving God and not having any idols the most important.

I believe that to commit serious sins indicates that despite all other appearances of success and importance, that we don't love ourselves as we should, by desiring the highest good for ourselves while being accountable to God and other people. This is a hard lesson to learn, one that I have had some difficulty with. To not love yourself does not mean that you look like a homeless person. On the contrary, you may have all the trappings of success: good looks, expensive clothes, a big house, an expensive car, public acclaim, sporting or business success, and the list goes on. But if, despite these signs of success, you are anxious, jealous, sexually promiscuous, drug or alcohol addicted, then I suggest that you do not see yourself as God sees you, and that you pursue these external signs to compensate for your lack of self-love and accountability. In this context, the highest good is measured by your seeking the same for your intimate family and friends and your community, for the longest possible time that you can envisage. The opposite extreme position involves becoming a narcissist—someone who loves a false image of themselves and looks for relationships with people who they are able to manipulate.

If you love yourself wholeheartedly and want the highest good for yourself, the discipline by which you will discover what this requires is the Golden Rule, since this leads you to love yourself, your neighbor and God in the type of relationship for which you were designed.

Solomon's despair

An example of narcissism is King Solomon, who is characterized in the Bible as being the wisest, wealthiest, most powerful, most prolific builder and most successful King of Israel, if not the whole world. Despite all of this, he is presented in the book of Ecclesiastes complaining about the vanity and unfairness of life, railing about the uncertainty of eternity, despite his strong seeking of it. As a remedy for his despair, Solomon takes a total of 1,000 wives and concubines into his harem, which of course eventually brings him to disaster and personal despair, alienated from God. I think that many of us in this age of wealth and apparent freedom to do almost whatever we want are like Solomon: seemingly able to make any choice that takes our fancy, but deeply frustrated and discontented with our lot in life. Solomon's conclusion is very instructive. At the end of the book of Ecclesiastes, after he has described his misery and frustration in detail, he comes to the inescapable conclusion:

Treat others as you would have them treat you

> *Now all has been heard; here is the conclusion of the matter: Fear God and keep his commandments, for this is the duty of all mankind* (Ecc 12:13).

This is the point at which we are hopefully ready to obey Jesus' command, to keep the Golden Rule. If you do love yourself as you should, then the Golden Rule will be satisfying if you persist to apply it to yourself. If the Golden Rule is repugnant to you, then you are a long way from being ready to begin.

What to do when it all goes wrong

> *Cry as much as you need to, then...*
> *When you're sad and when you're lonely*
> *And you haven't got a friend*
> *Just remember that death is not the end*
> *And all that you held sacred*
> *Falls down and does not mend*
> *Just remember that death is not the end*
> *Not the end, not the end*
> *Just remember that death is not the end*
> *When you're standin' on their crossroads*
> *That you cannot comprehend*
> *Just remember that death is not the end*
> *And all your dreams have vanished*
> *And you don't know what's up the bend*
> *Just remember that death is not the end*

Bob Dylan - Death Is Not The End Lyrics | MetroLyrics

7

…AS YOU LOVE YOURSELF?

"Love the LORD your God with all your heart and with all your soul and with all your strength and with all your mind'; and, 'Love your neighbor as yourself" Luke 10:27.

Loving ourselves involves the same objective as loving somebody else: *to seek the highest possible good for yourself.* The highest good cannot be an impetuous desire or whim, just for the moment or for selfish reasons. It must be seeking the highest good for yourself for the longest possible period. This is difficult to describe in more specific terms other than to say that the highest good is always life-giving from God's point of view. We will eventually realize this not because of choices inspired by our selfish nature, but according to our transformed mind, renewed by God's Spirit. This, by necessity, involves my relationships with other people because I discover that when I love others, I love myself more. This, however, is not just altruistic idealism as love always works the same way, even when I don't understand the theory. It could be said that to seek the highest good for another with no regard for yourself, leads to the highest good for you in any case, but there are many circumstances, such as a parent caring for a baby, where the highest good for a child is for the parent to preserve themselves so that they will be able to provide care for the child in future. Parents on aircraft are advised to get their own emergency oxygen arrangements worked out before they try to arrange their children's oxygen. This kind of decision making is difficult and guarantees that in some cases we will make mistakes of judgement while we work out for ourselves the purpose and limits of self-love and self-sacrifice. However, while we love ourselves and remain accountable to God, we will continue to learn how to love him and others.

Love as cosmic glue

I propose that the Golden Rule is the tip of the Love ice-berg. This concept has caused me to do a lot of soul-searching because what I am saying is so different from what so many other teachers say, and I could be wrong. At the end of the day though, I like to think that all I am doing is agreeing with what Jesus is said. There are, of course, many ways to eat an elephant, as the old joke goes, one bite at a time. In this case, a more relevant metaphor would be there are many ways to eat an ice pop; one lick at a time. What I mean is that Jesus is offering us a place in his Kingdom and if we look at what the various Christian churches and traditions tell us, there are as many ways to enter the Kingdom as there are churches, sects, cults and religions, which could be true, to some extent. I am not so much interested in the distinctive differences, other than to try to find the through-line which I suspect might be discovered in the historical creeds of the church, particularly the Nicene Creed. Most of all, I prefer the idea of Beautiful Orthodoxy, so well-articulated by Mark Galli of Christianity Today magazine as the true, the good and the beautiful that might be discovered in all genuine Christian traditions. This leads me to say that there is one Church and many churches which Paul describes as a body with many different parts, each with a different function (1 Cor 12:12) which all belong to one another. (Rom 12:4). Putting aside the functional differences for another day, my interest is in the common denominator which I believe to be the New Covenant of Love, to which the Golden Rule is our point of entry.

Before I begin, I would like to take another step to explain what I think love is and is not, and how we experience it as legitimate self-love. I propose that in the interests of clarity, there is only one love which is from God. All other things that we call love are subsets of love, or poor imitations. In the worst case, they are malevolent deceptions, designed to put us off the trail of what love is. Love is not abstraction, such as an emotion that we conjure up to make ourselves or others feel good. Nor is it an acceptance of an intellectual concept. Rather, love is a tangible and measurable power, force or energy emanating from God that must be experienced relationally, because love is the nature of what God is and has made available to bond us to him and to each other. AN Whitehead described it as concrescence, something that is growing as part of a process of real events. Love is not material as God is spirit, not a being limited by time and space. Love is our encounter with and accountability to the highest reality and greatest truth possible for us to experience. It is, I believe, nothing less than the glue that holds the Cosmos together, a Divine force much greater than gravity which God has called his creatures to share. More simply and more profoundly, love is seeing ourselves as God sees us as individuals. Since before the creation of the world he envisioned as fully functioning members of his family, to do his work in his Kingdom.

The Nicene creed

The Nicene creed, in my view, alludes to many of these essential elements:

> *We believe in one God, the Father, the Almighty,*
> *maker of heaven and earth, of all that is seen and unseen.*
> *We believe in one Lord, Jesus Christ,*
> *the only Son of God, eternally begotten of the Father,*
> *God from God, light from light, true God from true God,*
> *begotten, not made, one in Being with the Father.*
> *For us and for our salvation he came down from heaven,*
> *By the power of the Holy Spirit he was born of the Virgin*
> *   Mary and became man.*
> *For our sake he was crucified under Pontius Pilate;*
> *He suffered, died and was buried.*
> *On the third day he rose again in fulfillment of the*
> *   Scriptures;*
> *He ascended into heaven and is seated at the right hand*
> *   of the Father.*

He will come again in glory to judge the living and the dead,
and his kingdom will have no end.
We believe in the Holy Spirit, the Lord, the giver of life,
who proceeds from the Father (and the Son)
Who with the Father and the Son is worshiped and glorified.
Who has spoken through the prophets.
We believe in one holy catholic and apostolic Church.
We acknowledge one baptism for the forgiveness of sins.
We look for the resurrection of the dead, and the life of the world to come. Amen.

Contemporary Version (Prepared by the International Consultation on English Texts)

The Nicene Creed is important in my view because it provides the "through-line" I am looking for plus it is a conceptual framework for Mark Galli's *Beautiful Orthodoxy*. Several observers including Mark Galli and Paul VanderKlay, a Christian Reformed Church pastor from Sacramento California, have noted a trend toward what they call "re-sacralization" as an aspect of the so-called "Jordan Peterson effect" where young men have become interested in Peterson's retelling of Bible stories from a Jungian "archetypal" point of view. This means a reactivation of interest in the sacred and mystical aspect of biblical stories and the creeds, and their implications for life as it is expressed emotionally, intellectually, in ministry and preaching, in art, politics and in the purposeful re-assertion of religion into the public square due significantly to Peterson's clarity in retelling Bible stories and his courageous position against political correctness. This is paralleled by my own experience in the change from a Baptist church, to St James Old Cathedral, an evangelical Anglican congregation where the historical creeds are recited every week, to remind us that we are encountering the overwhelming majesty of God, whom the Bible claims to be underneath, over and above all other spiritual, social, religious, scientific and political claims.

Although God offers his love to us, we cannot experience it until we submit our minds to be transformed to know what love is, what it is not and how to receive it. Our personal experience of love is forged and tested in the real world of intentionally getting along with our neighbor and everybody else with whom we have a relationship. Love is defined as to seek the highest good for another, but that is insufficient because even in our own experience, love is far more costly, multi-faceted and nuanced than just saying "best wishes" or "good luck" to someone. Love is the beautiful essence and character of God about which we learn only when we take an active part to do all we can for another to ensure the best possible outcome for both of us, limited only by our capacity and the circumstances of a relationship. Our encounter with love begins with the recognition that to be a properly functioning person, we must love and want the highest good for ourselves. Self-love in its fullness, is the realization that God has loves us individually and has prepared a place for us in his Kingdom, since before the creation of the world. As we begin to experience this self-love consciously, we recognize that it is from God, who requires that we share it with others, causing it to grow in us by our obedience to the Golden Rule. However, we need to keep self-love in check as it can easily turn into a subtle proud distortion of what it is intended to be. Then there is an unanticipated chicken and egg confusion as to how the Golden Rule works that has caused many of us to be unsure about the difference between God's law of the Old Testament and his New Testament Grace. This confusion is the result of the unrelenting human need to earn credit for our good behavior, plus some ambiguity in the biblical text which has become exaggerated by some doctrinal specialties among Christian sects, enabling several different mistakes to become entrenched as traditional sectarian views. My Brethren view was a confusion of both extremes where on one hand we would criticize hierarchical churches for being bound by law or tradition, while we established new laws and dogma of our own relating to a refusal to observe the creeds or to have ordained or paid clergy and the enforced silence of women, amongst other things. While we rejected the creeds as being too legalistic and superficial, we created new laws about lay leadership and dogmatic eschatology to the extent that our pre-occupation with speculative "futurism" became a distinctive characteristic.

Another common misunderstanding suggests that because we are no longer under law, therefore God's grace allows us to do what we want. The other extreme is that because nothing has really changed between the two eras of Old and New, that we still earn favor with God by our compliance with the Old law. In fact, it is our experience of God's gift of love that eventually enables us to keep God's law; not because of duty or fear, but because of love. When our human instinct to break God's law is eventually replaced with new attitudes from God's heart and mind, then our desire be law-breakers slowly leaves us and is replaced with a desire to please him. This is what Jesus means when he says, *My food…is to do the will of him who sent me and to finish his work.* (Jn 4:34) Jesus then directs us as to our role in this new kingdom when he says; *A new commandment I give to you that you love one another, as I have loved you.*(Jn 13:34). However, this is not a situation where we can just correct an intellectual error that makes everything clear. Although the Golden Rule looks like a simple law for our diligent application, it is not. It is a process of learning about ourselves in relationships with others where we depend on them, to learn about ourselves. Therefore, it is an interdependent, symbiotic, systematic process that involves our whole being, heart, mind and soul, responding to an invitation from God.

To change pace slightly, in my role as the training manager of Beaurepaires, a national tire retailer, I was also responsible for organizational development where I was free to explore any kind of organizational innovation that may have been useful to the company. During that time, Peter Senge's book, *The Fifth Discipline* was published, which I thought was manna from heaven. Senge became famous for what he called "systems thinking," or more simply, thinking in an informed and orderly way. However, Senge's voice was only one of many in that era, which was still digesting ideas from the likes of Peter Drucker who began writing about the concepts of Management by Objectives and Human Resources Management in the 1930's. I was also influenced by W Edwards Deming and Joseph Juran whose statistical process control ideas of making decisions on the basis of data had made such a difference to the quality of manufacturing during WWII and in the post-war recovery of Japan. Behind these great minds, was the idea that humans need to think systematically and intelligently about human behavior to succeed in achieving shared goals in organizations. For instance, Deming is famous for saying that quality of a product cannot be "inspected in", by which he meant that no amount of checking something, improves it. Quality and value must be designed in to a product and the manufacturing process, which must then be followed exactly by everybody at every point of the process to ensure high quality and low cost. These principles have become universal requirements upon which modern businesses depend. I was so enthralled by systems thinking, that I commenced a university course in systems thinking to become an expert. While I remain convinced about the elegance of this and many other theories of human behavior and organizations, I learned that to try and make *myself* think systematically, let alone an organization, was impossible on any big scale in the short term. However, many elements of this revolution of human organization have become part of our modern language, such as Drucker's ideas of delivering customer satisfaction, eliminating waste to achieve value for money and Senge's mental models which remain as maxims of good business practice. As I have noted elsewhere, systematic non-contradictory thinking was one of the first jobs humans were given in the Garden of Eden, when God asked Adam and Eve to name the animals. This duty has led to the many scientific and other developments and revolutions in human progress. Of all the discoveries of systems thinking principles, common logic is by far the most important as this is the basis for all rational thought, intelligence, reasoning, assessment, decision making and behavior without which we would have made no progress. Of all of the applications of logic, I believe that the most important is to think about our relationships intelligently and systematically, by beginning with ourselves as our reference point as the Golden Rule requires. The reason for this is because no matter how successful we are as individuals, if we don't enjoy good relationships then all of our accomplishments amount to nothing. Proverbs 17:1 puts it so elegantly; *Better a dry crust with peace and quiet than a house full of feasting, with strife.*

If my claim about the importance of love and the Golden Rule is true, then why is it not practised as a discipline in all relationships in the same way that quality management, cost reduction and shared organizational goals is compulsory in modern business? I believe it is because individually, we resist thinking intelligently and systematically unless we happen to agree with the answer that such thinking inexorably leads us to. If we don't like the answer, we will do anything to avoid thinking logically, including confusing the issue by going to great lengths to prove that white is black and black is white.

Looking at love

To demonstrate that the Golden Rule is a process that requires us to think systematically, the most important biblical texts seem to me to have a clear meaning, depending on how carefully you read them. For example; *'Love the* LORD *your God with all your heart and with all your soul and with all your strength and with all your mind'; and, 'Love your neighbor as yourself.* Luke 10:27 (plus similar texts from Mt 22:34-40 and Mk 12:28-31. If I read this text as a sequence of: *1. I must first love God. 2. Then I must love my neighbor. 3. I must finally love myself,* then I think I may have come to the wrong conclusion before I begin by starting on the wrong foot. I believe that the Golden Rule specifies the outcome of a process, not the pre-requisite required of me to begin one, because it makes no sense to specify an input that is identical to the output of a process. 1 John: 4.20 says, *"whoever claims to love God yet hates a brother or sister is a liar. For whoever does not love their brother and sister, whom they have seen, cannot love God, whom they have not seen."* John suggests that what we believe to be true is not revealed by what we say we believe, but by what we do. These strong, unequivocal words prevent me from saying that because I love God, therefore, I love my neighbor and myself, unless it is already true. The only people I have ever heard make this claim to love God so comprehensively, have either been very young or very old. This is because most of us, if we are truthful, would say that while we know that we should love God with all our being and our neighbor as ourselves, we don't. Yet.

Jordan Peterson frequently discusses how the self-consciousness of the human ego and super-ego had to be replicated by artificial intelligence for robots to work. Robots could not be made to function in any situation that required semi-autonomous movement until their intelligence was located in a physical body by which the robot themselves becomes their own reference-point to be able to sense their environment. I am perhaps drawing a long bow in making this comparison, but it seems to me that to be perceptive of our surroundings, we need to consider our own embodied intelligence first, which I think of as being analogous to self-love proscribed by the Golden Rule. https://www.youtube.com/watch?v=uL0uIJf3aN4

I believe it is necessary to read the biblical text backwards, as this is how its logic is constructed, guided by the reality that from our point of view, our bodily existence precedes the development of our soul and our spirit, determining the way we grow and learn. Logically, if I genuinely love myself, then it is only reasonable that I also love my neighbor, because he has the same status before God as I do because we know that God loves both of us in the same way. When I genuinely love my neighbor, either out of intuition, inspiration, or obedience to Jesus, then I will begin to love God more as I see him more clearly. *(and follow him more nearly,* to quote the musical *Godspell)* As I engage in this process, then I also learn to love myself even more in an interdependent and symbiotic relationship because I am doing what I was designed to do which I will experience as goodness. Even then, this is not exactly straight forward as though we get ourselves sorted out first, then we sort out our relationships with others, then we are hunky dory with God. What I mean by *"Interdependent and symbiotic,"* is that this is a process where we alone do not call the shots. We do take the initiative to respond to God's offer, in my view, but then we must exercise faith to put ourselves in the hands of other people and God, trusting that God always gives good gifts and that the process will be beneficial to us without our controlling it. It is intelligently systematic and risky in the sense that when we have played our first card, we have taken a risk of being wrong and must wait to see how the game flows before we know what to do next, hoping that we will end the game with a shared benefit, still on good terms with God and others.

The Golden Rule, then, involves us embarking on a path of obedience to Jesus, by which I will begin to learn things that I cannot know otherwise. Certainly, I will learn more about God and my neighbor. But most importantly, I will begin to learn about myself—not through someone telling me things I don't want to hear, but by teaching myself about the unpleasant things that prevent me from loving my neighbor and God.

What does it mean to love yourself?

Despite my explanation and the apparent simplicity of the statement about obedience to Jesus, the notion that we should love ourselves remains problematic. I have heard highly respected church leaders say that it does not mean we should literally love ourselves. So what does it mean, to love yourself? My approach to understanding Jesus words and the Bible in general, is not the approach of a scholar. In the absence of expert explanation, I prefer to try to understand the text in terms of how it has affected me. I realize that this method has its limitations, so I will look for good scholarship that makes sense to me, but if I can't find it, then I go my own way. The Apostle Paul later adds detail to Jesus' statement about loving your body and provides a comparison between our self-love and Christ's love for the church.

> *After all, no one ever hated their own body, but they feed and care for their body, just as Christ does the church—for we are members of his body* (Eph 5: 29-30).

By this play on words, I think he means that because self-love is of the utmost importance, we should care for our bodies (and souls) as Christ cares for his body, which is us. I believe that self-love is necessary if we are to survive, because the opposite of self-love is despair, which leads to death. Self-love is required for self-preservation, both now and into eternity.

This concept of self-love, however, introduces many problems for our contemporary culture. Often, Christians hold up the ideal of self-sacrifice as a Christian standard. It is assumed that extreme selflessness is a requirement of all Christians, often expressed in terms of being *"self-forgetting."* My concern is that some Christians in their zeal to become "righteous" in God's eyes, want to be credited for their righteous relationships without having taken the preparatory course. I agree that selflessness is the position we finally take as an outcome of learning, but if we adopt the position of selflessness as an input to this process, then I believe that we are at risk of being self-deceived about our intentions and our emotional state. To say that we love our selves, in my view, is a necessary first step of being honest about ourselves and being in the right state of mind both emotionally, intellectually and spiritually, which, may require some growth and experience of God's grace, before we begin to love ourselves. Self-righteousness is the delusion of "earning" righteousness or earning God's grace by our good works, which we know to be a contradiction in terms because it is impossible to earn a gift (Eph 2: 8-9).

Strength from weakness

The Bible has an ironic way of describing this process of loving another, which often will seem to be acting in weakness rather than in strength, which in most situations will seem more natural. Paul, in recounting a mystical experience by which the Lord spoke to him, quotes Jesus as saying;

> *"My grace is sufficient for you, for my power is made perfect in weakness." Then Paul replies; "Therefore I will boast all the more gladly about my weaknesses, so that Christ's power may rest on me"* (2 Cor 12:9).

Both Paul and Jesus are saying that it is in the weakness of our faith in God, that we become strong in ways that we cannot anticipate. Mainly, I believe, by the diminishing influence of our impulsive ego causing us to do things that are not good and by increasing our repertoire of good actions we can take toward ourselves and others.

My experience is that over time, as my weaknesses become more obvious and as I overcome my doubts and fears, my weaknesses become strengths as long as humility remains. My behavior becomes more congruent with my beliefs and I become more integrated, more transparent as I become a more useful and wiser person. And yes, I become more intelligent, because I make better guesses about things I was unsure of as I stop making the same mistakes. As you make progress in following the Golden Rule, you discover even more reasons why you should love yourself — because we see that our life is being transformed by the renewal of our mind, just as Paul said it would be;

> *Do not conform to the pattern of this world, but be transformed by the renewing of your mind. Then you will be able to test and approve what God's will is—his good, pleasing and perfect will* (Rom 12:2).

Did the Golden Rule encourage the self-esteem movement?

We need to recognize the down side to self-love—when it becomes selfishness or, what is worse, narcissism.

During the past 40 years or so, there has been a major debate in the Western world which emerged out of popular psychology and which has massively impacted upon society. It concerns what became known as the self-esteem movement. Some self-esteem theories have had a deep and significant effect on social policy regarding parenting, education, the law, mental health, psychological treatment and other areas. Among these, many groups affected by the self-esteem movement were Christian churches who adopted its theories to determine how they presented themselves and the Christian message.

The importance of self-esteem among churches was supported by the idea that since we are made in God's image, God values us highly and loves us unconditionally. These principles were assumed to be biblical and were then often extended by the rationale that if God loves us unconditionally as individuals, then so should we love ourselves the same way. This notion is perhaps best characterized by Robert Schuller's weekly greeting to his globally televised Crystal Cathedral church, "God loves you and so do I," which became popular in churches across the world. However, I think Robert Schuller was drawing too long a bow in saying that he loved me in the same way that God loves me. Plus, in my opinion, it is too much to love myself unconditionally as this implies that I will love myself, no matter what. I believe that my sense of guilt and shame is a very important aspect of an active conscience. If my conscience is working properly, when I do something inconsistent with what I say is right or inconsistent with what I have experienced of love, then I ought to disapprove of my actions or thoughts that led me to this point of transgression. On the contrary, if my conscience and experience of love are strong enough, they will lead me to repentance and to the confession of my sins.

It seems to me that the self-esteem movement scared some Christians off teaching the Golden Rule because they associated the words, "*as you love yourself*" with the faulty self-esteem concept. Unfortunately, this association caused some people to lose confidence in this most important aspect of Jesus' teaching because it has been trivialized by the self-esteem movement. Another related effect of the self-esteem movement on churches was a general departure from forthright statement that we are all *"sinners in need of a savior"*, as preached by Billy Graham. The emphasis on protecting self-esteem dictated a much softer approach that only ever encourages people with kind words of God's unconditional love, mercy and grace, known as the positive gospel. This message avoided making the accusation that we are sinful either by explaining sin away as an outmoded idea, or by saying as Robert Schuller did, that people knew they were sinners and didn't need to be reminded of it, so the soft approach of mentioning the emotional and psychological benefits of the gospel were emphasized, rather than the consequences of faithlessness and sin. Similarly, many Pentecostal and Charismatic churches emphasized God's gifts of generosity and health, wealth and prosperity, leaving only the few the "Bible" churches displaying messages on their public notice boards quoting Bible texts that mentioned sin, hell and damnation, together with promises of salvation and eternal life in heaven, often in King James English reflecting out-of-date communication methods and message. None of these extremes are helpful, because they are all a distortion of self-love which ignores the obvious, that we are all sinners in need of a savior.

Feel-good faith

The self-esteem movement is now widely regarded as being bankrupt by most sectors of society, although it seems to have put on a new face as part of the post-modern political correctness, as we will see. Self-esteem is now seen by some churches who previously supported it, as having done more harm than good, including in the internationally prominent Willow Creek Community Church and the now-defunct Crystal Cathedral. I believe it is a salutary lesson to consider how this movement came about and how a truncated version of the Golden Rule was co-opted as part of its rationale. This is noticeable, in my experience, by church mission statements that say Love God and Love Others as their mission statement. On one hand this is troubling because it is a mistake made with a high motive; to make Christian faith and church experience more palatable for an unbelieving consumer society. On the other hand, it is a reminder to me that the key messages of the Bible are not to be trivialized as there will always be a consequence to any attempt to make the message of Jesus Christ less demanding and more acceptable. However, I am not advocating a return to the hardline fundamentalist gospel of literal dogmatic interpretation of scripture. The main characteristic that I believe should be noticeable, is a prevailing sense of gratitude, awe and wonder at the grandeur and wonder of God's absolute power, expressed in his mercy, compassion and justice held in an exquisite balance that mere mortals don't seem to be able to replicate. If I find this attitude toward God in any Christian tradition, then I imagine I could find my place in the church.

Meanwhile, I believe that a critical review of the self-esteem and seeker sensitive movement is necessary and important, just as a review and shaking of the Roman Catholic church is necessary in view of historical sexual abuse by its clergy. In all cases, a comparison of doctrinal theories should be made to the Golden Rule which may indicate that the Bible continues to hold profound insights into human behavior that are misunderstood and misappropriated if they are neglected. I am greatly encouraged by any movement toward reformation based on a reconsideration of what the Bible actually says in its most simple terms because it reinforces my belief that the teachings of Jesus recorded in the Bible are profoundly true and reliable to an extent that consistently exceeds our limited understanding and expectations.

In my view, financial prosperity, material success or an easy life should not be the goal of faithfulness. Prosperity and abundance, in the wholistic sense of blessing in each person's body, soul and spirit, should be, provided it embodies a complete definition of love, that includes the need for self-sacrifice. Even so, the experience that we might call "prosperity of spirit," indicated by a very complete sense of righteousness, peace and joy, despite our personal, financial, physical and even emotional state, must be offset with what Jesus describes in the Beatitudes as *poverty of spirit* (Matt 5:3). This, in my view, means a deep humility toward God and one another in recognition of our sinful state and need for salvation and continued transformation. This is an example of what I call the necessary tension between our humanity and our spirituality where if any true principle is slightly misused, it has the potential to give rise to delusions of self-importance, especially when the principle seemed so reasonable and apparently beneficial. This reminds me that we are not in a physical, intellectual or emotional battle so much as a spiritual contest as Paul reminds us in Eph 6:12, that ...*we wrestle not with flesh and blood but with powers and principalities...* This picture resembles to me, a football player (Aussie Rules, that is) being bumped slightly off course by an opponent by an illegal push-in-the-back, rather than an obvious head-on confrontation. It seems to me that the only antidote to being deluded and bumped of course by an opponent, is to remember that God gives grace not to the wise, wealthy, powerful or successful, but he resists the proud and gives grace only to the humble. If my point about the need for spiritual tension is correct, then potentially, the greatest untruth is a purposeful but slight deviation that sends us off in the wrong direction, because of our willingness to trust a view appealing to our ego, intellect or status, rather than trust in the dusty old Bible. Many contemporary churches are now returning to the personal and shared discipline of Bible reading as their strategy for discipleship. Whether this will be enough of a change to avoid the destruction being experienced by some mega churches at present, including the Roman Catholic church, remains to be seen. When I think of my own experience, I conclude that there have been many blind alleys and positive influences in my Christian journey, including important relationships. But when it comes to my personal growth, the thing that has made the difference over the longer period is my consistently reading the Bible and related texts, trying to integrate their words into my life. That, plus my reasonably disciplined experience of prayer is the key, I believe, to carefully making room for the Holy Spirit to act on my heart over the longer time so that I am increasingly aware of God's love for me, reminding me of my need to love myself as God loves me.

The self-centered Golden Rule

The Golden Rule is very obviously self-referential in that to follow it, I must begin by thinking about how I feel about myself. This gives rise to objections from figures such as Emmanuel Kant, who said that it therefore imposes on the receiver the view of the giver, which of course ought not be the case because freedom, to which we aspire, cannot come as a result of manipulation, coercion or the abuse of power. But this exchange does not stop with us trying out an imperfect idea of what is good for another. The giver has only himself to refer to at the beginning, with perhaps a guess at the interests of the receiver. But if this is a sincere attempt to establish good relations, then the giver is watching for the receiver's response while the giver is conscious of God's scrutiny. Even when God is not present in the mind of the giver, then at least they are trying to do the right thing at the beginning. If not, it is not the Golden Rule being applied. If the giver's motive is awry, which it may be, then all they have to go on is the response of the receiver. Even with a bad reaction, if the giver is at all open to the possibility of the good, then they must also be open to learning about themselves. If the giver persists in their attempt to do good, then they can learn a great deal about what might be a better way of dealing with others because they have provided they accept evidence as to their faulty thinking. This experience of learning by observing our own mistakes is, I think, a key building block of the Golden Rule process of learning to love yourself, others and God. While I am sure that there are other dynamics at play that I will cover elsewhere, my experience suggests that this is the major learning step.

When my family were very young, we attended a Uniting Church near or home where I was constantly amazed by the behavior of couples of my own age, who seemed to be more inspired by relationships in TV soap operas than by any Christian view. My growing criticism was set back when I read Matt 7:5 where Jesus warns us to remove the plank (an irritating speck) from my own eye, before I try to remove a speck from another's eye. This is not to say that I have learned this lesson so well that I have not made the same mistake again, but all I have to do when I feel a criticism coming on, is to remind myself of this deeply convicting experience.

Maslow's hierarchy of needs

As an aside, one aspect of the self-esteem debate is related to a theory of human motivation developed by the American psychologist Abraham Maslow, who popularized a model of the hierarchy of human needs, suggesting that self-esteem (or self-actualization) is a basic human need or motivation. A leading figure of the movement was the psychologist Nathaniel Branden, who was quoted as saying, *"[I] cannot think of a single psychological problem – from anxiety and depression, to fear of intimacy or of success, to spouse battery or child molestation – that is not traced back*

...as you love yourself?

to the problem of low self-esteem". The Psychology of Self-Esteem. Nathaniel Branden.

Maslow's hierarchy of needs stands as one of the most enduring theories of human behavior. Maslow explains that after the most basic human needs for food, shelter and relationships have been met, we ultimately desire self-actualization: the fulfillment of our most idealized and integrated personal potential. Later in his life, Maslow came to see that it is not self-actualization, but rather self-transcendence that is the highest source of motivation. However, Maslow's theory has done significant harm in Christian teaching by suggesting that higher order needs such as self-actualization cannot be addressed until lower order needs are satisfied.

However, the self-esteem movement has run out of self-esteem.

During one of my exchanges on the on-line academic discussion forum, *The Conversation*, I enjoyed an extended conversation with La Trobe University psychologist, Patrick Stokes. At one stage, when I mentioned Maslow's hierarchy, Stokes expressed his despair by saying, "I don't know what it is about Maslow. All my students love him and quote him all the time." My amateur explanation to him was that Maslow's schema is so memorable because of its simplicity and apparent elegance because it seemed to describe how people feel about their own motivation. Like so many sociological or psychological fads which start with an enormous flurry of activity and receiving highly credible intellectual support for a few years, until they start to run out of steam when the data comes in. Wall Street Journal reviewer Kay Hymowitz discovered after analyzing about 15,000 self-esteem studies, that self-esteem doesn't improve grades, reduce anti-social behavior, deter alcohol drinking, or do much of anything good for kids. In fact, telling kids how smart they are can be counterproductive. Many children who are convinced that they are little geniuses tend to not put much effort into their work. Others are troubled by the latent anxiety of adults who feel it is necessary to praise them constantly. In my view, Jordan Peterson puts the final nail in the Maslow Hierarchy of Needs coffin when he points out that it implies that both self-actualization and self-transcendence are not possible until lower order needs such as food, clothing and shelter, relationships, sex, creativity and other needs are satisfied. This is obviously not true, both from an experiential, psychological and theological point of view because all the evidence is to the contrary as there are countless examples of people who are spiritually fulfilled while remining in poverty and ill-health, deliberately in some cases. Maslow's Hierarchy then, is an example of a common pseudo-scientific belief that has no basis in evidence of any kind, a condition I think is far more prevalent the any of us would credit.

Personal sovereignty

As I have mentioned, I believe that to love God means to surrender our personal sovereignty to the ultimate Sovereign. The difficulty is that while we can say that we have surrendered ourselves to God, we almost certainly have not unless we have done so slowly, over and through the incidents of life and have experienced a transformation by the renewal of our minds. In so doing, we slowly relinquish ultimate control of our life and give it to God because we trust and are prepared to learn from him in the events of our lives over which we retain some limited control. Eventually, as we become more conscious of him and know that our purposes and behaviors are substantially aligned with His purposes, then we have become conformed to his image to the extent that we are no longer anxious about our security or destiny as a member of his Kingdom.

Desire for self-transcendence

It is not so well known that Maslow went on to criticize his own legacy, when, later in life, he discovered that self-transcendence, rather than self-actualization, is by far the more important source of motivation toward the good, which in my view is to consistently chose to do the things that are life-giving, of which the first and foremost is to choose to obey Christ's instruction to love one another as we love ourselves. According to Maslow, self-transcendence is the realization that we are not the center of the universe since we are each accountable to God, the highest of all authorities. From this accountability flows our awareness of our need for God's grace to experience the highest and best that life can offer. If this need is properly identified and fostered, it can become a primary source of motivation, like how hunger and thirst indicate our physiological need for food and drink. Jesus repeatedly, and uniquely points to the significance of our relationship with God, enacted through our relationships with each other, as the highest goal and the most satisfying experience we can have. This concept is further explained in the Lord's Prayer:

> ...and do not bring us to the time of trial, but rescue us from the evil one. For if you forgive others their trespasses, your heavenly Father will also forgive you; but if you do not forgive others, neither will your Father forgive your trespasses (Matt 6:9-15).

The Lord's Prayer, combined with the Golden Rule, is, I believe, a summary of Jesus' teachings from which we can determine the attitude we must have toward others to be able to implement all of Jesus' teachings:

> ...and forgive us our debts, as we also have forgiven our debtors...

If we want to enjoy God's goodness and grace, then we must first learn to offer others the same goodness that we seek for ourselves. This is identical to the commonly accepted biblical definition of grace: to humbly accept God's freely given gifts, which enable us to become His "Blessed Ones". The Golden Rule does not teach that superficial self-esteem should be encouraged. It does imply, however, that self-esteem, or self-love, is an instinct like all other human instincts, and one that needs to be recognized and constrained. As we see Paul's endorsement of self-love in Ephesians 5:29, he understands the Golden Rule in the same way that Jesus taught it. Paul also says;

> I discipline my body like an athlete, training it to do what it should. Otherwise, I fear that after preaching to others I myself might be disqualified.
> (1 Cor 9:27 NLT)

This suggests to me how we are to relate to the Golden Rule.

As I have mentioned, the Golden Rule should be a process of teaching ourselves to be self-disciplined and self-aware of our egotistical attempt to always put ourselves first. Rather, we should learn from our experience and from God's spirit how be more effective both in our mission of sharing the good news of Christ while we *"work out our salvation in fear and trembling"* to quote Paul. (Phil 2:12) As we share the gospel, do we have any choice than to regard ourselves and those who we are trying to reach as sinners in need of a savior?

We should, however, also continue to learn from science and from the modern world to at least try to address the hearts and minds of people who we want to listen to our message, as the Golden Rule suggests. If we are to do this, we must return to the Bible as a guide to life, particularly the Ten Commandments and Christ's sermon on the Mount. Rather than present them as God's angry threats, I suggest that we must consider the law and Jesus' New Testament teaching both as guidelines of what we should believe, think and do, and then as outcomes of the transformed life that conforms to the image of Jesus as a result of our obedience to him. As Paul suggests:

> *Don't copy the behavior and customs of this world, but let God transform you into a new person by changing the way you think. Then you will learn to know God's will for you, which is good and pleasing and perfect* (Rom 12:12).
>
> *For God knew his people in advance, and he chose them to become like his Son, so that his Son would be the firstborn among many brothers and sisters* (Rom 8:29).

This view of scripture (which I learned from Dallas Willard's book, *The Divine Conspiracy*) makes sense of Jesus' claim that *He has not come to replace the law, but to fulfill it.* Nor did He come to condemn the world, but to save it from itself.

Compliance as outcome

One of the unexpected outcomes of our commitment to keeping the Golden Rule is that we also begin to keep the biblical law, often as an unintended consequence. This experience gives meaning to Jesus' promise to not replace the law, but to fulfil it. If this is the case that the law is fulfilled by our transformation by love, then, we must at least return to the Ten Commandments as guide as to what we should expect to happen to us, and as the basis of what we teach our children. I believe that the Ten Commandments are guidelines that describe what we should aim to become and set the limits to both our belief and behavior, as inputs to a good life. However, when we try to keep them, we often fail because we cannot pull ourselves up by our bootstraps. Rather, fulfilment of the Ten Commandments is an outcome of our transformation into the image of Jesus as we start to become *"transformed into His image, by love."* This begins when we are *"born again of the spirit"*, and it continues for the rest of our lives as we learn about our shortcomings and our need for grace.

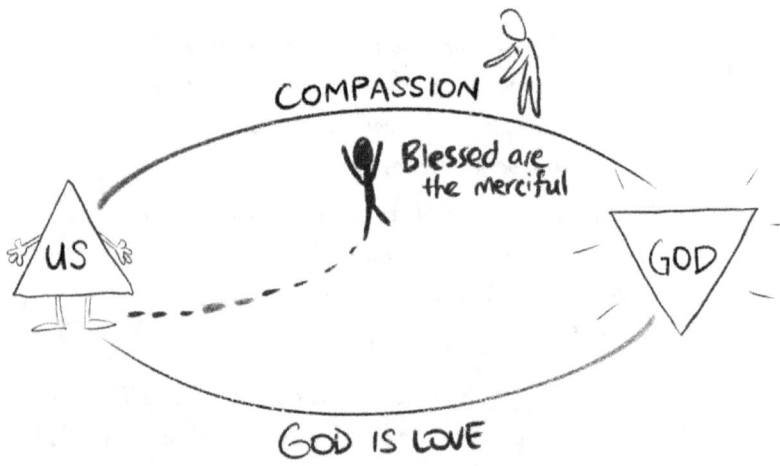

From the Ten Commandments to transformation into the image of Christ
Christians are called to respond to each of the following laws, not by our compliance, but as God's love transformed by his grace.
1 We have no other gods before me Reject all other gods as pretenders and deceivers promoted by the forces of evil to lead us into sin. This applies to the modern deceptions of faith in science, political or social idealism and all abuses of power.
2 We have not made any idols Monitor and prioritize your values. Do not value anything more than you value God, even good things such as your own family.
3 We do not take the Lord's name in vain Our words are of absolute importance. Never misuse your words to devalue God's name by demeaning him, or by exalting anything in his place. The unforgivable sin is to attribute evil to the genuine presence of the Holy Spirit.
4 We remember the Sabbath and keep it holy Prioritize and allocate your time and energy to what you value most. Work hard for 6 days to support yourself and your family, then relax for one day giving thanks to God and enjoying the fruit of your labor.
5 We honour our father and mother Enduring gratitude to your parents is a touchstone for life. You don't have to think they are perfect, but you are to love them despite their imperfections as they gave you life. If you don't get this right, all your other relationships will be more difficult.
6 We do not kill or murder All life is sacred. As your life is no more important than the next person's, you are prevented from exercising judgement of another person as this is God's prerogative.
7 We do not commit adultery Sex is sacred, to be enjoyed in marriage between a man and a woman for relationship and bringing children into a loving family.
8 We do not steal Property is important. Don't take or wish for anything that is not yours. You are only entitled to what you work for or are freely given.

9 We do not bear false witness against our neighbor Don't tell lies. Your word reflects your values and your character. Telling lies causes a loss of self-reliance and trust among others. Handle the truth with great care.
10 We do not covet our neighbor's wife or property You shall not covet your neighbor's wife, property or anything that does not belong to us. We are not jealous of what others have, that we do not have.
Our compliance with the law does not ever achieve what God wants for us because even with the best intentions, we fall short of the mark usually because of a sense of entitlement. When we are gradually transformed by grace, we are remade in God's image to both bring His Kingdom here on earth and to prepare ourselves for a time yet to come, when God's Kingship will be undisputed and we will be agents of His rule.

How then should we teach our children?

As the Ten Commandments clearly affirm, we should not tell lies, most of all to our children. Rather, we need to give everyone appropriate messages that treat them as we would want to be treated if we were in their situation. This means, from a biblical point of view, that to "*speak the truth in love*" (Eph 4:15) is a requirement for all the followers of Jesus. To become the agents of truth, we must always consider the impact that our words will have on another, and always choose words, expressions, emotions, examples and stories that have the maximum beneficial effect on the listener.

In church this morning, the day after I had written these words, the speaker spoke from his text, James 1:22: *But be doers of the word, and not hearers only, deceiving yourselves.* This reminds me that to be faithful to the word requires action, not just speech, ideas, or intellectual assent. This means that God's word, the Logos, is manifest in us as software for our soul, and for our body and spirit too. Truly, this is the meaning of the Logos becoming flesh and dwelling in us. Paul describes this as; *Christ within you, the hope of Glory.* Collossians 1:27, facilitated by our obedience to Jesus'

Golden Rule. The outcome of righteousness, peace and joy in the Holy Spirit is shorthand for the fruits of the Spirit from Galatians 5:22-23; *But the fruit of the Spirit is love, joy, peace, forbearance, kindness, goodness, faithfulness, gentleness and self-control. Against such things there is no law.* In both cases, the Holy Spirit is the agent who effects this transformation in us. Transformation is confirming an outcome of grace, not to be credited to our account, but is received as a free gift from God as a reward for our cooperation with him.

8

EGO DEATH

Neurosis is always a substitute for legitimate suffering.
— Carl Jung

There are far, far better things ahead than any we leave behind
— C.S. Lewis

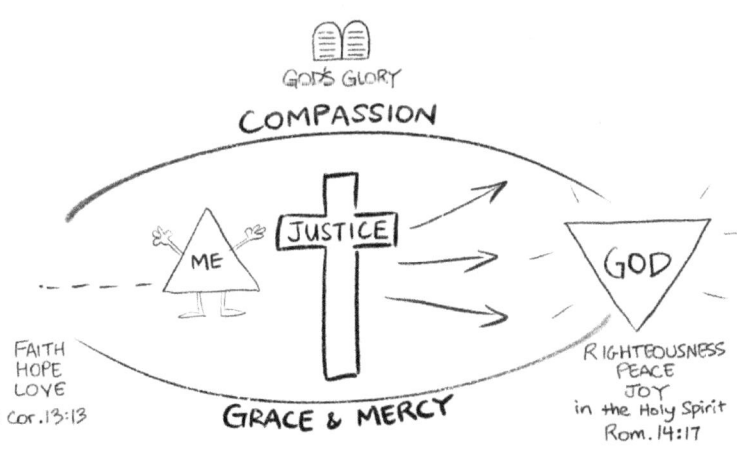

The concept of *testing our faith to prove ourselves worthy* is alien to most Christians in Western democracies because we think our financial, technological and social success has insulated us from the need to suffer for our faith. Many of us are in such privileged positions that we can seem to protect ourselves from the trials experienced by our Christian forebears. Consequently, we have not been *"refined by fire"* described by 1 Peter 1: 6 nor have we *"suffered for Christ"* according to Philippians 1:29. However, in this day of comfort, the suffering we must do is not (yet) in the hands of our enemies so much as in our own heads. In our affluence, even the poor amongst us enjoy wealth that is unimaginable to most people of previous generations, except for the wealthy and powerful few. This, in my view, is a major problem. We are among the first beneficiaries of such wide-spread wealth, that like King Solomon, we are spoiled for choice to the extent that we are fat, having far too much of a good thing, especially when it comes to freedom of choice and our decision not to take the narrow path through life. The suffering we must do, however, is the most difficult of all, because our inflated ego is the problem. We must deflate it by accepting an inconvenient reality that we are deluded at such a fundamental level, that it is almost impossible for us to act alone. To begin to see ourselves as God sees us, we must begin by at a more mundane level. It is here where we can learn from modern psychology, perhaps even more than our predecessors of the New Testament.

M. Scott Peck's best-selling 1978 book *The Road Less Travelled* begins with the line, *"Life is difficult."* [1] This is, I think, a powerful truism that is best recognized by looking back over one's life at some of the challenges and avoidable difficulties we have created for ourselves and seeing that there were changes we could have made much earlier, if only we knew what to do. Evidence of life's difficulties is the fact that we all experience suffering of some kind that we would like to avoid. If I accept Carl Jung's advice that avoidance of suffering leads to neurosis, then we may agree that suffering is not only inevitable, it is also necessary for our emotional and psychological growth. Scott Peck's solution to the difficulties of life is to apply the self-discipline of delayed self-gratification.

---

1 M Scott Peck, *The Road Less Travelled*, Rider &Co.

Ego death

My solution goes another step further into what I believe is the result of our application of the Golden Rule to ourselves where our ego must die to itself. This, I believe, is suffering of a most exquisite kind which we cannot even contemplate, let alone accomplish by ourselves. My discovery of Scott Peck's work in the late 1980's had a similar effect on me as my recent discovery of Jordan Peterson, both of them being highly regarded Jungian psychologists with a deep interest in the Judeo-Christian religion. I found this combination of interests to be very helpful for developing my understanding of myself as a Christian man, husband, father and other—not because they were great Christian teachers in the conventional sense (although Peck claimed to be a believer), but because they both helped to lift the lid on the way I understand myself and how I behave in response to what I believe. For instance, my neighbor Sheridan Bajada, had previously introduced me to Carl Jung's ideas of archetypes. Jung explained the need to be transformed through suffering, as typified by Jesus Christ's suffering for the whole of creation to reconcile the world to himself. Both Peck's and Peterson's writing led me to change how I thought of myself as an integrated person: body, soul and spirit. Although I thought I understood the theory of suffering, it is only in later years that I have come to understand its function experientially by looking back at the major events of my life where moments of crisis had taught me new things, for better or for worse. For example, Sherri observed that my conflict with an old mate suggested co-dependency, that I needed to be needed by him. I once asked my employer for leave of absence to travel overseas for six months, which they refused. My reaction was highly indignant, leading me to think, *I'll show those bastards what a mistake they have made.* Even then, I knew enough about unresolved inner bitterness to know that I would be harmed if I maintained my rage against the company, but I did it anyway. This is a pattern I have repeated—where I reacted with entitlement to a situation as I refused to properly think about my behavior. My regret is not that it has taken me so long to understand Jungian archetypes, but rather, how long it has taken me to become obedient to the explicit teachings of Jesus, who I claimed to follow as they would have taught me the same thing much sooner. Such is life.

Another truism that I discovered through reading Scott Peck is that "*all behavior is overdetermined.*" This means that the things we do have many complex and interrelated causes, often beyond our own comprehension, rather than a single cause. We often hear that a single mistake is provided as an excuse for someone who has committed a crime, despite the claim of friends and family that "*He really was a good person, who made a bad decision.*" Just as I might do if I am feeling sorry for myself and inclined to think of myself as a victim of some circumstances. Although I might, at different times, have wished to be different to what I was, I have learned the hard way by suffering from my emotional and spiritual immaturity, which I have begun to accept as my need for continuing transformation.

To thine own self be true

One principle that Elaine and I agreed to practise early in our relationship was to be honest with each other. But this is much easier said than done as it is difficult not to deceive ourselves. My approach is to apply William Shakespeare's maxim;

> "*To thine own self be true, and it must follow, as the night the day, Thou canst not then be false to any man*". William Shakespeare, spoken by Polonius in *Hamlet.*

This is not a perfect answer, as I can attest, but a commitment to truth is a beginning that eventually allows light to penetrate the darkness we live in, as Shakespeare suggests. I observe that most of us do the same thing to excuse our bad behavior.

Ego death

We either approve and normalize what we bring with us from childhood, or alternatively, we reject our immature selves by becoming conscious and make this the new foundation upon which we build our adult lives. Most of us require a strong disrupting force, such as a deeply positive learning experience or a trauma of some kind that causes us enough pain to force us to reconsider our prejudices and presuppositions to awaken us. For this reason, we often need to hear an unfamiliar voice to bring us to see reality from another point of view. This is, I believe, an example of legitimate suffering that helps us to prevent the development of neurosis predicted by Jung, that was also predicted by Jesus, who said:

> *For whoever wants to save their life will lose it,*
> *but whoever loses their life for me will find it*
> (Matt 16:25).

But what does it mean? Is to deliberately harm ourselves by some act of penance such as wearing a hair shirt to "*mortify the flesh*" to subdue our human passions? Or is it to make ourselves deliberately obnoxious Bible Bashers who do the opposite of what the Golden Rule requires so that we suffer as social outcasts? I don't think so. I know enough about my own religious impulses to know that my worst moments have often had some pretentious religious motivation, such as self-righteousness. My conclusion from these experiences is that it is often the unexpected events from which we learn the most about suffering or "*losing our lives for Jesus.*" I now understand this to mean that I must unhappily give up my delusions and misapprehensions and replace them with a revelation of truth about myself for my greater good. Many of us are unwilling to experience this type of ego death or *poverty of the spirit*, as Jesus calls it because it requires a type of suffering, perhaps unique to this modern age when we spend great effort, time, money and technology to insulate ourselves from any slight discomfort, let alone a major upset.

The suffering that I call ego death is a phase of self-surrender and transition from a state of self-delusion, to a new state of conscious reality that continues in cycles of fundamental transformation of the psyche, according to Jung.[1] In my personal experience, it is accompanied by tears of despair, resignation, hope and finally, tears of joy as we eventually leave what is false and partial behind and move toward something better, more life-giving, more satisfying and fulfilling. More human. The challenge for Christians, is that many of us think that by reading, interpreting and applying Bible stories that we can automatically solve the problems of humanity, especially our own spiritual and emotional problems. This allows enormously intelligent, articulate, successful, well read and capable people like John MacArthur (from Chapter Two) to excoriate other Christians for their "wrong belief," while giving himself a free pass in the "correct belief" stakes, oblivious to the possibility of self-deception or the idea that a human science like psychology could be helpful to a Christian as he discounts the possibility out of hand. I am not saying that John MacArthur is totally deluded, or that M Scott Peck is the source of all wisdom, over and above the Bible. On the contrary, we are so familiar with what the Bible teaches that we insulate ourselves against its insights to the extent that when it says, *"all have sinned,"* we think it is talking about someone else, other than us.

Although many of us do need to hear another voice, like Balaam's ass who sees realities to which we are blind, I am not saying that we all must be disassembled, as it were, pulled apart and rebuilt from the inside out. I am saying, however, that we must be renewed by Jesus who will strip away the falsehoods and delusions within us as we engage in a conscious process of renewal and transformation, enabled by the Holy Spirit working through the Golden Rule and our obedience to Jesus Christ, as we discover the meaning of his love which never ends.

---

1 Wikipedia.

Ego death

The occasions in my life where I have felt devastating grief have been mercifully few, but each of them has caused a profound shift in my attitudes to my own deluded self-importance. The term Ego Death is appropriate as death suggests something we avoid with every ounce of our being, to escape what feels like the worst thing that could ever happen to us. Each incident had to do with what I thought was the meaning of my life: my family, my business career and financial security, my faith and my accompanying behavioral roles. In each case, what I thought was a massive failure was a new beginning where circumstances changed as my perception of myself also changed.

Ego death means, I think, something the same as Jesus' other obscure teachings about cutting off our hands and plucking out our eyes and leaving families for the sake of the Kingdom. These statements are intended to provoke a strong reaction within us, of either rejection or acceptance following many years of struggle with the issue at stake. An example is the question that Jesus asked of Peter who had gone back fishing after the crucifixion,

> *Simon, son of John, do you love me more than these? (fish)* (Jn 21:15).

I believe that each of us will at some time in our life, have a crisis of loving God, or loving the lesser, ordinary benefits of life when the question will be asked of us plainly, "Do you love these false passions, or even these real people, more than you love God?"

Do you love a false image of yourself?

Narcissists are often very intelligent, clever people who rise to the top of organizations or society. They are remarkable, not for their achievements so much as the way they treat other people to gain high public status and success in their own terms. The question we must ask ourselves, is *what would happen to me if the whole false edifice of my life came crashing down like Job, standing before God?* If today, I stood before Jesus for his evaluation of my life on his terms rather than mine, how well would I stand to such scrutiny? If I was to apply the tests given to the Seven Churches in Revelation Chapters 2-3, I would have to say, not so well, because none of us is sinless, we have all fallen short of the Glory of God, despite how well we can selectively quote Bible texts to convince ourselves otherwise. I suggest that this delusion is so insidious, that those of us who are most successful and have the most public acclaim, are those who are most at risk of being narcissists. The difficulty for accomplished people is that they can't tell if they are deluded unless they see themselves from another's point of view and accept their judgement rather than our own approval.

The reason we must "*lose our lives*" as Jesus said we must, is because we are so hard to teach about what is ultimately good, as against what our egotistical nature wants for itself. According to a Native American Indian myth, it is as if there is a continual war within us between a black dog who is selfish and a white dog who is sociable. Whichever dog we feed the most wins. When we avoid criticism and continually approve of ourselves, we risk becoming blind to our shortcomings. However, when we relate to others who have our best interests in mind (or even our enemies who don't) then we have a greater opportunity to learn about ourselves, from them. This includes our relationship with God, who created us for his pleasure and expresses his love towards us for our mutual benefit. Genesis 1 begins with God declaring his pleasure in his creative handiwork, which he has initiated for his own purposes and enjoyment and declares it to be "*very good.*" God's pleasure is displayed in the story of Adam and Eve, who he created for company and with whom he walked in the cool of the evening. At the other end of the Bible in The Revelation of St John, the writer concludes with the declaration:

> *You are worthy, our Lord and God, to receive glory and honor and power, for you created all things, and by your will they were created and have their being* (Rev 4:11).

In this statement, John recognizes and extols God for his accomplishments, as he ascribes unique greatness to him, which is a recognition of God's love foreshadowed.

> *I will proclaim the name of the* LORD. *Oh, praise the greatness of our God! He is the Rock, his works are perfect, and all his ways are just. A faithful God who does no wrong, upright and just is he...* (Deut 32:2).
>
> *And he passed in front of Moses, proclaiming, "The* LORD, *the* LORD, *the compassionate and gracious God, slow to anger, abounding in love and faithfulness, maintaining love to thousands, and forgiving wickedness, rebellion and sin. I will give compassion to those to whom I am compassionate* (Ex 34: 6-7).

These texts combined suggest to me that God who is love, receives his enjoyment from the fulfilment of his desire to share it with another being who would enjoy it with him, resonating with the quote from C.S. Lewis; *There are far, far better things ahead than any we leave behind.*

Love as a universal force

Isaac Newton's discovery that gravity is a universal constant revolutionized science and unlocked countless other related principles of science that continue to drive the modern world. Similarly, I propose that love is an even greater universal constant than gravity. Herein lies the difference between science and faith as it is an aspect of love. Science is a study of objective facts and the intricacies of the material world of time, space, energy and matter. Love is just as evident as gravity and arguably, just as important, because human consciousness and relationships cannot function without it. Like faith, however, love is not a force whose existence can be proven scientifically because it only exists on a spiritual level of relationship. It is never independent of human relationships between each other and God because that is how it is designed: to be available only to those who seek God himself, rather than his power, and are prepared to put all of their trust and hope in the possibility that he rewards those who seek him. It is, I believe, evidence of God's mysterious spiritual presence and life force in us.

Love is so important and precious that there are many counterfeits and counterfeiters, who use the concept of love to sell cosmetics, cars and snake oil without the slightest hint of irony. This counterfeiting is especially true of those who sell religion for reasons other than love. Love is one of the first words that we say to children, which they seem to immediately understand and use to express their relationship to their parents. It is also the most powerful and intimate word that can be expressed between two people, who intend to share their lives together. Because of its great value, love is a word whose meaning is corrupted perhaps more than any other. Consequently, when the word love is used to describe relationships, especially with God, it must be carefully defined to prevent its misuse. Even the dictionary definition: a *profoundly tender, passionate affection for another person,* is misleading and woefully inadequate, which is why I prefer Thomas Aquinas' definition, shared also by M Scott Peck, that love is an act of the will, to *seek the highest good for another.* This definition encompasses all other legitimate possible uses and definitions of the term. I propose then, that life in the Cosmos continues to exist because we are the apogee of God's handiwork, who he loves and sustains for his pleasure.

Love is measured as pleasure

God's love is fulfilled and experienced as his pleasure, just as it is also is with us. The problem comes when any of us take pleasure or a sense of accomplishment of any kind into our own hands as self-congratulation. Pleasure should always be an outcome of purposeful fulfillment in a relationship which we must attribute to the other, which I describe as righteousness, peace and joy, in the Holy Spirit. The other extreme is narcissism, where we fall in love with our own false self-image, or worse, develop the contemptuous indifference of a sociopath, whose pleasure comes from inflicting harm on others.

I propose that finding satisfaction in relationships is a normal outcome of an ordinary life, lived with reasonable faithfulness and accountability to each other and to God. I say "reasonable" because none of us is perfect. We are, however, forgiven for our unfaithfulness and failure if we genuinely seek each other's mercy and forgiveness for our failings. Those who were least likely to ask for forgiveness were not just those upon whom we would often like to heap condemnation, such as the woman caught in adultery who was presented to Jesus as a test of his conformance to the law. Rather, Jesus saved his criticism for her self-righteous accusers.

Pleasure, self-satisfaction or happiness alone should not be the objective of our lives. Rather, they should be outcomes of doing the right things in the right way, not accomplished goals for which we give ourselves credit. However, when satisfaction becomes a goal that displaces relationships for which we were designed, I believe we have an insurmountable problem of having an unachievable goal. Not only is it unachievable, it will not lead us to make the sorts of discoveries required by the complexities of life. Self-satisfaction is therefore, a cheap counterfeit of the real thing that the ego desires for its narcissistic self as an alternative to the fulness of God's love revealed as the highest fulfillment of all relationships, including between two people.

The ego's ability to create this delusion, is why it must be restrained to the point of death, so as our ego may be reborn into a transformed state, where it may return to doing its proper job, of seeking to achieve the highest possible good.

The inward and outward journey of love

I remember a discussion I heard in my church as a child about the evils of the "social gospel." This discussion continues today as an increasingly polarized debate about whether Christians should be predominantly inward looking, as evangelicals usually are, or outward looking, as progressives are more inclined to be. My experience is that these positions are usually more political than spiritual, rendering them unhelpful in any discussion about faith in Jesus Christ or our place in the Kingdom of God. In my view, this impasse can be resolved by the proper application of the Golden Rule, but first, we need to understand the competing positions. Evangelicals have been traditionally concerned with the salvation of souls by their personal acceptance of Jesus as Lord and Savior as the solution to all human and social ills. Progressives are concerned with achieving universal salvation by the reform of social issues relating to justice, equity and fairness, usually by changes to the law or by overturning social structures. Both positions have apparently strong biblical support. Evangelicals quote as their key text:

> For God so loved the world that he gave his one and only Son, that whoever believes in him shall not perish but have eternal life (Jn 3:16).

Progressives like to quote the Lord's Prayer:

> ...your kingdom come, your will be done, on earth as it is in heaven...(Matt 6:10) and Jesus' statement: ...if anyone gives even a cup of cold water to one of these little ones who is my disciple, truly I tell you, that person will certainly not lose their reward (Matt 10:42).

The extremes are reflected on the one hand, in the eschatology held by some evangelicals who say that Jesus will return and take the faithful to heaven before the world is destroyed in the Apocalypse. Some progressives, on the other hand, believe that Christ will not return until Christians have ushered in God's Kingdom by changing Earth into paradise as a result of social actions and legal reform. I believe that neither of the extreme positions is even reasonable, let alone true to the message of the Bible or historic Christianity. I think it is true to say that the gospel of Jesus includes social welfare, but it is not the gospel.

My yardstick in this debate is to consider how Jesus related to his disciples by asking them to follow him despite their personal faults, which we know were eventually ironed out over the longer period of their lives. Certainly, Jesus said that we must be *"born again of the spirit"* to have a place in his Kingdom, but whether this is a single moment in time or a process of learning is not so clear. It seems to me from both the examples of the Bible and the heroes of faith of Christian history, as well as from my own life, that the journey of faith is never an either/or situation. It is always a personal inward journey as Jesus and his Spirit occupy my consciousness, displacing my selfishness. Once the Divine presence is within us, it is always expressed by an outward movement, as we learn from him that no one is saved by their inward journey alone. We are saved by love which must now express itself through us toward others. (I hope that this is not defined as "works righteousness" but that is how I understand it). Certainly, the journey begins with a moment of obedience to Jesus and the initial confrontation between God's love and our selfishness when we are justified by our faith in him. But then we must immediately apply what we have learned about ourselves to our relationships with others, in an outward movement.

This is precisely what is accomplished by the Golden Rule as we become conscious of our selfish ego, which must then die and be resurrected to do good works toward others before we make real progress as disciples of Jesus.

Discovering levels of love

This diagram represents the experiences we have of love as the triangle, ME, which is my physical body, with its strengths, skills and abilities. I am encircled by my soul, which includes my mind, knowledge, emotions and will. And my spirit—the power and influence of my will to do and act.

Ego death

As I grow, I learn about the four main kinds of love (as discussed in Chapter 4) through my relationship to others, beginning with the highest form as my mother's unconditional self-giving love for me, experienced at her breast. This love is called *agape*, a reflection of God's self-sacrificing, unconditional love for me. As an infant becomes a brother, sister or a friend, we experience empathy, called *storge* and *philia*, which is love for a friend or family member. Through further development and achieving greater intellectual, emotional, physical and sexual maturity, the child becomes an adult and experiences new dimensions of love within another set of boundaries. *Eros* is expressed as romantic love, and then as erotic sexual love toward another.

The ultimate form of love is *agape*, as it embraces the range of possibilities included in a purposeful relationship between, for example, a man and a woman who join to make a family. In this ideal state, the full range of *eros*, *philia* and *agape* are realized within the boundaries of respect and fidelity of a monogamous and productive marriage. To not have those elements of love and the relevant boundaries in the fullness of a relationship results in a couple having a sub-optimal experience of love and a reduced capacity to enjoy life and confront its sorrows. When people in an optimal relationship experience loss and despair, there are two to encourage one another back to a normal state, perhaps by accepting a new reality. If it is an individual with no relationship with another person, then they are often more vulnerable to the difficulties of life, unless their purpose and meaning is projected to a cause greater than the individual in which their full potential for love is realized would be a godly, transcendent cause.

As I develop, my experience of love becomes more integrated with my whole being, body, soul and spirit. *Eros* moves from being self-gratifying toward the gratification of my beloved, within very clear boundaries about who that person can be. For instance, it cannot be a family member, or an intimate partner of another person. As I become more independent, *philia* becomes the legitimate expression of love toward family and friends. *Eros* provides the motivation for the creation of my own family where ego is sublimated by responsibility and a growing sense of *agape* toward my spouse and my offspring and extended relationships.

As we make progress doing what we think we are supposed to do, we tend to go in one of two necessary but opposite directions.

The inward journey

At first we go on the inward journey. This is necessary to discover over time, who we are, what is our place in the world and who we are in our important relationships. We accomplish this by projecting the assumptions we have inherited from our family and culture to see if they are reliable. If our assumptions are realistic, then we flourish and make further progress. If our assumptions are wrong, we founder on the rocks of life. If we are really deluded about our self-importance, we end in ever-decreasing circles until we disappear into insignificance.

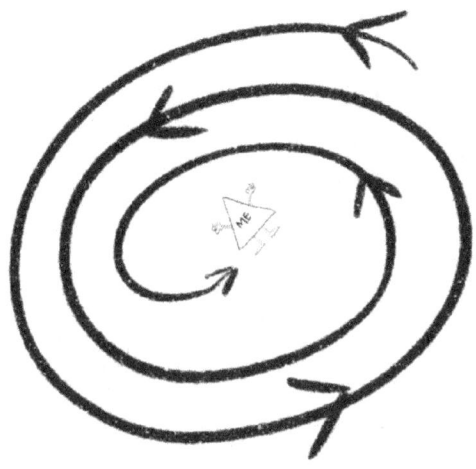

The outward journey

The other alternative is to become so outwardly focused, that we become dissipated like the beauty queen, who says she loves everybody and just wants everybody to be happy, like her.

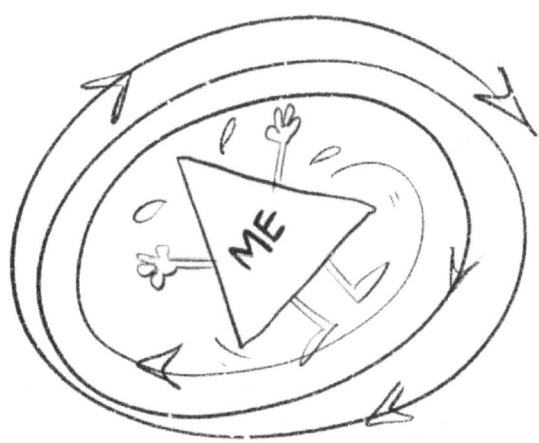

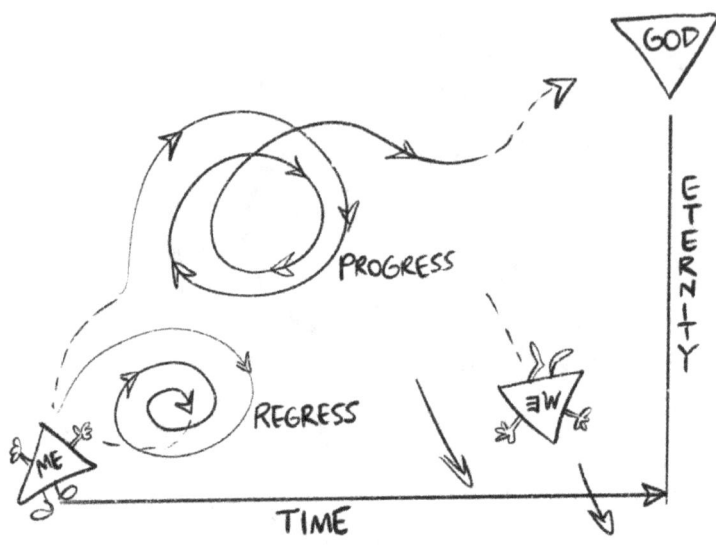

Transformation toward the image of God

The Golden Rule journey is when our inward and outward journeys are focused on and directed by God in a continuing cycles that avoids regress by making steady progress. My use of the term "Transformation toward the image of God" and the illustration above is my very rough heuristic for personal spiritual growth toward God. I am transformed toward Christ-likeness as I grow in love. We make necessary progress toward God with the inward journey by becoming conscious of our relationship to him, which we resolve by accepting his offer of grace. This is called justification that satisfies God's demand for justice, by my acceptance of Jesus' sacrifice on the cross for my sins. My act of faith in him commences my becoming "spiritually born again" as his spirit invites me into his Kingdom and then begins to infiltrate my being. If I reject his invitation, I remain in an unchanged state of separation from God. My claim to be "Christian" means nothing if my practice of faith has not led me to increasingly love my neighbor as myself. This is the outward journey toward God, via my relationship with others. If I have not become more like Jesus, who I claim to follow, then my "faith" may be in vain. According to Paul:

> *Though I speak with the tongues of men and of angels, but have not love, I have become sounding brass or a clanging cymbal* (1 Cor 13).

Born again

I believe that most of us, if not all, must admit that our inward journey is usually somewhat irregular, as our un-transformed ego is engaged in this process of transformation, always seeks to re-assert itself over and above any other source of power or allegiance to God. I have depicted this as a circular battle where the skirmish is rewarded by making further upward progress. I know of some people who have displayed great religious promise only to decline into the oblivion of rebellion and bitter despair because they have mis-used their privillege. Nor am I suggesting that the battle is regular as the straight diagonal line indicates. Speaking for myself, my born-again moment was as a 12-year-old, petrified by the prospect of being left behind if my family were "gathered up" into heaven in a pre-millennial rescue by Jesus. Although I believe that my salvation began on that day in 1959, I certainly don't think that it was complete by any means as I have wavered, lost faith, regained it, made progress and slipped back many times. However, seen over the longest time, I have made steady progress toward God's kingdom and toward sharing the mind of Christ in many ways. Admittedly, I cannot claim that I love God with all my being, and my neighbor as myself in any complete sense. I would not, therefore, claim any sort of achievement of great holiness because I know myself to well. Plus, I have far greater faith in God's grace and mercy that he will treat me justly, rather than in my own righteousness.

My progress toward God's kingdom is derailed most of all, when I am not willing to give up my familiar illusion of being in control and retaining ultimate authority over myself. In the worst case, we are subject to the presence and power of another spirit that is not of God. In its mildest form, it is the malign Spirit of the Age, also known as the Zeitgeist. Just as our human spirit is already in a fallen state, so also, is the Spirit of the Age as it is rebels against the Divine Presence of God as it has done since the Fall of Man in the Garden of Eden. If our initial struggle is resolved by us submitting our sovereignty (right to self-determinations) to God's sovereignty, then we have made progress indicated by another circle of struggle forming as new issues present themselves. If we have resolved to engage in this struggle obedient to Christ's command, then we apply the Golden Rule as this is the test to determine which dog wins the next round. The extent to which we stay the course of obedience to Jesus, is the extent that our body, soul and spirit is strengthened by the struggle and the more our mind is transformed to share the mind of Jesus. If we have allowed the black dog of our ego to win, then we make no progress, or we regress backwards.

If we continue to allow the spirit of God to be the prevailing force within us, then we begin to form a symbiotic relationship of interdependence, where we continue the outward journey of relationship to others and God, that was begun by our practising the Golden Rule.

Moving from ME to US

The key to my understanding of the Golden Rule is that when we treat our neighbors as we would like to be treated, so the inward journey of transformation begins. As we are confronted by our delusions of egotistical selfishness, which must be overcome by the death our ego, so our conscious minds are renewed. We then become aware that our progress is dependent, not on our saying that we love God, but on our love for others to the extent that we can make this conscious choice. Transformation is manifest in our relationships as righteousness, peace and joy in the Holy Spirit which we experience as pleasure, because it is only due to God's presence that his fruits become apparent in us.

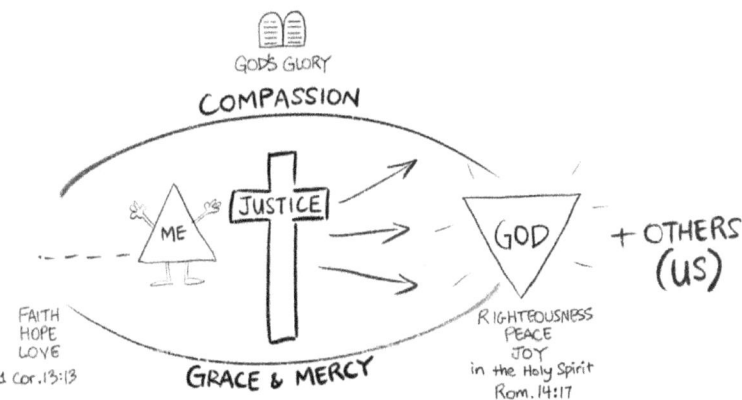

INTERLUDE 2

During November 2018, we visited friends who live in a Baptist monastery called the Community of the Transfiguration at Teasdale, a two-hour drive from Melbourne. The next day, I attended an event called the "Awakening: Australia for Jesus" at Marvel Stadium across the road from where we live in Docklands. With no planning on my part, I could not have experienced a greater contrast of Christian expression and witness if I tried. The monastery is a unique Baptist order of people who make a life-long commitment to live, contemplate, worship and work together in one of the most beautiful sanctuaries I have ever seen, filled with icons and deep symbolism. I found the experience powerful because my visualization of their shared worship of God was tangible. As attractive as this was, though, it did not compel me to want to join with them as their spiritual expectations are far higher than mine and I know that I would not fit. The event at Marvel Stadium, on the other hand, demanded my participation.

My interest in this event was piqued because Bill Johnson, the speaker in the afternoon session, is one of my heroes of faith, having attended his conferences, read his books and watched his videos for the past few years. Bill, the senior pastor at Bethel church in Redding, Northern California, was named by his pastor father after Billy Graham, in the hope that he might emulate the great evangelist, as he has, although in a slightly different manner. Bill Johnson is the unappointed global leader of the "apostolic reformation" movement within Pentecostalism, which emphasizes the spiritual gifts of power as the peak of Christian experience. Bill was true to form during the service and made several appeals that Christians' lives should be oriented to *"Heal the sick, raise the dead and drive out demons."* I assume by this Johnson means that all Christians should take literally Jesus' words to his disciples about performing miracles, as this is Bill's own life mission. When I attended the Awakening earlier in the week, I was concerned with the Workshop Schedule of activities which ran at the same time as the main event claiming to be *"For everyone who wants to grow and learn about evangelism, healing, business and worship...speakers from around the world training and equipping you in a practical way to live like Jesus in your daily life"* This is an impressive list of priorities that does not mention the first and most basic duty of all Christians, to be obedient to the teachings of Jesus. I wonder how it can be that there are millions of Christians busy with worship, healing or evangelism, that have not yet learned how to be a Christian or how to become transformed into his image by the renewal of our minds as an act of simple obedience.

Christianity seemingly by necessity, always ends up with a religious specialization such as Orthodox, Catholic, Protestant, Calvinist, Armenian, Baptist, Methodist, Pentecostal, Apostolic, Brethren, Seventh Day Adventist or some such that emphasizes one aspect of Christian faith while de-emphasizing many others, to say nothing of pseudo-Christian religious innovations such as Mormonism or Jehovah's Witnesses. Of course, it would be worse to aim at nothing and end up with spiritual apathy, which is how most of this generation of young adults have approached religion. The worst of all, in my view, is to take it upon yourself to condemn all the others, as the Jehovah's Witnesses do while they blindly elevate themselves to be the only ones with the truth that they have based upon a very peculiar interpretation of scripture, that no-one else shares.

To Do List Christianity

I would much prefer that we tried to get to the essence of what faith in Jesus Christ is and to see our specializations for what they are; usually a corrective footnote to history rather than a new

Interlude 2

religion that answers all the religious problems of humanity. I am reminded of this universal duty to be obedient to Jesus every time I recite the Nicene Creed. While I am aware of the potential for corruption that surrounded the Council of Nicaea under Emperor Constantine, the Nicene Creed is an artefact of church history that is worth preserving because it is widely recognized. But here is the thing. When our religious traditions don't have a specialization such as spiritual gifts, healing the sick, celebration of the sacraments or aggressive evangelism, we seem to accommodate every secular trend ending up with liberal progressivism and universalism where the only good thing you can say is that they don't reproduce themselves and die a slow religious death. Nor is the antidote to try to cover all bases as some evangelicals try to do by being a contemporary and welcoming church, responding to the needs of "seekers". What I also notice is that some Christian groups without a specialization end up with what I call a shopping list or a To Do List approach to Christian faith. They usually have a highly disciplined approach which includes: baptism, daily Bible reading and prayer, living by "Christian principles" (no sex outside marriage, no smoking, drinking or dancing) separation from worldly activities, hospitality and service to others in your community, no political involvement, regular church attendance, giving to the missions and to the poor, giving tithes to the church, respect for church leaders, encouragement of youth leadership, honour for the traditions of your faith, putting family first and to a lesser degree, systematic Bible interpretation with reassuring apologetics, accompanied by denominational theology, doctrine, dogma and so on. Some of my best friends have written books that contain these lists, or they organize their ministry and their church around such disciplines. This leaves me, according to my wife, as a constant critic who finds fault and picks nits with the traditions and priorities that I don't like.

The problem is that I agree with most of what they say; all these things are important and necessary in their place, but these lists are usually not differentiated or ordered into high or low in importance, simple or complex, advanced or beginners, as inputs to growth or outputs from growth. Plus... Can you see that I have just compounded the problem by creating even more lists?

Hot Rod ministry

The solution, I believe, is the begin again by learning to be Christians by doing what Jesus said to do by teaching the Golden Rule as the first order of business, always, in every undertaking of the Christian church, for ever. I hope this book has provided a reasonable account of why this is so, and what the process is, but I cannot say anything with any more force than it is the Great Commandment of Jesus Christ, for his church. What I do know for sure, is that discipleship (or apprenticeship as Dallas Willard describes it) is necessary for us to begin to learn how to be Christians and how to begin to sort out the difference between what is secular of the world, and what is spiritual of God.

One of my heroes is an American drag racer, *Big Daddy* Don Garlits, about whom I have written an as-yet unpublished book called; *The Power of Love: The Life and times of Big Daddy Don Garlits.* Garlits has been my hero since I identified with him in my early teenage years. He was a pioneer of the clandestine sport of drag racing which emerged out of the post-war boom of returned servicemen and women as they sought to reintegrate into civilian life, particularly in sunny southern California. Garlits, though, in true underdog style, was not from California, but from the everglades of Florida, where he and his brother Ed, built hot-rods out of junk (called swamp rats by their competitors) and went racing on the streets and dis-used air fields, of which there were many. Garlits inherited some of his father's alternative beliefs and engineering genius and became a gritty competitor who thought

Interlude 2

nothing of crossing the USA to compete against the best dragsters that California had to offer, accompanied and encouraged by his wife, Patricia. Mid-career, while recovering in hospital following an accident in which an explosion cut his car in half, taking part of his right foot with it, Garlits had an encounter with God that changed his life. Subsequently, he was inspired to redesign his dragster so that an engine explosion or fire would be behind him, rather than in front. Some time later, while contemplating sponsorship arrangements for a new car, Garlits imagined putting the cross and the words *God is Love* on the cowl, just ahead of the cockpit, in recognition of his revitalized Christian faith that he shared with Pat. While Garlits was well known for his engineering brilliance and his hard-nosed competitiveness, his faith had not been explored to any degree, so I decided to present him as a model, not of a perfect Christian, but of a drag racer whose faith overarched his success. To edit my book, I chose another hot-rodder that I had known since the early 1980's, a magazine publisher named Larry O'Toole, from Castlemaine in central Victoria. During the editing process, Larry told me that as a young man, he had considered a role as a Roman Catholic priest but had implausibly transferred what he thought was a call to a religious life, to a call as a hot-rodder. Even as I write these words, I carefully check what I am saying, as if to be sure that I mean what I say. Yes, Larry O'Toole's godly mission is to be a hot rodder. To bring enjoyment, fun and meaning and purpose to people's lives, to be a responsible, reliable authority bringing order and legal compliance to an activity that would otherwise be illegal and harmful. Not only is Larry an excellent hot rodder, he is an accomplished writer of books on topics other than hot rods. Predictably, he is also an excellent citizen who with his wife Mary has created a major publishing business that serves many interests. Larry has served as chairman of the Castlemaine Economic Development Committee and as a board member of the Rural Water Commission. He was also a Board Member of the Castlemaine

State Festival for 18 years and a constant promoter of his region and his industry. Currently he is chairman of the Castlemaine Hot Rod Centre Limited, a not for profit organisation responsible for an ambitious project to fulfill Castlemaine's boast of being the hot rod capital of the world, employing hundreds in a local industry worth millions of dollars, exporting parts and information globally. This organization is currently establishing an extensive resource centre for everything to do with the Specialty Automotive market including education and training, an active interpretation centre, tourism and retirement living. I know that the evangelists and fundamentalists among us will be saying, "Yes, but does he preach the gospel of Jesus?" My answer is that this is the gospel of Jesus Christ, that we take his words seriously and *treat others as we would like to be treated.*

I think this story about hot rods and drag racing is important enough to mention here, because I believe Christians need to have a clear view of the purpose God has for our lives, so that we can continue on the journey with measures of our progress toward a goal for which we provide our own motivation, clearly in view. It is not that we live perfect lives by any means, a mistake I made of idealizing Don Garlits before I met him. However, I consider that both Garlits and O'Toole have had a significant influence on many thousands, if not millions of young men, encouraging them toward what our vicar, Matt Williams calls "righteous relationships" where they are very conscious of the influence they have on others. I consider Bill Johnson's purpose of the restoration of the Apostolic mandate to *"Heal the sick, raise the dead and drive out demons"* as a special, rather than a general calling. Hot-rodding is another, perhaps less ambitious specialization.

I certainly do believe that we should all have very high expectations of ourselves as we seek to do what God wants of us, especially where we intersect with the lives of others. Some of us will have very specific ministry roles where we teach, preach and pray for others to be released from spiritual death, disease and disorder. But this is not our primary mission. We are called to give our hearts and minds to Jesus by obedience to his commands for the purposes of God's Kingdom to serving one another with our legitimate passions and abilities that we are called to share.

Some of us will heal the sick and cast out demons. Some of us will become pilots, doctors and nurses, while others, like Elaine and I, will teach kids, fix cars, write books about hot-rods as our day job. Of all Jesus' instructions and commands, none are so clearly unequivocal as the Great Commandment, *to love God with all our heart, mind, soul and strength and our neighbor as ourselves.* It seems that if I replace this one imperative with the alternative of religious activities, such as miracles and wonders as my primary goal, then I am at risk of doing what Paul warns us of in 1 Corinthians:

> *If I speak in the tongues of men or of angels, but do not have love, I am only a resounding gong or a clanging cymbal. If I have the gift of prophecy and can fathom all mysteries and all knowledge, and if I have a faith that can move mountains, but do not have love, I am nothing. If I give all I possess to the poor and give over my body to hardship that I may boast, but do not have love, I gain nothing* (1 Cor 13:1-3).

Moreover, I certainly do not want to be constantly condemned for my lack of hyper-faith, in which so many in the Pentecostal/Apostolic movement seem to specialize. Rather, I want to learn to be like Jesus, who fulfilled his Father's wishes perfectly, because the father loved the son and the son loved the father in return. Following this simple act of obedience, if I am strongly called or motivated to become a miracle worker, then I am all for it – provided that a foot-hold toward a Divine achievement is not actually a stumbling block.

My life experience is one of almost unbroken enjoyment from my childhood, through my teenage years into adulthood. I met my wife, Elaine, at church when I was 19 and she was 16 years old. The 50 and more years that we have been together have been characterized by fun, excitement, adventure and enjoyment, not because we didn't face any challenges, but because we faced them together, full of optimism and hope. Soon after we were married, Elaine resigned her teaching job as we relocated to West Australia for a work opportunity with my employer. Back in Melbourne a couple of years later, we bought our first house without having saved a deposit by both taking second jobs and living with Elaine's parents for a few months. When we bought the house, we realized that if we sold our car and lived on bread and water for a while longer, we could save enough to travel overseas for six months, which we did. When a couple of years later our first child arrived, we automatically assumed the hardship of just scraping by financially and living from each pay day to the next because we had confidence for the future in each other plus the support of our families and friends. Two years later, the adventure of life together allowed us to build a new house just as our second child was born. Then our third child, two and a half years after that. The middle years of family life were full of fun with our kids and friends, long distance car trips, camping, and church and business adventures along the way, including another short-lived interstate relocation

Interlude 2

for work, and a return to our family home after 20 months on a farm and in a Christian community in Sale, Victoria. This is not to say that it was all plain sailing, or that I don't regret having made some bad decisions in business and with other life choices. But as a couple and as a family, we have thrived. I have had some great successes and some equally great failures in business. Elaine has had a magnificent career as a teacher, which she considers to be her ministry. I fulfilled a life goal by designing and building a racing car to satisfy my creative urge and need for speed. Our kids are all married and have presented us with five grandkids and counting. Elaine resumed her teaching career after ten years as a mum, which culminated in her becoming a school principal for the last six years of her working life. My forays into business have given me great satisfaction and great anxiety; but my role as a husband, father and grandfather have become deeper, more purposeful, more satisfying and fulfilling every year.

I have enjoyed the many benefits of being born into a Christian family in a Western democracy based on the Judeo-Christian tradition. This is prevenient grace that is available to everyone who inherits these benefits as a foundation to life. In all cases, however, this huge advantage of inheritance is consolidated by the personal choices we make – to continue with the Christian faith we inherited culturally, with a very personal decision to accept Jesus as Lord, and to recognize His Lordship in every area of our lives. This is the necessary decision that enables us to experience personal grace – a gift of God only available to us when we are humble enough to ask for it and to accept it. As I became more aware of the benefits I have enjoyed, I commenced a ministry to men with David Wraight called "BunchOBlokes" based on our shared life experience of the Golden Rule. The point we stressed is that if we make the decision to practice Christ's teaching seriously, and stick at it however imperfectly for long enough, then we begin to experience the benefits of greater fulfilment and satisfaction in our family lives, in particular. This experience seems to be very uniform among many Christians that we know, despite the difficulties and mistakes we make, predominantly, because we can come back to refresh our purpose and obtain renewed guidance every day with the continual promise that even as our days begin to count down, the best is still yet to come. Our experience is that God is the giver of good gifts and His commands are not burdensome.

9

ARE WE THERE YET?

Whoever finds their life will lose it, and whoever loses their life for my sake will find it. Matt 10 39

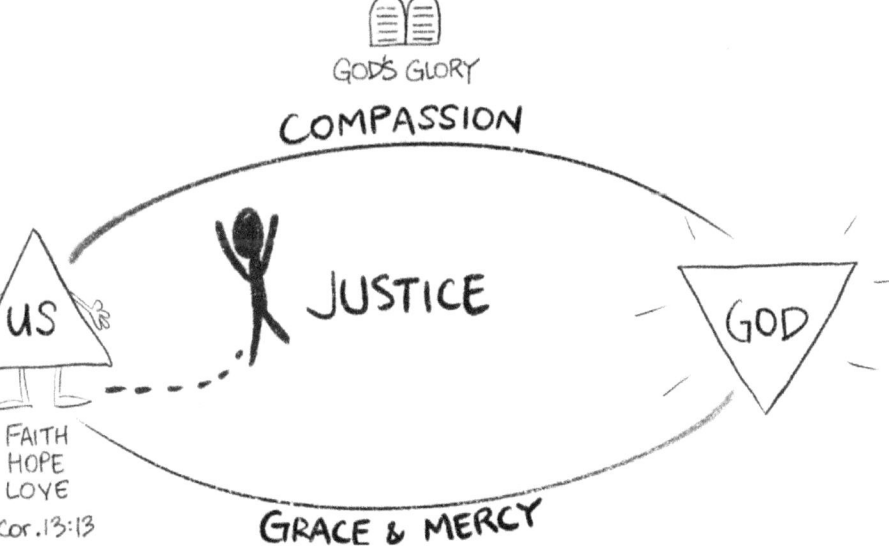

We began a journey together in pursuit of two related goals. One was to share a dream about a place called Paradise, which is found in a Kingdom so fantastic that it is almost unimaginable. If you have begun to wonder about your place in Paradise, then that is real progress. The other goal was to learn about the Golden Rule, which I believe to be a map of how to get to Paradise with instructions as to how to learn its unique language from someone who has been there before us. So far so good. Despite the obstacles we have overcome I hope we are closer to our destination. To some extent, the obstacles are milestones that indicate the necessary tests that we have taken to show that we are learning the skills required to complete the journey.

Some obstacles are useful because they warn us about what not to do, provided we see them as tests and do not become distracted from our goal. Obstacles often appear as criticisms from others who do not share our goal or even see the barriers that must be overcome. In any case, we should take these tests with confidence, because the worst thing that can happen to us on a journey such as this, is to discover that we have gone down the wrong road or a wrong direction that took us from the right path. Both diversions can be corrected.

Our greatest source of inspiration for the journey is to continue to dream about Paradise, and our clearest instructions are from the Bible. We have discovered that with these two combined, and with the help of friends, we experience not just some illusory "pie in the sky when you die," but real food and drink to sustain us on the road, because our guide is none other than Jesus, who has made the way possible and has sent his Spirit to teach, comfort and correct us along the way. As we have learned to read the map and have followed his instructions to watch out for one another, so we have begun to learn the language of the Kingdom. It is called the Language of Love, and we learn it according to the Golden Rule. The Language of Love is the *lingua franca* not just of Paradise, but of humanity, and without it, we cannot exist anywhere in any fully satisfying and sustainable way, because it is how God speaks and relates to us. Even if we are completely lost on the journey, to learn the language of love will get us back on track.

Perhaps to our surprise, we have seen that versions of the Golden Rule are common to many of the histories of humankind – usually in a diluted form where the real meaning has been watered down over hundreds of generations, except for the Jewish nation, whose religion demanded that the secrets revealed by God were written down and preserved in the Bible for our benefit.

I recently watched Bob Mumford discuss what he calls The Road Makers,[1] which he explains is about preparing the way for the Lord, just as John the Baptist did for Jesus when he said that he is:

> *A voice of one calling in the wilderness, 'Prepare the way for the Lord, make straight paths for him. Every valley shall be filled in, every mountain and hill made low. The crooked roads shall become straight, the rough ways smooth. And all people will see God's salvation* (Lk 3:5-6).

Mumford suggests that this text is for all fellow travelers who are tasked with "preparing the way" to the Kingdom, both for themselves and for others in a continuous, present act of faithful obedience. Of course, I would like to add that this task is enabled

---

[1] https://youtu.be/eVBr9Y6WuIc

by the Golden Rule. This leads me to ask several questions: what does the Golden Rule require of us? What does it teach us about the values of the Kingdom? How do we know if we are speaking the language of love fluently?

Often, it appears that we need to re-learn the meanings of words beyond what we thought they meant. I believe that the *zeitgeist* of popular opinion in our democratic culture can have an enormously harmful effect upon our individual thinking, even as Christians – so much so that we may not be aware of its effect until we contrast what the Bible claims as reality with what our culture says it is. The question of sexual behavior is an example of this when what the surrounding culture says and what Jesus says are opposed to each other. If this is true, we need to re-learn what he says, in sharp contrast to what people say he says. Not just by studying words either, but by looking at the harmful effect of ignoring Jesus' instructions compared to the positive effect of obedience to him. The other thing we learn from the Golden Rule is that our thoughts, words and deeds need to be consistent with both our goal and our behavior. Beyond simple inconsistencies, whatever I think is good for me must also be good for you as this is the most basic test of what is acceptable. If this is so, then I must test anything I think is good to see if it is also acceptable to you. Likewise, any good that I want for myself I must also want for you. This is a glimpse into God's Kingdom where there are not a lot of rules. Just two in fact, like the rule that God gave to Adam and Eve in the Garden of Eden, not to eat of the tree of Good and Evil, put in the positive sense rather than the negative. As we have travelled, we have left our first-hand knowledge of evil behind, consigned to the dust of the road. The one rule of the Kingdom is two that are both the same:

> *To Love God with all our hearts, souls, minds and strength and our neighbor as ourselves.*

Have you noticed that systems of law created by humans have lots of rules? Every new problem seems to result in new laws that eventually overlap and contradict each other. The Kingdom of God is not like that because the one new law is written on our hearts because of the new beginning that Jesus gave us, and the way he taught us how to apply the law of love by thinking it through ourselves.

In answer to the question posed by this chapter; "Are we there yet?", the answer is *no*. We have made some progress toward our goal, but the fulness of the Kingdom exists in a time yet to come for which we are being prepared. At best, we can say that we experience the Kingdom of God *now but not yet,* because it is both present and future. As John suggests:

> ...*we have passed from death to life (1 Jn 3:14). He also says later: And so we know and rely on the love God has for us. God is love. Whoever lives in love lives in God, and God in them. This is how love is made complete among us so that we will have confidence on the day of judgment: In this world we are like Jesus* (1 Jn 4:16-17).

Meanwhile, we are strangers in our present location because we don't quite fit in, but we are preparing for a land that is also strange to us because it is so different from what we are used to.

Strangers preparing for a strange land

The more we have come to know about our destination and about our journey, the more we have discovered that everything there seems to be inverted, somehow. Things are not always as they appear. For instance, we are already in this Kingdom, but we are not fully conscious of it; which is why we must learn its language – to become more aware of our presence in it. There are many details about this place that are unfamiliar to us. Things have a different feel about them. They are still real enough though – it is not as though our experiences are not real – because righteousness peace and joy is utterly tangible, but there is another quality about everything, an essence, a transcendent *spiritual* quality that is real and elusive at the same time. Yes, that's what it is; it's a spiritual place for which we had to become spiritually re-born to find our place in it.

The difficulty is that we cannot possess this spirituality; we can only be possessed by it; so we must be very careful to be sure that what we have found is the genuine article, the Real Deal, as there are always plenty of counterfeits. Can we tell just by looking at the effect this Spirit has on us? Are we experiencing any change? What is it? Are we becoming more like God, whose Kingdom this is? And anyway, how do we know? What the Bible calls the fruit of the Spirit is the best evidence. These fruits are the distinctive outcomes of what we believe and do as a result of our transformation – which, by the way, are the same as the *Competencies of the New Covenant* that we discussed previously. They are things that we learn to become and do, and the attitudes that produce *love, joy, peace, patience, kindness, goodness, faithfulness, gentleness, and self-control* that I summarize as a state of *righteousness, peace and joy in the Holy Spirit.*

As I write these words, I am reminded that I first heard the term righteousness, peace and joy in the Holy Spirit from Bob Mumford at a conference in 1984, and I have been thinking about it ever since. RPJ, he called it.

It is when we experience the initial euphoria of Divine love that we begin to understand this fruit and desire more. However, just like Spirit that gives us gifts, the gift is elusive. It is something I can receive and give to others in the same way, but I can make no demands upon it. Having tasted of the fruits of love, I want more, realizing at the same time that while my desire is good, I must bend toward the Arc of the Universe, toward God and his Kingdom, toward Jesus as Lord and savior, waiting patiently on the Holy Spirit if I am to receive more of what I now desire so much. But I cannot demand it or buy it with money or favors. There is, in fact, a price to pay. I cannot enter the Kingdom with my un-transformed mind intact. To allow my spirit to be re-born, my ego must die and let my *mind to be renewed by transformation of my spirit* to receive God's gift of grace, as it is available only when we are humble and poor in spirit. Before you get disheartened with all that there is to know and do, I would like to remind you that although your knowledge about the Kingdom, your place in Paradise, and even your knowledge about the Golden Rule is important, none of it qualifies you or prevents you from beginning your journey, as it is possible for you to learn on the road. If you have not yet taken your first step, may I encourage you to begin without delay and accompany me?

The loser who wins

When I was a child at Sunday School, we sang *Running over, running over my cup is full and running over...* It has taken me a long time to understand what this song means – that the greatest measure of success and fulfilment in life is not material. Running over alludes to the extent to which we are blessed ones who are being slowly transformed by faith in Jesus Christ, leaving us overwhelmed with a surprising sense of completeness and joy. The best description is to say that we are filled and running over with a sense of being blessed with holiness and joy. Normally, I don't like to use such religious language very much, because I object to its frequent misuse. But in this case, I have nothing better to say. As it turns out, I am in good company. CS Lewis, the literary scholar who, as an adult, was transformed from being an atheist to one of the best greatest Christian apologists ever and wrote a book about this experience called *Surprised by Joy*. Lewis began an intellectual journey for which he was very well equipped. But it ended up as a discovery of his whole being, body, soul and spirit, not just his mind.

In keeping with my suggestion about strangeness, our progress on the journey toward Paradise is not always measured how we first think it will be. Increasingly, we tend to agree with the thinking of Friedrich Nietzsche (who infamously declared God to be dead), whose ideas have permeated our culture. That is, we hold that human success is the realization of our *will to power*, as measured by our achievements, ambitions, and our striving to reach

the highest possible position in life. That, plus some Epicurean delights and post-modern ideas about social justice overlaid upon a much-diminished Christian model of relationships that we will consider later. I strongly protest Nietzsche and his destructive influence upon modern culture, as he thought Christianity was inherently weak and an abandonment of essential human strength. For myself, I claim that my greatest successes are now realized in the things that are different to the usual expectations of modern life. They include my faith in God, my wife and my family relationships, my friends, my church, and my citizenship, much of which are the fruit of that privilege, freedom and prosperity that I have enjoyed as a Baby Boomer. It is worth remembering, however, that many of these privileges and freedoms were won by generations of faithful people, some of whom died for them. But still, none of these fruits compare to what I have experienced of life as a *blessed one*, which I believe to be the greatest experience I can have, because every other experience is greatly enhanced by this one almost inexplicable thing. It is deeply ironic, though, that this form of success, if I could call it that, is measured inversely to any remaining *will to power* in me. Progress of this kind is not measured by what you get, so much as by what you give, and it has far more in common with those who gave their lives for freedom than those who insisted on their right to be free because they are powerful. This irony is compounded by the realization that this is both how this reality is experienced and how it is achieved. For example, relationships such as marriage can be measured by such a tangible thing as endurance and having kids. But who wants a marriage that just endures or counts the number of kids as a measure of its own quality and success? What if, instead, you could have a marriage that is filled with an overwhelming abundance of shared pleasure, enjoyment and satisfaction because of what you had contributed to it? This is the reality we can anticipate from our application of the Golden Rule, which requires us to take the initiative in doing good to others. Even in such everyday relationships, we must begin to use such obscure measures of success, because the ingredients of true fulfillment and progress are hard to pin down. If we still think that we achieve success in a relationship by the assertion of rights, then we must recalibrate our thinking, because true joy must be shared with our intimate partner, family and community. According to Jesus, in this upside-down reality, it is the winner who loses and the loser who wins.

How do I measure success?

Success, I have discovered, is not about getting more stuff – especially not money, sex, or power. They are important, but they are pathetic compared to this experience of a superabundance of God's goodness as a blessed one. I know this will sound like a predictable outcome of my Golden Rule theory, but that is exactly what it is. The more you give away, the more you get. This concept is what hucksters, crooks, snake oil salesmen and TV evangelists in white suits have been trying to get you to buy since the Prodigal Son left home. However, these things that we desperately hope are true are not "magic" as my granddaughter Sara insists, they are. They are the *substance of things hoped for, the evidence of things not yet seen* (Heb. 11:1). Nor are they discovered by taking huge leaps of faith, but by taking small steps that the spirit invites us to take as he gently proves *...the world to be in the wrong about sin and righteousness and judgment:* John 16:8.

For good measure, as you too ponder your concept of success, I would like to add a couple more ironic sayings that characterize this upside-down Kingdom:

> *Jesus saves, but we must do the work of accepting what he offers us for nothing and not take the credit.*
>
> *We live in an imperfect world, so we cannot expect perfection. But the worst possible result would be to discover at the end of my life, that what I had succeeded doing caused more harm than good.*

If you are thinking that I have departed from the rational mode of evaluating life, you are right. Since I have begun, I wonder if you would mind further indulging me a moment for a little bit of my opinion. Most certainties in the modern world are verified by the concept of "peer reviewed science" based upon what can be measured. However, so much of science is based upon unprovable assumptions, just like the belief in God, except that they are different categories of knowledge. Science, by definition, is limited to the observable material world of time, matter, energy and space, none of which can be defined in absolute terms as to what they are, let alone why or how these things exist. We just know that they do exist and can be *measured or described* in terms of what they do, but they cannot be defined absolutely. In the absence of proof, assumptions are required that we accept without question, and *a priori*, as a pre-supposition, based upon probability or the best explanation to fit the data. Belief in God, by comparison, requires our pre-supposition of his existence as creator of the universe, not because it can be scientifically proven, despite the overwhelming evidence. This is because we are dealing with matters beyond the limited scope of science and our ability to "see" or measure by conventional means. To say, as many do, that the material world and science are all that exists is to limit oneself to the measurable material world which we already know is not the full extent of reality. Theism and theology, then, are a much grander field of knowledge and experience because they include the world of mind, spirit, passion, emotion, faith, hope and love to which our souls respond, perhaps even more than our minds. Although none of these things of faith in God can be proven, life without them would be unbearable even if we ignore their relationship to the spiritual realm completely. Moreover, theism is not reliant upon the changing opinion of peer review. It is verified by the Bible, plus the unchanging word of God confirmed by thousands of years of human experience that we can personally put to the test with our small steps of faith, confirmed in our relationships.

This underlies my question to myself, "How do I measure success?" To answer this question, I need to tell you a story about my biggest failure, which became my greatest success.

After being self-employed for about five years in CR Management Systems as a consultant to the automotive industry, I happened to be in the right place at the right time to respond to an Australian Federal Government scheme to control used car imports from Japan. Previously, used cars could be imported by people who could convince the government that a car complied with Australian Design Rules (for safety and performance) by giving a "personal assurance" of compliance. The problem was that some of the people giving the personal assurances were dishonest, and the cars coming into Australia were not what they were supposed to be. In response, the government introduced the Registered Automotive Workshop Scheme (RAWS) which required that importers met the requirements of an international standard for quality, called ISO 9001, in which we had established expertise. Being first up and best dressed, we followed the government roll out to importers across Australia and signed up the majority of the aspirants for the new scheme. This was a bonanza for us. At one stage we had over 300 participants who had paid deposits on RAWS ISO 9001 packages for either $5000 or $15,000 depending on the level of service they required. Then I got greedy. Each of the participants needed an additional Australian Design Rules (ADR) evidence package, for each car make and model they wanted to import. As we did not have the required expertise, we needed to engage an engineer who did. One was a Christian guy from Queensland, who agreed to work with me for a 10% margin, which I rejected, because I had 30% in mind. Another of them was a Melbourne engineer, with a dubious reputation, who agreed to my proposal for 30%. Guess which one I choose? After we had taken several deposits for the $15-20,000 ADR package, the Melbourne engineer failed to honour his commitments, so I had to find another supplier, as the Queensland engineer now had his books full. The only supplier available was of unknown reputation. But I was desperate, so I sent him a commissioning check for $86,000, as I recall. But this was money from deposits for payment for an audit process with Australia's largest ISO 9001 auditing body, SAI Global. It was that or liquidation. When I had signed the check, I rang SAI Global and told them what I had done because I was technically trading while insolvent, as I could not pay my creditors if payment for all of the audits fell due at once which I thought would not happen. Fortunately, SAI Global trusted me because of my good track record as they knew they would eventually get their money from withheld commissions they would normally pay me. So they agreed to a moratorium on the debt, provided all future payments from clients were made direct to them, if I would forgo future commissions from the on-going annual audit fee.

So began a weary 3 years of trading out of a potentially ruinous situation. Not only had we lost much of our goodwill in the industry, but I had to pay double for the ADR evidence packages while we ran around pacifying irate customers to avoid legal action. In total, I estimate we lost about $1,000,000 gross margin by paying for evidence packs twice and having to pay full price. Plus lost future commissions and the total distraction from new business until the debt was repaid.

Would I regard this experience as a success or a failure?

Success is normally defined in terms of achieving our set goals, which I had miserably failed to do. Looking back with hindsight over that experience, would I have been better off to have taken the smaller commission for the ADR packs? Of course. I would have enjoyed a regular 10% margin from the ADR evidence packs, plus future retained commissions and sales, all while avoiding the many losses I had accumulated. The Christian engineer from Queensland went on to dominate the market because he was honest and realistic as he would only agree to what he could deliver. Following that setback, we developed new products for different markets, but the halcyon days were over.

In part to heal my wounds, I busied myself with designing and building a racing car, as you do. This was also the fulfilment of a life-long goal, which I am glad I had the opportunity to do because of what I experienced and learned. But did it give me the ultimate satisfaction I sought? Maybe a bit. After completion of the project, Elaine and I had another five years of club runs and competition before I decided that I preferred to go to church on Sunday, so I sold the car. We humans are strange creatures, full of contradictions and conflicting emotions. However, we must play the cards we have been given in the games we choose. Some of my choices have been excellent. Some, not so much. However, this series of choices led me on a very circuitous path, which, as it turned out, is now running over with a kind of joy that an extra $1,000,000 would not have delivered.

Fulfilling human desires

Many people, especially high performing business and sporting types exist by fulfilling goals that most of us cannot imagine. Their success and achievements often bring them great rewards of money, acclaim, status and power, which often facilitates sexual achievement, if that is what they seek. These accomplishments can bring happiness in the short term; but with this comes a risk that their ego is so bound up in success that they allow nothing else to intrude preventing other possibilities of satisfaction of desire to remain undiscovered. As I look back now, it is with very mixed emotions that I review what I had accomplished. When I sold my car, I said to Elaine somewhat grandiosely, "I wonder what I will do next?" From the time I began with the car, just after my 50th birthday, the project took nine years to complete due to other priorities of family, work, church and a return to study. Another factor was Elaine's successful job application at a school on the fringe of Melbourne's CBD, which led us to sell our family home, since our kids had left, and buy another house close to the school, causing me to question whether I would continue with my car or not. Deciding to continue was a new beginning which I am glad I made.

For the motor-heads amongst you, my 777 Clubman is a scaled up version of a Lotus 7 design, from the mid-1950 era. It weighs 750kg and has a Nissan 2litre turbo SR 20 DET engine with a bigger turbo and intercooler producing about 300 BHP, a 5 speed transmission, an LSD with De Dion rear suspension.

Following our relocation, the car design and build took another five years, plus five years of driving it in club runs, race events, hill climbs and related activities that consumed me. Sitting in church during that period, I would come up with many new ideas for my car, which had become central in my life. Was it time well spent? No and yes. Yes, because I resolved my concept of my self-worth as a competent person doing what I loved most. No because I discovered that my car was not of ultimate importance and therefore, not worthy of my commitment. But the opportunity to explore my place in the world by building the car was important. It is now obvious to me that ultimate satisfaction is not to be found in material things, important though they are. Nor is ultimate satisfaction to be found in human relationships alone as our ultimate relationship is reserved for us to discover in our encounter with our maker and his design purpose for us. When this is my goal and when I can relate all my desires, accomplishments, attributes, relationships, property, competency and aspirations to it, then my cup runs over with purposeful satisfaction, enjoyment, gratitude and pleasure. In hindsight, this whole experience was a win after what was a great loss initially Too bad it took me so long to get there but I have learned an important truth: to enjoy real success, that I must learn how to deal with failure.

Trust God

Whoever has will be given more, and they will have an abundance. Whoever does not have, even what they have will be taken from them (Matt 13:12).

Could I have come to the same conclusion without going through the agony? After much pondering, I came to the conclusion, *yes*. This is one reason why I am writing – to stop myself from making the same mistake again and to maybe help you from making the same errors that I have made. The question is finally resolved by trust: Do I trust God, my maker, to allow me to be human? Or rather, are we even supposed to have a choice in our human desires at all? This pondering brings me back to the Calvinist/Arminian argument as to whether we are free to make our own decisions. The answer is yes, we are free to choose; but the best choice is to choose him. Then he immediately releases us to fulfil our legitimate life-giving human passions, for which we are made.

> *For I know the plans I have for you," declares the* LORD, *"plans to prosper you and not to harm you, plans to give you hope and a future. Then you will call on me and come and pray to me, and I will listen to you. You will seek me and find me when you seek me with all your heart* (Jeremiah 29:11-13).
>
> *Keep your lives free from the love of money and be content with what you have, because God has said, "Never will I leave you; never will I forsake you." So we say with confidence, "The Lord is my helper; I will not be afraid. What can mere mortals do to me?"* (Heb 13:5-6).
>
> *Because he turned his ear to me, I will call on him as long as I live* (Ps 116:2).

Be patient

We are promised Oak trees, but we are given acorns.

So many mistakes are made because we don't understand how valuable time is. Apart from love, time is perhaps the most valuable thing that we are given for our exclusive use to waste or to invest. Time is a necessary dimension of love. As we love something or someone, we are expressing the extent and quality of our love by the length of time that is inherent to our decision. If our love is for five minutes, then that's how valuable that type of love is. If it is for a lifetime, then that's about as much as we can ever claim for sure because not having been to eternity yet, we take it in faith for the time being. Of course, we can be certain about eternity because we can rely on the promises of God, so we put our hope in Him and invest in relationships and other things that we hope will last for eternity.

> *Give, and it will be given to you. A good measure, pressed down, shaken together and running over, will be poured into your lap. For with the measure you use, it will be measured to you* (Lk 6:38).

To be fully alive as human beings, our humanity needs to be expressed, not suppressed. We are body, soul and spirit living in a material world that is less than it could be, because our humanity is infected with rebelliousness against God. We have fallen short of his purposes for us. I know that this sounds like religious melodrama, and it *is*, since I am guided by Romans 3:23: *For all have sinned and fall short of the glory of God*. Interestingly, sin is the one religious belief for which faith is not required. We can see it in society every day and, if we are honest, in ourselves. Perhaps the greatest mistake any of us make is not to indulge in our sins, but to pretend that we are not sinners. We see this in Christ's condemnation of the Pharisees of his day as they set standards for others that they could not keep for themselves. We do the same thing with what we think of as our own righteousness. But this is not what we pretend it is. It is hypocrisy, whereby we project

Are we there yet?

our self-righteousness by criticizing the faults we see in others. This is why Jesus says, *You hypocrite, first take the plank out of your own eye, and then you will see clearly to remove the speck from your brother's eye.* Matt 7: 5.

As I sit here, warmed by the autumn sun watching the fog recede from the city, I feel the tug of my sinfulness competing for my affections once more, as it often does. Where is this influence from? To some extent it is an agent of evil distracting me from my task. If I am fully conscious, I see the deception for what it is because I already know it will not bring any satisfaction. That impulse, however, is not sin. It is sin only when I accept its invitation. This is an irony because we normally think of sin as sex, drugs and rock and roll, or money sex and power, depending upon your age. However, sin is at its most diabolical when it is expressed in religion: My attempt to justify myself with religious self-righteousness, rather than to accept God's offer of justification and reconciliation with him is the basis of inevitable perdition.

My soon to be published book, *God is Love: The life and times of Big Daddy, Don Garlits,* deals with this conundrum. Don Garlits was the man who professionalized the sport of drag racing in post WWII America. Against insurmountable odds, he became 17 times world Top Fuel champion; the greatest innovator and champion in the most contested and dangerous class of a most dangerous sport. When I went to Florida to interview him in 2014, I was a fan, and hoped to discover a deeply mysterious man that would inspire me and my book with his deep insights. I had wondered for many years what had led him to famously display the words "God is Love" and the cross of Jesus on the machines that nearly killed him, several times over. But when I arrived at his Museum of Drag Racing in Ocala, he was ready for me, having met many of my type of idolizer many times before. Almost without introduction, his opening sally was, "Your government has taken our f.....g guns away from us," revealing another of his many passions. This was Don's pre-emptive strike against me for which he had given me a previous warning when he said by email, "I am not who you think I am." He was bringing me down a few pegs by referring to an Australian gun buy-back, instigated by our Prime Minister, John Howard, following a massacre in Port Arthur, Tasmania, where 35 people were massacred by a madman with an automatic rifle. My surprised reply was, "Well Don, that was a difficult time for me. I had brought some guns to go hunting with my son and I had to surrender them. But I'm glad I did. There have been no more mass shooting since." During the next two days that my travelling companion Eugene and I were with him, Don gave me several more hard lessons in the great problems all humans must face: our mortality and fallen humanness, as against our hope for eternity, can only be resolved when we declare that God is Love. Not that he put it so elegantly as it has taken me several years since then to unpack what I think Garlits was saying, which is why that book is not published yet. I have come to recognize this as an impossible task. We cannot separate our highest aspirations from our fallenness by ourselves. We must surrender the struggle to God and rely upon his great compassion and mercy, believing that he will treat us justly because his son Jesus has paid the price for our reconciliation with him. This is what God is Love means. Not that I am I justifying Don Garlits' or my bad behavior. It is for us to acknowledge it and to seek forgiveness from those who we have offended, beginning with God. However, I have learned bitter lessons from my own fallen humanity and from Don Garlits, for which I am glad, and which I now offer to you for your consideration.

The need to be fully human

This chapter is about a pretty abstract concept that many Christians struggle with, and atheists would dismiss out of hand. It is, however, one of the most important topics to get our minds around if we are to have any real idea of how God's love is fulfilled in his

kingdom that he has prepared for us. Our prevailing idea is that God's kingdom is in heaven, and exists in a time yet to come, rather than on earth. This is not incorrect, but it is insufficient. God's kingdom is present all around us and within us. If only we could open our eyes and see it, we could become conscious of our ability to be in it every day. It is, however, not by being super-spiritual or religious that we realize our close proximity to God's kingdom. It is rather by being fully human. I can explain this best by telling a couple of stories about Jesus and his engagement with women.

The one I like best is the story of the Woman Caught in Adultery because it demonstrates the irony that I have come to love and expect from this wonderful, timeless book, The Bible. The story goes:

> *The teachers of the law and the Pharisees brought in a woman caught in adultery. They made her stand before the group and said to Jesus, "Teacher,*

> this woman was caught in the act of adultery. In the Law Moses commanded us to stone such women. Now what do you say?" They were using this question as a trap, in order to have a basis for accusing him. But Jesus bent down and started to write on the ground with his finger. When they kept on questioning him, he straightened up and said to them, "Let any one of you who is without sin be the first to throw a stone at her." Again he stooped down and wrote on the ground. At this, those who heard began to go away one at a time, the older ones first, until only Jesus was left, with the woman still standing there. Jesus straightened up and asked her, "Woman, where are they? Has no one condemned you? "No one, sir," she said. "Then neither do I condemn you," Jesus declared. "Go now and leave your life of sin. (John 8:1-11).

There is a very compelling back story to this account in an earlier reference from Jeremiah 17:13, where the prophet, alluding to Jesus, says, *Lord, you are the hope of Israel; all who forsake you will be put to shame. Those who turn away from you will be written in the dust because they have forsaken the Lord, the spring of living water.* The conjunction of these two stories is irresistible to me – that Jesus wrote the actual names of the woman's accusers in the dust, causing them to slink away bearing the shame they tried to use to accuse both Jesus and the woman of sin. This is an ironic example of *being shot with a ball of your own shit*, as my old boss used to say.

John 4:10 recounts a similar story, known as The Woman at the Well. A woman from Samaria met Jesus at Jacob's well on a hot day. Jesus did not have a rope and a bucket to draw the water, so he asked the woman for a drink to quench his thirst. In discussion with the woman, Jesus said, *"If you knew the gift of God, and who it* is who says to you, 'Give Me a drink, you would have asked Him, and He would have given you living water.'" Jesus was ready to give this woman, who he knew to be sinful, the living water described in this chapter. "Whoever drinks of the water that I shall give him shall never thirst; but the water that I shall give him shall become in him a well of water springing up to eternal life".

These stories are excellent examples of Alfred North Whitehead's "actual occasions" or ordinary events in which Jesus demonstrates another reality, other than our limited view of time and space in which the events occur. According to Whitehead, this method of deriving theology from ordinary events is unique to the Bible. In both cases, Jesus is taking ordinary encounters with ordinary people to tell them that they are not seeing the full picture of reality. Although Jesus confirms their sinfulness, he does not condemn them. Instead, he offers them an insight into another reality which only he can grant access to.

Rowan Williams, previously the Archbishop of Canterbury, has written a book called *Being Human* in which he argues a similar case to the one that I have just put, namely, that if we focus too much on one aspect of humanity over another, then we do ourselves great harm. Regarding how we learn, Williams notes "...the tension between children acquiring easily checkable skills in strict succession and tested relentlessly on the one hand, and a focus on the "embodied mind" of the developmentally rounded child in which play, leisure, music, sport and drama (each) have an important role on the other."[1] I propose that this applies to adults in the same way - especially the sense of "embodiment" which suggests that we must acknowledge and provide for our physical needs, so we can become a complete being. My point is this: our faith in Jesus introduces us to an entirely different way of evaluating success and seeing the reality of the human condition. Although Jesus acknowledges that humans are sinful, he does

---

1 Rowan Williams, *Being Human*, SPK London, 2018.

not concede that we should be resigned to sin. Rather than hold a despairing view of our weaknesses, described as the world, the flesh and the devil, *the three enemies of the human soul*, Jesus paints a picture of the future to which anyone can aspire (Mk 4: 15-17). To be human is to admit to our shortcomings and then to transcend them. This is accomplished by our conscious engagement with the power of God to transform us from our fallen state into an abundant life where our cup runs over. Jesus offers us an alternative to constantly giving into miserable, deceitful, attachments to our human desires that we know to be harmful.

Go deep

Having the right expectations of success enables us to value everything that we experience in our lives for what it teaches us – provided that we don't take ourselves too seriously, but we do take our relationships with God and others very seriously. Among many other things, our trust in God and engagement with the Golden Rule teaches us about our:

- Hypocrisy and sinfulness
- Need for reconciliation with God and with others
- Need to experience real humility
- The availability of God's mercy and grace as he transforms us by the renewal of our minds
- Destiny of becoming more like Jesus
- Place in his Kingdom
- Anticipation and experience of abundant joy
- Present and future role as the chosen sons and daughters of the Most-High God in his creative process

Does this mean that we should not have high goals in our search for success and happiness? No. The problem, I believe, is that our goals are not high enough. We expect too little from our faith, which promises to transform us into new creatures while we are happy just to get by, living as insufficiently changed people in a fallen world.

Spiritual transformation begins with seeing new possibilities promised to us by Jesus and desiring them by hungering and thirsting, as a man dying of starvation and thirst desires food and water, and then a decision to be obedient according to Jesus' command to observe the Golden Rule and to put our ego to death.

> *Trust in the LORD with all your heart and lean not on your own understanding; in all your ways submit to him, and he will make your paths straight* (Prov 3:5-6).
>
> *Jesus replied, "Anyone who loves me will obey my teaching. My Father will love them, and we will come to them and make our home with them* (Jn 14:23).

The recipe always seems to be the same. On one hand, we have what has become known as "Beautiful Orthodoxy" that I mentioned previously. On the other hand, we have an intellectualized and somewhat materialized form of religion, including Christianity, that appeals to our intellect and our ego. The "orthodox" reference is to an updated version of CS Lewis' famous book, *Mere Christianity*, which became so influential following his conversion from atheism to becoming perhaps the greatest Christian apologist of the modern era. Lewis' influence is due mainly to his seemingly inexhaustible knowledge of classical literature, and to his being convinced by his friend J R R Tolkien and others as to the essential truth of the Christian narrative, woven as it is into human history and the human psyche. We are so easily seduced by an appeal to something other than to trust and obey Jesus, as I was guided to do by a childhood Sunday School song whose refrain is:

Trust and obey, for there's no other way
To be happy in Jesus, but to trust and obey.

It has taken me many years to join the dots of my experience and to say with absolute assurance, and no fear of ridicule, that this simple instruction is all we need to know in order to begin a journey toward a faithful and satisfying life. If I am to pursue the highest good for myself as an integrated person who recognizes the necessity for his soul to win over his reason alone, then I must trust and obey, for there's no other way to be happy in Jesus.

10

Conscious Transformation
19 Nov

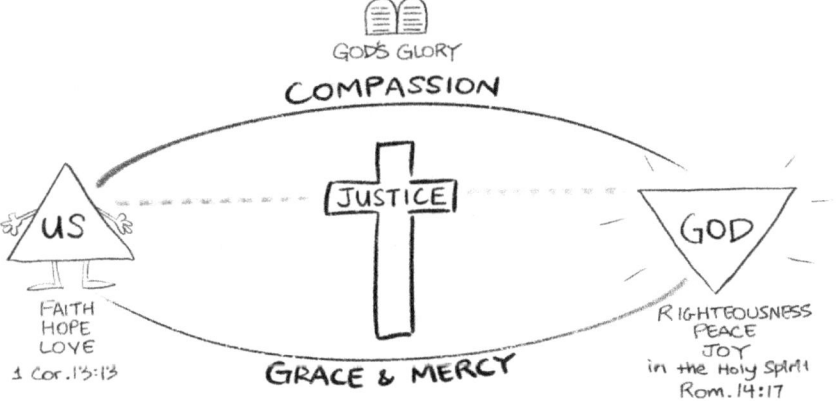

> *I would not give a fig for the simplicity this side of complexity, but I would give my life for the simplicity on the other side of complexity.*
>
> —Oliver Wendall Holmes Jr.

Once when my youngest daughter was about 12 years old, she and I were in the car together as she waxed lyrical about her philosophy of life. My attention was suddenly focused when she told me that she thought I was "lecturous" because "I lectured people all the time." She was right, of course, as she had inherited from me her inclination to often explain in detail things she didn't fully understand. From my beginnings as an automotive mechanic in an experimental engineering workshop, I graduated to a role in which I was able to combine my curiosity with my want to explain things to others as a professional workplace trainer. According to my wife, my specialization became "difficult topics that nobody understood because I liked the challenge" of helping automotive businesses to comply with occupational health and safety laws applicable to dangerous farm machinery and similar subjects. This strange proclivity, coupled with my engineering training, led me to wonder how risk management could fulfill its legal goal of enabling employers to take the "reasonably practicable" steps required by law to help people protect themselves and others in a workplace. My brilliant friend Manuel, a Doctor of Architecture student from Germany who read early drafts of this book, pointed out the link between my professional role and my interest in the Golden Rule. Workplace safety is about protecting people from harm while enabling them to be responsible, productive and fulfilled at work. The Golden Rule is wonderfully designed to protect us from harm in relationships and from ourselves. It also enables us to live productive and fulfilling lives, full of righteousness, peace and joy for all eternity.

During the 20 or so years that I was self-employed as a workplace trainer, I would lead groups of somewhat hostile farm machinery dealer business owners through explanations of what the law required of them to protect themselves from prosecution and their customers from injury. Before long, I realized that some of these highly successful and competitive men had not sat in a room together with their competitors from whom they were divided by the color of their product: green for John Deere machinery, red for Case, blue and yellow for New Holland, orange for Kubota and so on. Safety was not a topic they felt much passion for, nor was it going to give them a competitive advantage. It was about legal compliance and avoiding prosecution, something that they knew had sent some business broke. So, to break the ice and prepare them to learn what they would rather not have to know, I learned a few red versus green jokes to at least get them talking.

In this process, I applied one of the great principles of learning: that a teacher prepares students by not taking difficult subjects head-on, but rather by taking them on a journey from unconscious incompetence to conscious incompetence, through to becoming consciously competent, then finally to unconscious competence – in this case, competence in the important area of legal compliance.

Becoming conscious

As I have previously explained, my purpose in writing this book has been to encourage you to take a journey with me – on an adventure of discovery to uncover the meaning and the delights offered by the Golden Rule.

In this final chapter, I would like to summarize my thesis. It is that the Golden Rule is the means by which we learn the language of love so that we can receive our inheritance as sons and daughters of the Most-High God. In keeping with Oliver Wendall Holmes Jr's maxim, I hope I have provided enough complexity to convince you that I can now move to attempt a distillation into simplicity, for which Holmes said he was prepared to die.

The irony in Holmes' statement is that we will all die physically, but whether or not we die spiritually depends upon the simplicity of our faith and how we lived our lives in response to it.

If we have not been reborn spiritually during our allocated three score years and ten we have not yet begun to live in eternity present because we have not chosen to accept the reality of God's spiritual kingdom and his offer to us of abundant life. The offer extends to all the parts of my body, soul and spirit as essential parts of my humanity, to be fed, nurtured and disciplined to ensure that my potential as a person is realized.

I hope this does not sound like a threat of God's anger being meted out in the fires of hell, as this is not what I believe to be the case. Rather, I believe that hell is a place that we create for ourselves by our hard-heartedness and rebellious against reality and against God, who desires only to offer us good things for our acceptance. This is right, isn't it? You have already seen this in your own life or in others' lives, where the choices we or they make are stupid, because they were not the best that were available to us. Hell, in my view, is when time and space come to an end and we see the Kingdom of God clearly, realizing it was around us all along, but we are not in it. Then we will say, *"How could have I been so stupid?"* Not that I expect to convince you about heaven and hell so simply, as my sympathies are with Jake Blues, who didn't want no *"jive-assed preacher"* lecturing him about such things.[1] In fact, my sympathies are really with Solomon, who says despairingly that we all share an uncertain future: *Who knows if the human spirit rises upward and if the spirit of the animal goes down into the earth?* (Ecc 3:21). Perhaps this is the best time for me to begin to explain this. I believe that human life is eternal from the time that an embryo is viable, because we are made in the image of God and we belong to him, regardless of whether we believe it or not. This means that our souls have the potential of becoming conscious of God while we are living in time and space, because when it ends, our full consciousness begins. If we have refused God's invitations of grace, then he will not force us to accept him, but rather, God will respect our decision to refuse his offer.

As there may never be a better time than now, I must tell you that you are his, made for relationship with God for your shared pleasure. God's goal for us is not just to get us to believe that our souls will live for eternity, because, according to Jesus, we already do. *Very truly I tell you, whoever hears my word and believes him who sent me has eternal life and will not be judged but has crossed over from death to life* (John 5:24). The question is whether we will enjoy the fullness of life that is intended for us, both now and in eternity. What I am suggesting, however, is not something for which you must take a huge leap of faith to believe something

---

1 *The Blues Brothers* movie directed by John Landis.

that you think is impossible. Rather, I am proposing something that is utterly provable, whereby you examine my suggestion that the Golden Rule is good for you and prove it to yourself today by testing it in the reality of your own relationships, beginning with the bloke next door. This, I believe, is the beginning of wisdom and reconciliation with God.

Conscious competence

The process of becoming consciously competent happens to all of us in most areas of our lives, often without us becoming aware of it, because it happens gradually. When there is an important topic that we must concentrate on to understand, then we might observe our engagement in the process of learning, as I had to when I became painfully conscious of what would happen to me if I failed to convince those tough machinery dealers of their need to become consciously competent about the safety of used machinery they were selling. In that case, I had to very quickly become competent myself in how to engage them in an important subject that they hated. This is a lesson I will never forget.

My experience with the Golden Rule is similar. As a young adult, I knew of it as a teaching of Jesus, but I would come up with objections to it (such as: "you can't allow yourself to be a door mat for others to walk all over you") in order to find reasons not to apply it to all areas of life. However, as I realized that there was no other way to maintain a workable relationship with my intelligent and assertive wife, I became more conscious as to how it applied to my marriage and then to other areas of my life. I also realized how often I made mistakes of judgement because I didn't apply this principle. Over my lifetime – more as a result of my mistakes than my successes – I became more competent as I also became more conscious of the need to be obedient to Jesus in applying his great command. My consciousness was further enlightened when I began to see my past mistakes more clearly and decided I did not want to continue to repeat them. If only I had seen more of them sooner...

I contend that many Christians, including me, have become lukewarm and ineffective as disciples of Jesus because we have not taken his greatest commandment seriously. We have, at times, allowed ourselves to think that we are automatically competent to represent him, almost regardless of what we say and do. This is a sanctimonious sense of entitlement, and an example of arrogant complacency in some instances. I became more aware of this in my own life as my men's group discussed the concept of our potential rejection by Jesus, who said, *depart from me, I never knew you* (Matt 7: 23). If we are aware of this potential, we may recognize that we have become guilty of the same sins of complacency as the church of Laodicea, who were threatened with being spewed out of the mouth of Jesus in his judgement, predicted in Revelation 3.

> *I counsel you to buy from me gold refined in the fire, so you can become rich; and white clothes to wear, so you can cover your shameful nakedness; and salve to put on your eyes, so you can see* (Rev 3:18).
>
> *To the one who is victorious, I will give the right to sit with me on my throne, just as I was victorious and sat down with my Father on his throne. Whoever has ears, let them hear what the Spirit says to the churches."* (Rev 3:21-23)

Did you notice Jesus' counsel to buy gold from him refined in the fire? I prefer to think of this as an oblique but clear reference to the Golden Rule.

This type of consciousness is remarkably like workplace safety, as I have suggested above. It is not by unthinking compliance with the letter of the law that a workplace becomes safe. Similarly, it is only when the spirit or the essence of the law permeates our thinking and the way we behave that we can say we have truly learned to follow its requirements. As I have become a student and an exponent of the Golden Rule, studying its history, biblical importance, and its social meaning, I have become increasingly confident regarding its imperative role as a foundational teaching of Christian faith. I have also discovered that it has a built-in antidote to the smug satisfaction of know-alls like me, in that it leads us toward self-applied humility as an alternative to humiliation because it allows us to see the patterns of our mistakes in the privacy of our minds. If we become aware of this possibility, it can prevent us from making big mistakes publicly in which our short-comings are on full display. However, our compliance with the Golden Rule does not save us. Rather, our acceptance of it is an act of obedience that enables us to learn about ourselves and our relationship with God and each other. God wants us to accept positions of responsibility in society and in his kingdom, for which we are not yet ready. He wants to prepare us to assume responsible roles as his emissaries – for we are pre-destined and called by the title "The Elect." By the way, this does not mean that God imposes his will on us. It simply means that he has a job ready waiting for us as soon as we are ready to accept it.

Our simple obedience to the Golden Rule provides the opportunity for us recognize our need for change and repentance, and then humbly allow God's spirit to permeate us and renew our minds so that we become more like Jesus.

Jesus' explicit teaching

I have found that the great characters of the Bible and church history have had a lot to say about this principle of entitlement, although not always overtly and certainly, and not always in the way we might have expected. For instance, many of the heroes of the Bible such as Abraham's wife, Sarah, Moses, Rachel the harlot, David and Solomon are just as remarkable for their mistakes as they are for their successes. When they treat God as he wants to be treated, we see the fulfilment of God's purposes in them. On the other hand, we see disaster and chaos reign when relationships are overlooked for some other priority. Solomon, for instance, was incredibly wise, powerful and rich, but he ultimately destroyed his kingdom because he seduced himself with his harem of 1000 women. If he had been able to treat just one of them as he would have wanted to be treated himself, the destruction of his kingdom may have been avoided. Clearly, the theme and principle of the Golden Rule is established in the Old Testament, which Jesus then adopts and implements at the commencement of his ministry. I propose that the Bible presents the Golden Rule as a learning principle of conscious transformation that lasts a lifetime, preparing us for new purpose and satisfaction in relationships now, and unimagined new responsibilities in the far reaches of the cosmos in a time yet to come.

I have a photograph in my office from, of a painting of Jesus standing in an archway, knocking on the overgrown door of my heart, with the words from Revelations 3:20: BEHOLD I STAND AT THE DOOR AND KNOCK IF ANY MAN HEAR MY VOICE AND OPEN THE DOOR I WILL COME IN TO HIM AND SVP. WITH HIM AND HE WITH ME. I love this image of Jesus holding a lamp under the statement "THE LIGHT OF THE WORLD", which is on the arch above him. This is my inspiration for the Arc of the Universe because it represents Jesus' invitation to bring me into light and life by my obedience to him with Jesus as my teacher and my guide.

From St Paul's Cathedral, London

The Golden Rule is an imperative in the sense that it is Jesus' explicit command. In fact, I doubt that there is a real alternative to this essential act of obedience because if we do not begin to *"Treat our neighbor as ourselves"* and to *"Love our brother,"* then we are liars and the truth is not in us as we have previously seen. Jesus' command is essential in the sense that the curriculum, the learning method and the assessment are all presented to us in detail. The course objective is for us to become *competent as ministers of a new covenant – not of the letter but of the Spirit; for the letter kills, but the Spirit gives life* (2 Cor 3:6).

My wife is an expert early childhood teaching specialist who has followed professional trends in teaching and learning with a critical attitude towards change for its own sake. Over the years of her experience, she has determined what works as against what is just another fad. One example is her resistance to the idea that it does not matter how children learn to read, as she insists on teaching children to read phonetically by requiring children to learn the sounds of letters so they can work out for themselves how to pronounce words. Phonics has become part of what is known as explicit teaching, where the teacher creates an environment in which children become conscious of the building blocks of their own learning of language, writing and speech in a rich environment where learning and practicing are a seamless whole. This teaching method not only leads to excellent literacy, but also relates to a learning intervention system called Reading Recovery. When a child is not keeping pace with reading and comprehension milestones, the teacher intervenes to find out where the blockages are by sitting with the child in a space with no distractions and observes the child in a range of listening, reading and speaking activities. The teacher then notices what the child does to distract themselves to avoid learning, such as their looking out the window, or attempting to change the subject to distract the teacher. She then requires the child to focus on the explicit elements and the process of conscious learning and practicing until the child can master the task and then explain what they have learned.

I know it should not surprise me that Jesus understood and implemented explicit learning 2000 years ago, but it still does. His skill as a teacher can be seen throughout the New Testament narrative, but most particularly in his insistence on the Golden Rule as an explicit learning method for his disciples. Not only did he explain to them in detail what the outcome of following the Beatitudes would be, but he also gave them homework to do and assessed whether they had applied the elements and principles he had taught them. Then, when there was an indication that they had failed, he gave them remedial classes, such as when they asked him who would be the greatest in God's Kingdom. In response, he presented a child to them to show an example of their misunderstanding and their need for self-imposed humility (Matt 18:1-4).

Confused by complexity

After the apostolic era and the reign of Constantine, the Golden Rule seems to have become obscured in the complexity of politics, religious power and theological narrative – particularly later, when the church had new priorities such as conquering the new world, winning wars, souls and political battles. According to the Catholic Encyclopedia, Augustine of Hippo, who was the major influence in the Christian West from the mid-5th century, established his "Rules of St Augustine" in which he focused:

> *"upon charity, poverty, obedience, detachment from the world, the apportionment of labour... fraternal charity,* prayer *in common,* fasting *and abstinence proportionate to the strength of*

the individual, care of the sick, silence, reading during meals..."[1].

While Augustine's rules were intended for his colleagues in religious vocations, nothing much has changed amongst sincere Catholics and Protestants who maintain similarly long "To Do" lists in their approach to faithful Christian life. 850 years later, my hero, Thomas Aquinas, is closer to my vision than Augustine, but he again muddies the water with philosophical and theological complexity resulting from his insistence on "natural law" and its relationship to "virtue ethics". Aquinas distinguished between natural virtues of prudence, temperance, justice, and fortitude that are binding on everyone, plus the theological virtues of faith, hope, and charity that were additionally applicable to Christians. Some of Aquinas' definitions and summaries cut through with me and are fundamental to my thinking because of their simplicity and elegance.

But let's not get too far ahead of ourselves. At the end of his ministry, Jesus redoubles his emphasis on relationships as the cornerstone of faith in God with his words:

a new command I give to you, that you love one another as I have love loved you (Jn 13:34).

Could he have been any more concise or clear? The reason for the confusion that soon emerged, I think, was the same then as it is today: his disciples had different expectations of the Messiah than Jesus had for himself. In his last days, Jesus knew what was before him: his betrayal and abandonment by his disciples, a determination by the religious rulers to kill him, and the expediency of his crucifixion by the Roman rulers of Israel, all of which sealed his fate on the cross of Calvary. Meanwhile, his followers still thought he would rescue their nation from political and military oppression.

---

1 https://en.wikipedia.org/wiki/Rule_of_St._Augustine

But they had seen him die pathetically on the cross and be buried in a tomb. Their hopes of liberation were shattered as they retreated in shame, sorrow, confusion despair and ruin, perhaps reflecting on what fools they had been for believing that Jesus was more than just another Hebrew dreamer. But then…the events of the resurrection further confused them. Some distraught women had gone to his grave to embalm his body, only to find him missing and a man they thought to be the gardener saying that Jesus had risen!

It took the disciples and followers of Jesus many days, perhaps, or even weeks, months, and in some cases, years, to hear the many accounts of Jesus reappearing, asking his disciples to confirm what had happened before his death. Now they saw him eating fish, suddenly appearing in a locked room, or talking to fellow travellers on the road, only to realize that something totally unexpected was still happening, something so incredible, so unanticipated, so other-worldly, that it was years before the stories coalesced to become the songs, poems and liturgy recorded in the Gospels and the Epistles of the New Testament. Unfortunately for us, these stories are now so familiar that they have become almost banal, and we suspect, even factually wrong – perhaps a delusion or just a metaphor for something else. If it is properly taught and practiced, however, Christian doctrine and Jesus' teaching in particular is always practical and deeply relational, just as it was when it was first recorded.

Of course, my own expectations have had a major influence on my life; some good, some not so much. However, I can confidently say that we are vastly better off when we become more rather than conscious of our expectations. As I learned more about my own attitudes and motivations toward the Golden Rule, I also found that Christians whom I thought might be interested in it were not. I was alarmed that very few capable Bible teachers shared my interest and conviction. They would say, "mmm, yes but…" or "What happens when…?" presenting questions that they would have answered themselves if they had given them any thought. Or sometimes they would agree, perhaps to shut me up. But when I asked them months later if they had acted upon what they agreed was an imperative of Christian faith, they would give themselves an excuse for not having treated it seriously enough to act on it.

On the other hand, there are many beliefs and behaviors that Christians do incorporate the principle of the Golden Rule into, though unconsciously. This is good, but it is not optimal, because Christian faith seems to have become divided and unfocussed in its mission and purpose when it is unconscious. The church is now subject to ridicule and derision; it is being forced to the edges of society with no voice in the halls of power or the public square. Perhaps this is a good thing, a necessary pre-condition to relearning what we have forgotten. Christians are not only disempowered as the voice of reason and love which shaped Western Democracy; they are slowly being declared irrelevant, blamed for the problems of society just as the original Christians were blamed for the burning of Rome. All the while, they are being replaced by other voices preaching universal love, tolerance, equity and social progress towards utopia. These voices, however, have been heard before, and have been found to offer nothing new apart from tyranny, because their source is not the God of love, but a false god of idealism and faithless materialism, masquerading in his place. To some extent, we Christians are to blame for our own demise as division and confusion have diverted us from the task of obedience to Christ's commands, to which we must now return.

How is it possible that we have lost the vital and central message of Jesus? Have we confused ourselves with religion, or with alternative beliefs that discredit the idea that Jesus did something totally new in the cosmos and invited us to be a part of it? Have we been so seduced by the material world that even Christians have materialized and rationalized their faith, so much so that faith is no longer the substance of hope? Faith, to many, has become a test of seeking material evidence to provide "proof" of seeing before we believe, suggesting that some of the Christian "faith" movements are not of faith at all. Augustine said, "When we believe, then we will see,"[1] illustrating the normal processes of faith and the way we perversely invert them. Some people and movements have become dogmatic in their assertions that God is obliged to "keep his promises" if only we will "speak the words of true confession" or that we will persist in "believing for a miracle" or be "faithful in tithing". It is a similar situation for some literalists who want every word of the Bible to be literally true, according to their understanding of literal truth, so they tragically pervert the lyrical prose, poetry, wisdom and theology of ancient writings to fit their facile view. The marvel is that faith is more profound, and the Bible is truer, more fantastic, than they can ever imagine. If only we would leave our insecurities and need for material, physical and intellectual certainty at the foot of the cross of Jesus, we would find that the greatest miracle is not healing of the body, it is healing of the soul that is achieved by our obedience – not by looking for material proof for certainty, but by the evidence of transformed lives that are being recreated as our minds are renewed. This is not to say that people who desire the experience of the apostolic age or miracles of healing, or even those who teach prosperity are necessarily totally wrong, as we are all wrong to some degree. The problem instead has to do with their emphasis on the outcomes of faith, which are the responsibility of God, rather than the inputs of obedience for which we are responsible. Of course, we should want to see the Kingdom of God come accompanied with spiritual power and prosperity, manifest in our lives. Of course, we should pray for and expect miracles of healing. Even churches that believe miracles have ceased to exist continue to pray for the sick because the Apostle James commands us to. I personally would rather be healthy than sick, and rich instead of poor. But first and foremost,

---

1 Augustine's *Confessions*.

I must allow for God's unique and utter sovereignty and not create doctrine out of every passage of scripture. Rather, I would prefer that my soul is healed of its illness, its despair, its alienation from God and its poverty. I hope I am then prepared for whatever I am called to do or to be – rich or poor, sick or infirm, wise or ignorant – because I will have found my place and my calling in God's eternal kingdom.

From the known to the unknown, from the simple to the complex

Another of the trainer's tools is to take students from the known to the unknown, from the simple to the complex, in order to make a lesson more palatable. If your objection is that the Christian message is bedeviled with complexity about unprovable and unbelievable ideas and laws that you have no hope of accepting, then I have good news for you: Jesus says that the whole of the law is contained within the two statements: *to love God and your neighbor as yourself*. That is as much as you need to know or understand to begin the process of transformation to become his disciple. We somehow expect that we should receive God's promises as soon as we become aware of them. Like the Prodigal Son, we want to claim our reward before we are ready to receive it. We have been promised an oak tree, but we have been given an acorn which we must plant and nurture. Earlier, I related my story about Peter Stone, who said the we cannot change ourselves; we can only choose the power by which we change by small steps of faith as we trust and obey. It is now time for us to accept this challenge and to become conscious of what the spirit requires of us.

Should we not now return to his commands and re-discover what always was and will always be true – that the Kingdom of God is entirely relational, from top to bottom, from beginning to end, from age to age? My goal is to make the Golden Rule conscious for every individual believer as a process of learning, because it is a command of Jesus to do so, and because it works to reveal God's Kingdom to us and to prepare us to take our place in it. My hope is that in maintaining a strong focus on the Golden Rule, we will:

- Be directly obedient to Jesus' commands
- Avoid unnecessary complexity
- Establish a foundation of love
- Experience improved relationships very quickly
- Directly enhance our experience of our essential humanity
- Mitigate against cultish theologizing and speculation
- Establish a hierarchy of principles based on love and obedience, that permits all other legitimate avenues for discipleship, principles of faith and works in the expression of the gospel of Jesus Christ

Freedom and liberation

Paul says, *It is for freedom that Christ has set us free* (Gal 5: 1). What does he mean? Freedom from what, exactly? Paul goes on to talk about returning to the bondage of the legalism under the corrupted Jewish system of religion. Then he summarizes his concern in verse 6: *...the only thing that counts is faith expressing itself in love.* It is tragic that 2000 years later we are still making the same mistakes with some subtle changes to confuse us. Paul summarizes again in verse 14: *The entire law is summed up in a single command: "Love your neighbor as yourself."* It is ironic to me that the "legalism" Paul is talking about is now disguised as the "progressive" politics of the socialist left, as social reform has been adopted as a "work of faith" by those who have abandoned Jesus' gospel of personal salvation and transformation to one preferring a Marxist postmodern narrative of social reform. Although this may not sound like classic legalism of the past, it is, as it shares many of the same characteristics, such as pointing the accusing finger at someone else for the ills of society and requiring change in anyone but oneself.

Liberation is profitable to humanity in the same way that Jesus means when He says:

What shall it profit a man, if he gains the whole world, but loses his soul? (Matt. 16:26).

To gain all the material objects, wealth and power of the material world is nothing compared with the survival and fulfilment of our soul, because our souls are the "real us" that transcends time and space. Profit in this sense, then, means the totality of good things that accrue to us when we inherit our share of God's family business. The immediate evidence of this inheritance and increasing liberation of our souls is the deposit of *righteousness, peace and joy in the Holy Spirit* that we experience progressively on our journey of *faith, hope and love* facilitated by the Golden Rule. The dynamic factor in the application of the Golden Rule to our ordinary lives is the promise of the Holy Spirit. This is the personal encounter with the numinous Divine person that you cannot predict. Nor can it be genuinely conjured up from within you or from any other source, as far as I can tell. The Holy Spirit is an elusive Divine personality that you get to know because he visits you regularly, and you begin to anticipate His presence. You already know who he is. He is the Spirit in the back of your mind who encourages, teaches and warns you. Perhaps it is some time since you have listened hard enough to hear his voice. I hope you now to begin to listen and to expect Him to speak when you when you are ready to act. For this to happen, we have to put aside our ego and our intellectual objections, which suggest that we already know all that we need to know for a satisfying life.

I want to remind you once again so that you can consciously engage in this experience of liberation and transformation by your adoption of the Golden Rule as the primary method for transformation that prepares you for a role in the eternal Kingdom of God. Of course, it is not the only way, because God can prepare us by other means, as he did with Paul on the road to Damascus. The following illustrations attempt to present this concept based upon thinking about the nature of the relationship between God and humankind, and how that relationship is determined by the process of our response to the Golden Rule.

What does transformation look like?

Many years ago, the then Prime Minister of Australia, Bob Hawke, compared the complexity of his political situation to trying to explain the Holy Trinity. Hawke, who is the son of a Congregational minister, Clem Hawke, should have known better than to compare his political situation with the complexity of God's family, as many of his misfortunes, especially his personal ones, were of his own doing, and easily explicable if he would have been so humble as to have admitted such. Despite Bob Hawke's appeal to impenetrable complexity, a serious attempt to understand the Trinity is helpful even if it is imperfect, because we can find our way to at least begin to think about the similarities we share with the One whose image we bear.

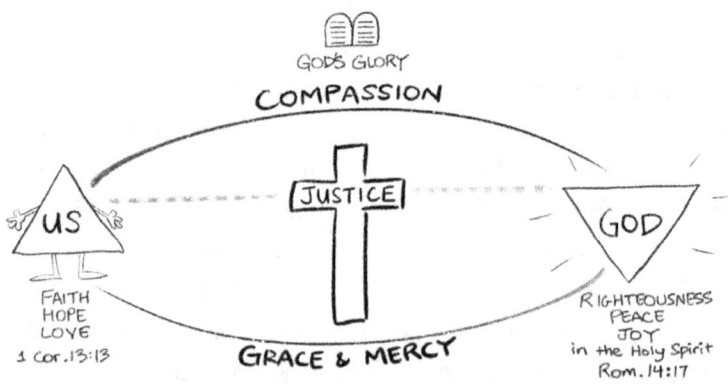

The process of transformation is where we rightly claim to begin to become like God. As with all concepts, illustrations, parables and archetypes, they are not a perfect description because, for one thing, God is the sovereign spirit: his ways are not subject to our understanding or intellectual approval of him. Although we cannot describe all the elements of the process of our relationship with him in detail, I will begin by making several assumptions about the nature of God and us human beings. Once again, as these diagrams present implied rather than direct instructions, since they are not all supported directly by scripture, you may choose to ignore them.

In Mark 12: 28-34, Jesus declares the absolute sovereignty of God and the nature of the relationship between God and Israel, his chosen nation. The relationship is then personalized to the religious scholar that Jesus was debating. This is very important because if we miss the implication, then we make the same mistake that has been made by organized Christianity over the centuries, namely, that the church can save us by its control of its adherents and by the magisterium of its authority and teaching. As much as we should regard all legitimate branches of the Christian church highly, it is painfully obvious that none of them is perfect. They have all failed and will continue to fail because they are human institutions, in my view. It is the individual that is responsible for their own accountability to God, not the church. The church is what we need for continuity, history, organization, teaching, fellowship and for engagement with the world. But the church will not save your soul. Jesus declares that the process of salvation applies in the same way to you and me as it did to the lawyer in Mark 12.

I hope that the following illustrations and dialogue will illuminate the dynamics of this relationship:

Who is God?

God is an absolute sovereign divine trinity comprising the father, son and spirit, and it is best summarized by the Nicene Creed.[1]

---

1   http://creeds.net/ancient/nicene.htm

None of the individual parts is the whole; but together, they are God, a Divine relationship, held together by love. To begin, we should notice that the trinity is a cooperative relationship wherein the Father authorizes the Spirit, who responds by empowering the Son, who acts to please the father. Together, in this dynamic relationship, they are collectively God.

1. The father is spirit, who loves his son, whom he begat.
2. The beloved son who has human form seeks only to please the father, whom he loves.
3. The Holy Spirit proceeds and emanates from the love between the father and son as their powerful agent between GOD and ME. The spirit then does what the son directs him to do. However, he is also a person, with a mind and will of his own.

God remains a mystery because he is not a man, but rather spirit, beyond the limits of time and space. God is therefore beyond our understanding, other than what scripture and the spirit reveal to us.

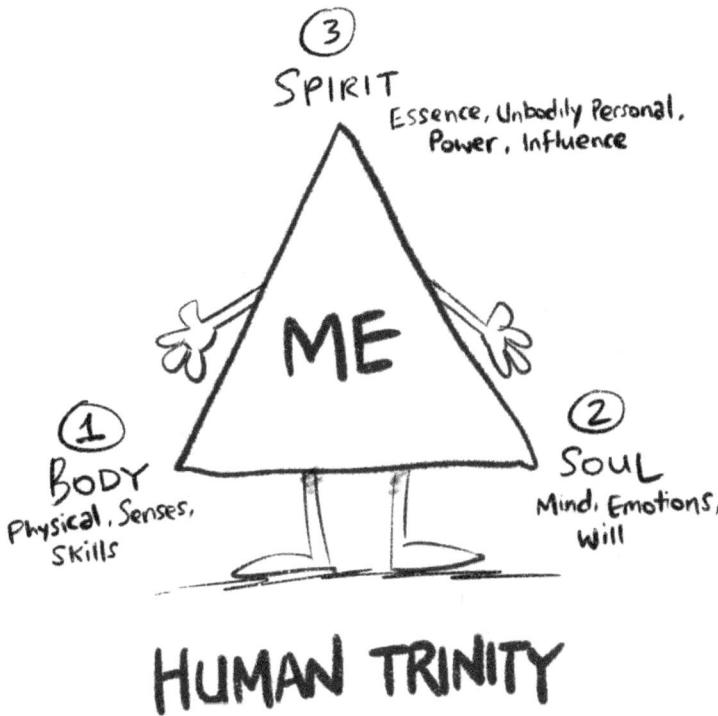

Who am I?

I am a human trinity of one person, body, soul and spirit, living in God's universe of time and space.

What is my relationship to God?

God, my creator and sustainer, has invited me and you to become his adopted children, not by force, but by the exercise of my will in response to Him.

My purpose is to love God and enjoy him forever

According to the Great Command, I am to love God with my heart, mind, soul and strength which combines the three aspects to become ME. The term "heart", as used in scripture, usually means the metaphorical center of a person's whole being, body, soul and spirit.

I am:

1. **Body.** I come into existence as a body, conceived through my parent's creative act. From conception, I am precious to God. My body is the aggregation of all my physical characteristics, my strength, skills and abilities which I have inherited and learned. My body is the physical expression of my existence.
2. **Soul.** (Also Heart.) My soul is my mind, emotions and will. My soul emanates from my body naturally, plus as I use my potential to learn from my experience in the world of time and space. It includes my self-knowledge and self-love.
3. **Spirit.** My spirit includes my soul. It is my un-bodily essence and extends from my body as my personal power and my influence, though it does not rely upon my physical strength or presence. My spirit is the part of me that most resembles God as it includes a deposit of his love, expressed as faith and hope. It is that part of me closest to God's spirit. He invites me into relationship with him when I hear God's word to me. If I respond, my soul exercises my will to pursue this relationship by my small expressions of faith, hope and love within me that resemble God, in whose image I am made.

Faith

Faith is my soul's yearning to be reunited with God. It comes by hearing from the word of God and the spirit's influence upon me. Faith reaches out for what I have not seen, but what I hope is true. To exercise faith is not a blind leap into wishful thinking. It is a series of small, informed and intuitive steps that I take in response to God's spirit beckoning me plus what I have learned. Nor is faith an increasing and persistent delusion, as it is confirmed by my tangible experience of personal incremental transformation. As I take a small step of faith, I learn more of my relationship with God, confirming that what I have hoped for was in fact true.

Hope

Hope is my anticipation or wish that my perception of God is true. Hope never fails; it keeps me going, leading me to take risks based upon the best opportunities I encounter and what I have experienced so far.

Love

Love is reflection of God in me. It is an act of will whereby I seek the highest good for myself and others. If I love myself, this love is not selfish because it always wills the same for others as it does for me. The reason for this is that this love is from God. Love seeks the best for me and others to whom I relate, particularly those who already love me. It also seeks the greatest good for the greatest number of people for the longest possible time. Anything less than this is not God's love, but rather selfishness, obsession, infatuation or something similar. I experience God's love in every part of my being, spirit, soul and body when I have begun a new life with Christ living in me.

Hearing from his word

Hearing the word of God from the Bible and from the spirit and other people grants us access to his dealings with patriarchs and prophets like Abraham and Moses, to whom he revealed himself and gave his law as archetypes for us to follow. Finally, he revealed himself in Jesus. We also hear God's word by the witness of others and by hearing preachers preach. On some occasions, even modern people have received direct revelation from God.

As I respond to him, God's word is made real for me by his spirit dealing with my spirit, reassuring me and inviting me into a more intimate relationship. My spirit must cooperate because if my will doesn't allow it to happen, my spirit cannot As my spirit engages with God's spirit, he enters me to the extent that I am willing to be indwelled by him. In so doing, my faith is rewarded as my will desires more of God's spirit, which I identify as righteousness, for which I hunger and thirst.

I have used my sovereign will to accept God's sovereign will. I have begun a conscious reciprocal learning process. I have become less cynical, skeptical and naive. If I continue to grow, I become as wise as a serpent and as harmless as a dove as tangible evidence of Jesus in me.

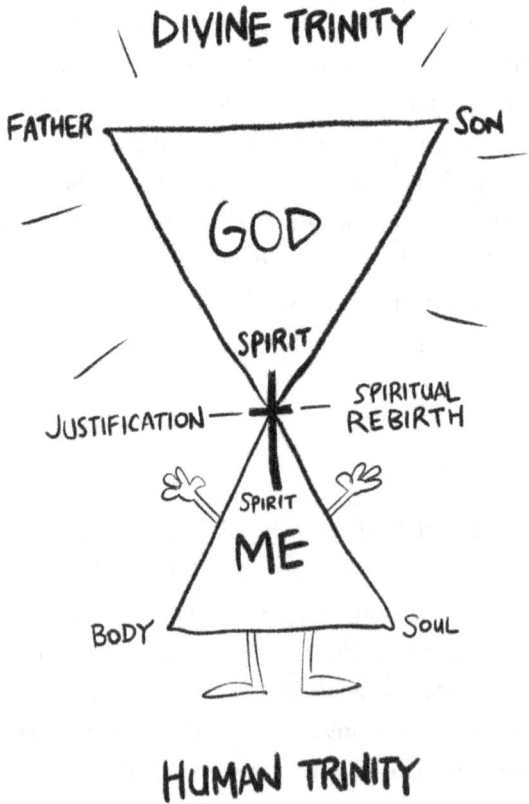

Process and sequence

As I accept God's offer of love and receive God's spirit, I am spiritually "born again" and justified by my faith in Jesus Christ. My mind begins to become transformed and to increasingly resemble Christ's as I trust him and seek to obey his commands, of which the Golden Rule is the greatest. The Golden Rule then guides me towards a dynamic symbiotic relationship between God, Me and You. This implies that my relationship with him depends upon my relationship with you. As we are transformed by love, so we begin to comply with all of God's laws, not out of duty or compliance, but out of our love for him.

First the natural, then the spiritual

There is an important principle applicable to human transformation contained in 1 Corinthians 15: 46: *First the natural, then the spiritual.* This re-occurring theme means that I must learn real things with my human capacities to prepare me to accept transcendent spiritual things. We can consciously engage in this process of growth first by responding to Christ's commands, then by becoming conscious of the renewal of our minds. This is a volitional process in which what we learn prepares us for the next steps of progress, to the extent that you cannot possibly anticipate where it will take you because you have entered a creative relationship with the creator. However, your humanity is not crushed, but rather enhanced. This amazing phenomenon is described by Jesus in the parable of the talents, where the one who has done nothing with what he was given has his talent taken away and given to the one who previously multiplied his gift (Matt 25: 14-30). It would be wrong to assume that we immediately become a mirror image of God as the diagram might suggest, but we do know the destiny and objective of our transformation, which we still control through our trust and obedience to God's offer of love.

Righteousness, peace and joy in the Holy Spirit

Righteousness, peace and joy in the Holy Spirit is an outcome of our faith, hope and love. The Holy Spirit acting on behalf of Jesus determines the outcome of our faith, hope and love for which we are responsible as sovereign beings. This means we are not responsible for the outputs of faith, but only for the inputs. This is why faith is so important. Without it, it is impossible to please God (Heb 11: 6). This in my view, is also what it means to be "predestined" or "elected", where we are called by God to fulfill certain generic and perhaps some specific roles which God has prepared us for, and which we are now able to undertake with great joy, even though they may be difficult tasks, because we have become increasingly more like God and we delight in doing his bidding out of love, not out of a sense of obligation or duty.

As I persist by seeking God and continuing to trust and obey him, so my experience becomes filled with right relationships with him and others that are peaceful and joyful, to the extent that we are ecstatic – not just at the initial experience, such as when we might speak in tongues or be involved in a healing, but as a continuous state, where we are conscious of God's presence in us, and of our place in his family and his Kingdom. We experience this as "running over" with gratitude and joy.

Obstacles to transformation

There are many things that prevent me from taking these steps of faith which Bob Mumford calls strongholds (of sin).[1] These strongholds are anything that keeps me back from making a positive response to God's call – the rebellious part of my un-transformed character (sin) that irrationally rejects God. This part of me is irrational because it acts contrary to what I would do if I was

---

1 https://youtu.be/Z9iNh70sgcQ

responding to my best interests, motivated by love alone. This is why small children love God until cynicism or rebellion sets in. Strongholds are not based upon reason, although they appear to be. They are based upon an illusion of reason and wisdom that is actually confusion and chaos. If my mind and will don't overcome the strongholds, I make no progress toward transformation or my full participation in the Kingdom of God. This is essential preparation in time and space for my eventual role in eternity as an adopted son of God. Similarly, my presuppositions either prepare me or prevent me from being transformed. The reason I can so confidently confirm what Bob Mumford says is that I have had plenty of experience confirming that his characterization is true.

When I respond to God's invitation, my spirit is released into God's Spirit by my will acting together with my mind in faith. I am vitalized and inspired to the extent that my faith allows. As my deposit of faith grows as a result of this encounter, I desire more of God's presence in my life, because his presence has a tangible effect upon me (Lk 22:29). As I begin a reciprocal learning process, God's Spirit teaches me, comforts and guides me into truth about the reality of natural laws of God's creation. As my souls allows my spirit to further engage with God's Spirit, he enters me and begins to transform me by his grace, by the renewal

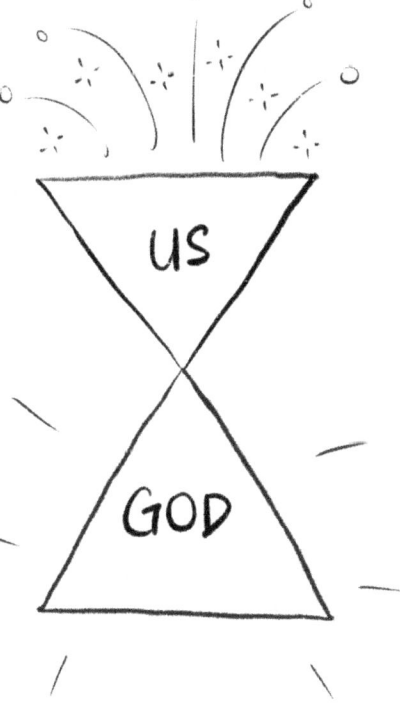

of my mind. (Rom 12:2). As I become transformed, I begin to resemble the one I worship: Jesus, God incarnate. However, when I stop being humble and awed by what is happening to me and am no longer consciously grateful, I also stop growing.

We risk becoming stagnant in our spiritual growth if we do not become conscious of this process of transformation. This is not just about theological knowledge, although a little bit always helps. This is a dynamic relationship between people like you or me in which we become changed by the presence of a friend who never leaves. Wonderful! However, if we do not become conscious, we forget how this miracle began and make no further progress due to strongholds re-asserting their control. Consciousness is the subject of the long discourse, presented below, that Jesus gives in John 14. In this scene, Jesus has just entered Jerusalem on Palm Sunday when he predicts his death and betrayal. But he first washes his disciple's feet to symbolize his role as the King who came to serve, not to be served. Then he comforts and prepares his disciples for what is to come just before he is betrayed by Judas. Jesus reminds them of the great mission that he is assigning to them by giving them these final instructions: *A new commandment I give unto you, That ye love one another; as I have loved you, that ye also love one another. By this shall all men know that ye are my disciples, if ye have love one to another* (Jn 13:34).

Then Jesus finalizes his mission by saying:

> *If you love me, keep my commands. And I will ask the Father, and he will give you another advocate to help you and be with you forever— the Spirit of truth. The world cannot accept him, because it neither sees him nor knows him. But you know him, for he lives with you and will be in you. I will not leave you as orphans; I will come to you. Before long, the world will not see me anymore, but you will see me. Because I live, you also will live. On*

that day you will realize that I am in my Father, and you are in me, and I am in you. Whoever has my commands and keeps them is the one who loves me. The one who loves me will be loved by my Father, and I too will love them and show myself to them. Then Judas (not Judas Iscariot) said, "But, Lord, why do you intend to show yourself to us and not to the world?" Jesus replied, "Anyone who loves me will obey my teaching. My Father will love them, and we will come to them and make our home with them. Anyone who does not love me will not obey my teaching. These words you hear are not my own; they belong to the Father who sent me. "All this I have spoken while still with you. But the Advocate, the Holy Spirit, whom the Father will send in my name, will teach you all things and will remind you of everything I have said to you (Jn 14:15-22).

Life is for living

My friend Graham Billings once reminded me during a very intense discussion about theology that "Life is for living." This made an impression upon me because of my tendency to look for new and interesting ideas rather than just get on with the job at hand using what I already know. His point was that we are not all supposed to be deadly earnest preachers, pastors or missionaries every moment of the day. We are supposed to be good citizens, good mums and dads, good mechanics, good school teachers and principals who enjoy life and are good at doing *whatever our hand turns itself to do* to quote Ecclesiastes 9:10. However, we are not always conscious of our various roles due to many human factors and our susceptibility to sin, which will always remain while we are human. Our ongoing awareness depends upon our willingness to listen to the spirit, especially when we catch ourselves thinking or behaving like we used to in our natural state, rather than what we know what we can be now when we listen to the spirit. Sin never leaves us. It constantly seeks to deceive us and pull us back. Jesus promises, *Remain in me, and I will remain in you.* Recently, when I reminded my friend Lucy Harris of our early discussions about the Golden Rule and asked why she thinks we don't respond to it as a command of Jesus, she said to me, "It's hard to trust our own motivations because we know that our hearts deceive us." To admit the possibility of our self-deception is our first step towards transformation.

Golden Rule—Lord's Prayer relationship		
The Golden Rule Christ's Command to us	⇨ Outcome ⇦	**The Lord's Prayer Our response**
Context & declaration		
...Hear, O Israel: The Lord our God, the Lord is one.	GOD / US	...Our Father in heaven, hallowed be your name
Process: command, petition & outcome		
And you shall love the Lord your God with all your heart and with all your soul and with all your mind and with all your strength.	GOD / US	This, then, is how you should pray: your kingdom come, your will be done, on earth as it is in heaven. Give us today our daily bread And forgive us our

The second is this: You shall love your neighbor as yourself. There is no other commandment greater than these. Mark 12:28-31	debts, as we also have forgiven our debtors. And lead us not into temptation (testing) but deliver us from the evil one for yours is the kingdom and the power and the glory forever. Amen. Matt 6:9-13

Outcome. Our place in God's Eternal Kingdom
For if we have been united with him in a death like his, we will certainly also be united with him in a resurrection like his. (Rom 6:5)

Christ in you, the hope of Glory (Col 1:27).
The Golden Rule is Christ's command to us. We are invited to consciously respond with the Lord's Prayer as the foundation of our hope in an interactive relationship to God and with each other where he forgives us as we have forgiven others. We are the elect, choosen ones of Israel, because we are in Christ as he is in us.

God is love

Love deserves our full confidence because love never fails nor is there is any law against love or any reason not to trust love, provided it is the real thing. If we are agents of God, then our job is to encourage each other to love and do good works. But first, notice the order. Love always precedes good works, not the reverse. The greatest love that ever existed is God's love for us, and this love caused him to send his son for us. Love is available to us when we accept Jesus' sacrifice for us. To say yes to him today, is to begin the greatest adventure that it is possible for a human being to go on, because we were made for this very purpose.

I do hope you have enjoyed this journey as much as I have, and that will continue with it, remembering that it is much easier and more enjoyable if you bring others along with you.

Postlude

My Joyful Place in the Cosmos

> *"If we find ourselves with a desire that nothing in this world can satisfy, the most probable explanation is that we were made for another world."*
>
> C.S. Lewis

Recently, the following sermon was preached at my church by Lay Minister Bei-En Zou from the text Nehemiah 12:27-47 as part of his penultimate talk in a series on Nehemiah.

Nehemiah was a Jewish exile from the city of Jerusalem, whose people had become subject to the Persian King Artaxerxes. He uses his privileged position as cupbearer to King Artaxerxes to petition to allow the rebuilding of the walls of Jerusalem, which were broken down by previous conquests, leaving the city defenseless. He was then appointed as governor of Persian Judea by Artaxerxes I during the Second Temple period. Bei-En also referred to the New Testament text from Revelation 21:1-5, 21:22-22:6a, which describe a future state of unending and ineffable joy because "*God is present among us.*"

Bei-En:

> *When was the last time you felt joy? ...*
> *...Then it's a sign that God is working in you.*

How Good is the Golden Rule?

...we come to a section of the Bible that is just overflowing with joy and celebration.

Back in Chapter 6 Nehemiah fulfils his mission
The wall surrounding Jerusalem is complete
And today he leads them in dedicating the wall.
And look at how the people dedicate the wall:

...So joy is our great and our challenging theme today...

What can we learn about joy from this passage?

1. Joy is commanded

2. Joy comes from purification – v. 30

3. Finally joy come from obedience

Do you associate obedience with thrills? With joy?
Obedience feels something that is complete opposite of joy.
It feels like a straitjacket –stifling my freedom and creativity, it's really pain. It's really boring.

I'm also one of these people who
If you tell me it's a rule,
Will immediately break it!...

...But the constant witness of the bible,
The testimony of Christians throughout the ages,
is that obedience is the key that opens all doors,
It's the gateway to joy.

My joyful place in the Cosmos

…Joy comes from obedience
Come to me, Jesus says,
Take on my burdens,
They're light, and my yoke is easy.
Learn from me,
For I am gentle and humble in heart,
And you will find rest for your souls.

Conclusion

In the book of Revelation, John has a vision:
He sees a great multitude that no one could count,
people from every nation, tribe, people and language,
    standing before the throne God and before Jesus.
They're wearing white robes
And they're holding palm branches in their hands.
And they call out the praises of God:
"Salvation belongs to our God,
who sits on the throne,
and to the Lamb."

…John sees of vision, at the end of time
Of believers doing exactly what the people in Nehemiah
    are doing
but on an infinitely greater scale.

The servants of God will surround his thrown
And there will be shouts of thanksgiving and songs of
    joy
As cannot be imagined.

We too, like Nehemiah and the Israelites,
Are looking forward to the future with hope

We too, are longing for the day
When we'll be in the new Jerusalem
Where our joy will be pure,
unalloyed by mourning, or crying or pain or death

Friends, And as we wait,
Let's not allow transitory griefs of this world,
Deep and real though they are, rob us of our eternal
joy...

...And finally,
When our hearts are cold and our souls are calloused,
hear the word of God and obey it![1]

I have included Bei-En's sermon because, as I said to her on the day, *"There may have been better sermons preached, but if there are, I am unaware of them,"* as she said exactly the right words for me to conclude my book. This sort of serendipity has become commonplace during the 12 months while I was writing. One of my original complaints and motivations for writing was that I could not recall the Golden Rule being preached. This complaint is now no longer valid as there has hardly been a Sunday as St James this year when the Golden Rule was not included or implied by the sermon, to say nothing of it always being in the liturgy.

I make no apology for this book being about me, as narcissistic as that may seem. At the risk of further self-indulgence, the best any of us can do is to tell our story as it is, warts and all, because to do otherwise means that we risk becoming self-deceptive and pretentious, both religiously and otherwise. I am not trying to say that I am something special, but just that I have become something that we all can be – rich or poor, intelligent or not, powerful or weak as there is no difference in status in the Kingdom of God.

---

1 From Bei-En Zou's sermon notes.

Certainly, there may be different potential outcomes of our role in the Kingdom, because some of us have risen to the high calling that applies to all of us. This statement of Jesus from Luke 12:28 can be summarized as follows: *With great power comes great responsibility.* Whether or not I have done my bit remains to be seen, but this book is an attempt – not for self-justification, but an encouragement to all of us, including myself, that there is a place and an important role for us in God's Kingdom if we are ready to accept it.

I hope to see you there.

After all

Whoever has my commands and keeps them is the one who loves me. The one who loves me will be loved by my Father, and I too will love them and show myself to them (Jn 14:21).

Yes and amen.

www.ingramcontent.com/pod-product-compliance
Lightning Source LLC
Chambersburg PA
CBHW051933290426
44110CB00015B/1960